Singapore Repulsed

by

Ordinary Seaman Ian Hay

Singapore Repulsed

by

Ordinary Seaman Ian Hay

The Pentland Press Ltd
Edinburgh • Cambridge • Durham • USA

01388 776555

© Ian C. Hay 1998

First published in 1998 by
The Pentland Press Ltd.
1 Hutton Close
South Church
Bishop Auckland
Durham

British Library Cataloguing in Publication Data.
A Catalogue record for this book is available
from the British Library.

ISBN 1 85821 542 0

Typeset by George Wishart & Associates, Whitley Bay.
Printed and bound by Antony Rowe Ltd., Chippenham.

Ian Hay

To the memory of the officers and men of Force 'Z' Singapore, Admiral Sir Tom Spencer Vaughan Phillips KCB in the Flagship HMS *Prince of Wales* and the Battle Cruiser HMS *Repulse*.

CONTENTS

FOREWORD
by
Vice Admiral Sir John Hayes

10 December 1941. Three days after the Japanese declaration of War by their sudden air assault on the American Fleet in Pearl Harbour and their Army landings at Khota Baru, the north-easternmost point on the Malayan Peninsula.

A few days before that, two capital ships of the Royal Navy had arrived at Singapore as a hopeful, but clearly abortive, deterrent to such Japanese entry into the War: the comparatively new battleship *Prince of Wales* and her sister, the elderly and graceful battle-cruiser *Repulse* of Jutland, days used frequently to take Royalty around the world.

On 8 December they had been despatched to the Gulf of Siam to try to interfere with the Japanese convoys of their landing army – but to no avail. The two big ships headed back to Singapore at speed and were off Kuantan, only a hundred miles away, when they were interrupted by a completely spurious report of further enemy landings there. While dawdling around to investigate a horizon empty save for some old barges under tow, the two ships were found by Japanese torpedo bombers and both sunk within the hour.

Ordinary Seaman Ian Hay of *Repulse* was at his customary action station as bridge lookout. Lieutenant John Hayes, Assistant Navigator, was rummaging around within his bridge and communication duties, naturally ignorant of the name of the lookout who, fifty-six years later, tells me that our beloved Captain 'Bill' Tennant and I once supported him from behind in a snow-storm!

When *Repulse* eventually could avoid no more torpedo salvos despite the brilliant combing of their tracks by her Captain, she sank quickly with over five hundred casualties. Hay and Hayes have recently discovered that they are fortunate survivors – and shipmates are shipmates forever. That is clearly one reason why this author of *Singapore Repulsed* pays me the compliment of asking me to write this Foreword as one who unwittingly shared his experiences on that historically fateful day. The other reason is coincidental and totally different.

Millions of words have been written over the years about the catastrophe which overtook the two ships and the eventual ensuing surrender of Singapore, by the highest, such as Lord Wavell himself as a late Supreme Commander, and the countless who shared personal experiences within the tragedy, including, I must confess, myself. Many military historians classify it as our major disaster of the war.

Some amongst us, and particularly the readers of this book, may be as impressed as I am that he who began naval life as a boy seaman aged fifteen and whose original rank target would have been modest, in fact achieved so very much more.

Ian Hay was first one of over a thousand in HMS *Ganges*, one of two such Boy's Training establishments. The other was HMS *St. Vincent* which I happen to have been fortunate enough to command some thirty years later, with another thousand of such impeccably enthusiastic boys of whom I was justly proud. I am therefore in a position to commend to readers my admiration and support of someone who is likely to describe his experiences and opinions from a different angle than, I dare to say, any such before.

After *Repulse* he served the rest of the war as a junior rating in some half dozen Battle of the Atlantic destroyers. He retired from the Navy in 1957 as a Petty Officer and immediately enlisted in the Merchant Navy as a deck hand and lamp trimmer. By the time he joined Cunard he had qualified as a junior Navigating Officer and ended his career at sea as First Mate of a Royal Fleet Auxiliary. He brought me up to date some thirty years after we were swimming together in the South China

Sea, by calling on me during my final naval appointment as Flag Officer Scotland, a rather different contact!

So, readers, after such background, you, like me, may well disagree with Ian's opinions; Lord Wavell's and mine. Who has not on this now historic disaster? All points of view are worth pondering. Nothing is permanent but change, and happily may it ever be so.

ACKNOWLEDGEMENTS

Admiral Sir John Hayes KCB OBE, President of HMS *Prince of Wales*
& HMS *Repulse* Survivors Association;
Alan 'Jessie' Mathews writer Marchwiel;
Captain R. McQueen, CBE RN, General Secretary, The Royal Naval
Association;
Sue Sullivan, *Navy News*;
Meinhard Janssen, President of the German Heavy Cruiser
Association;
Diana Fletcher.

PREFACE

The title of this book recalls the action of the battle cruiser HMS *Repulse* at Singapore. Through the bedlam on the gundecks could be heard at intervals the steady chant of the communication numbers at the guns: 'Barrage, barrage, barrage.' The events now taking place were critical, and seemed to be an echo from the long corridors of time immemorial in the Royal Navy's history when the enemy was at close range.

Time after time *Repulse* had 'Repulsed' very low torpedo-carrying Japanese aircraft, as they arrived in their wave after wave of squadrons of twenty-seven, at the same time as very high level bombing attacks. All at once they flew off, as suddenly as they had arrived, to give their undivided attention to the flagship of 'Force Z', where Admiral Sir Tom Spencer Vaughan Phillips, KCB, affectionately known by the ordinary seamen on the lower deck as 'Tom Thumb', was on his battleship HMS *Prince of Wales*.

HMS *Prince of Wales* had only recently been launched and was armed with ten 14-inch guns. It was one of the huge KG5 class battleships of 35,000 tons deadweight, like HMS *Duke of York* which had caught the *Bismarck* trying to escape after it had sunk HMS *Hood*, hitting it very heavily till it sank.

Now that the Japanese squadrons had left us to attack the *Prince of Wales*, we wondered if it was because we had put up such a strong barrage in defence, or because of Captain William Tennant's amazing seamanship. He had taken avoiding action, dodging 19 torpedoes out of 24, sustaining only 5 hits and had been missed by the high level bombing attacks, as he zigzagged the 32,000 tons dead-weight battle cruiser like a destroyer on Fleet manoeuvres, no doubt using the experience of his time spent as a young destroyer Captain.

Standing out on the bridge wings, and exposed to enemy fire beside him was the Gunnery Officer, Lt. Cdr. C.H. Cobbe, who was killed as he watched with Captain Tennant judging the bombs and torpedoes falling to take successful avoiding action. As this was an emergency, in the engine room valves were now opened that had never been opened before, to the despair of the Chief Engineer Officer Cameron, a Scot, as the engines built on the Clyde that had outpaced the 'wolf packs' in the battle of the Atlantic were ruined for ever. A huge cloud of black smoke belched from *Repulse*'s funnels, streaming aft and mingling with the blue of our gunfire smoke that blotted out visibility astern. *Repulse* was running for her life like some hunted wounded stag.

In the lull that followed the Japanese squadrons leaving us, the Bos'n's Mate's piercing high trilling pipe sounded, followed by his announcement, 'Do you hear there!' On *Repulse* this was only said on special occasions, and not for the routine pipes. Now the Tannoy said, 'The Captain is about to speak.'

Captain Tennant's voice came over in his usual calm steady manner, 'We are now going to stand by HMS *Prince of Wales*.'

From that moment on both ships' fates were sealed. On the gun decks we replenished ammunition and tended the injured, clearing away the many empty used brass cartridge cases from around the guns.

Their brassy bell-like sound as we raked them clear, still too hot to handle, and their merry clinking tinkling tunes seemed obscene after seeing our dead and dying mates around the guns being whisked away quickly to the first aid stations.

The ammunition hoist to S1 gun to starboard (on the right side) and P2 gun on the port (left side) had been damaged in enemy action, and this is where we from 'A' turret's 15-inch gun's crew came in. In the first onslaught there had been many casualties in the upper deck personnel, and only key senior rates were kept 'closed up' in the main armament. These were mostly junior seamen, ordinary seamen, and young ABs, $17^1/_2$ to twenty-year-olds who replaced the upper deck and guns crew losses. Michael, Blondy, myself and others supplied S1 and P2 guns by going below each time to the top of the 4-inch HA magazine which had a hydraulic lift from the magazine to the deck above where we collected the shells.

To give a picture of these guns' positions: look at the photograph of *Repulse*'s port side and you can see just below the foremost funnel and level with the upper deck P2 gun's shield, about six feet high and in a curved two-inch thick armoured plate. This gave a measure of protection, but the low flying torpedo bombers soon found out that we could only depress the guns so far. S1 on the starboard side was the same, and so the aircraft would come in even lower, dropping their torpedoes and strafing along the upper deck. At one time we saw the pilot's grinning face.

We had just arrived with 4-inch projectiles on our shoulders from below, when we saw to our horror Leading Seaman Jock Devlin dead with most of his crew. We had known him personally in our mess for two years, and would never know now if he was joking or serious in his signature call: 'You can sleep with me any time, Ian.' On the crowded messdeck where we ODs slept on the mess stool's table, myself under the table to avoid being trodden on, all the slinging billets having been taken by the senior ABs meant there was nothing untoward in his saying. The sight before us numbed us in horror.

We now loaded up S1 gun and were rooted to the deck in fear as we heard the communication number's desperate report to the TS repeating, 'S1 gun ammunition expended, S1 gun ammunition expended.' Were we to suffer P2's fate in not keeping our fire sector open? Then came the snarling voice of AB Scouse Bob Hewlet dancing in rage and pain with a bullet shattered arm, shouting at us, 'Don't just stand there, load up with fucking practice smoke!'

These practice smoke shells were stowed in the ready use armour plated water-tight lockers around the gun. We were immediately galvanised into action and loaded up with them and were soon back to normal as ammunition piled up at the side of the gun. Scouse went off for first aid and survived, and later sailed with me on HMS *Daring* when I was a Gunnery Instructor after the war.

The Flagship of Force 'Z' was in trouble as we went round and round her, trying to give her covering fire as she drifted helplessly, her steering damaged. It was an ironic fate as this is what she had done indirectly to the *Bismarck*, who with faulty steering had drifted helplessly so that the sister ship of the *Prince of Wales*, the *Duke of York*, could catch the *Bismarck* and sink her. The *Prince of Wales* however had suffered damage in that action with the *Bismarck* and now was paying the penalty as she still had dockyard mateys on board repairing the damage. She had also been hit extensively by the heavy cruiser *Prinz Eugen*, and she was badly mauled after they had sunk the *Hood*, but she fought back and was hitting the *Bismarck*, forcing her to turn and run when she was ordered to withdraw.

Now again she was fighting back, not in the cold Arctic waters but in the South China Seas and against overwhelming odds without air cover against Japanese squadrons, wave after wave of them. As some of her guns jammed in their racks, her Royal Marine guns crew, ever resourceful, courageously hauled their guns around to bear with deck tackles exposed to enemy fire.

The artist's impression of *Repulse* going round the *Prince of Wales* giving her covering fire is how most young seamen and officers of that time will remember it.

The introduction to my main story is now concluded.

xx

Chapter One

IN THE BEGINNING

Dad drove me to Glasgow's Central railway station, following the tram lines, though even this didn't help much. There was a heavy blanket of smog and you couldn't see your hand in front of your face. On his advice I buried my face into my old school scarf to avoid breathing the stuff. My clean white shirt was already grubby as our old Morris Cowley growled steadily on like a tank. If we hit anything I knew who would come off worse; they don't build cars like that any more.

I was joining the Royal Navy at the age of 15½ at the shore establishment, HMS *Ganges*, that had begun in 1901. At that time daylight in Glasgow started briefly at twelve noon and ended shortly later, so the lights in my school were kept on all day. We had just come out of that dreadful depression of the thirties, far worse than anything today, when my father said after every meal, 'It's always good to come away from the table feeling hungry,' as we always did. Now however Glasgow was enjoying for the first time prosperity. Every so often the sky at night would light up red, that's when you could see it, and this would be followed by a loud roar from the outskirts at Beardmore's Parkhead steel foundry. They were turning out gun barrels as fast as they could, and steel for our Clyde shipyards, their craftsmen having been known throughout the world at a time when Japan was only building canoes. The reason was that war was imminent, and later in that war it was a great consolation to me in a force 10 storm, as the ship took a dive in one of those forty-foot monster waves, the bows

1

In my first sailor suit.

seemingly digging themselves down in alarming creaks and groans in jerks as the plates were put under tremendous pressure to bending moments and stresses, to know that she had been built on the Clyde.

At Glasgow Central my seat had been booked, back to the engine, and I awaited Dad's return from the station bookstall that he'd suddenly remembered. Now he arrived back breathless and, to give you an idea of the age most of us were who joined, he gave me my favourite comics to read on the train: 'Oor Wullie', sitting on his upturned bucket, *The Broons*, *Hotspur*, and, I think, the *Beano*. He then stood below me on the platform giving me last minute advice that as usual went in one ear and out the other. At last came the guard's whistle and flag and the sound of slamming doors and the wavering shouts of farewells as the train agonisingly pulled out. As the distance widened between us, Dad shouted out, 'Ian, try and make friends with a bigger boy in the class when you get there!' He was thinking of my slim figure and at the minimum height for entry, 5 ft. 3 ins. The

2

HMS Ganges.

RN doctor at Bath Street Recruiting Office had said, 'He will grow.' I did.

I was alone in the carriage except for a motherly type lady, who I feared any moment would rush over and take me in her arms. I was the only boy from Glasgow, a fact due to the very rigid joining qualifications. At that period in Glasgow, owing to the terrible poverty and conditions, there were many boys with rickets, short in height, with poor eyesight, poor feet, and many other problems so the Navy did not want them.

The train now clacked and clicked its monotonous way, until at one time I could have shouted out, 'Is it ever going to get there?' only to be more depressed on finding it had only reached Waverley Station in Edinburgh. A crowd of noisy boys got in to my compartment, which now had a poster saying, 'Reserved for Naval Personnel'. This was the first indication that we now belonged to the Royal Navy for twelve years, though only from the age of eighteen. I now felt how the pressed men from the pressgangs must have felt.

The others were older at sixteen or 16½, not a great difference from my age of fifteen, but a great gap in the hierarchy of boys. They refused my timid friendly advances and left me alone in my corner seat. At long last, after the long nightmare of the train journey, we arrived at Harwich railway station, the end of the world, I thought, as we tumbled out more dead than alive.

Then we went by naval picket boat towards what appeared to be an island, and on the top of a high hill appeared a huge mast which we found out to be the old *Ganges* battle sailing ship's main mast, the highest in the Navy. It dominated the surroundings. We were not going to an island in fact, but to a headland jutting out that gave this impression, though for all intent and purposes it could have been Devil's Island. Meeting us at the pierhead were two smiling, friendly and immaculately dressed Petty Officer instructors, and we ambled and strolled along in groups, chatting to each other and pointing out places of interest. Trying to guess the height of the mast, laughter broke out, we were so happy and relieved to get off that terrible train.

HMS Bonaventure in the Chinese Boxer rebellion. My grandfather was Gunnery Officer.

How often we were to wish we were back on it. Now we were like tourists just off the boat or plane and approaching our hotel after sight-seeing. I turned to one of the boys I'd not noticed before and asked politely, 'I wonder if it would be at all possible to use those boats tied up at the pier?'

What a daft question that turned out to be. I met the eyes of the biggest boy in the class, a curly ginger-haired Southern Irish boy who had come a different route than us. There was no need to think further of my father's parting advice; I'd found him. His name was Michael O'Hern and he was to remain with me throughout my time in the service, like a continuous thread running through my story, holding it together, giving it perspective and balance.

We were first accommodated in the new entrants' block, then moved to the long low dormitories, seen in the photograph middle right hand side, at right angles to the quarterdeck, by the mast. These were called the 'Long covered ways' as they provided cover to the entrances to dormitories or messes. At the head of the main covered way was a placard that said, 'Fear God, Honour the King'; this was the entrance to the Holy of Holies, the Quarterdeck, and as we scuttled across with

BOAT PIER – SHOTLEY.

The Boat Pier.

6

a hurried salute to the White Ensign, we dreaded that shout if we were at all sluggish, 'Come here, that boy!' We were no longer Nozzers, new entrants, and did everything now on the double. What a shock after our stroll up the steps from the pier head that were called, 'Faith, Hope and Charity': the three sets that can also be seen in the photograph, beginning at the boat-house.

Entering the mess, you saw that the first section floor was of concrete and on the right hand side was a small toilet called the night heads that was used at night, saving us from going out in the cold and night to the main heads at the foot of each covered way. These square brick-built buildings were open to the fresh air, except for the actual cubicles that had half doors and were roofed. The sides had narrow slots like the arrow slits on old castles, so the Royal Marine sentries, on their patrol night and day, could observe any irregularity, mainly smoking for which the punishment could be very severe. The RN even as long ago as that were only too aware of the danger to health, only now forced by the government to admit and suffer the potential loss of tax revenue.

On the left of the night heads was the scullery with two large sinks, one for dishing up in, the other for rinsing off. We all took turns in pairs of being 'Cook of the Mess' a purely technical term as we did not cook, and would never do so throughout our service in the RN. We fetched the food from the galley at the pipe 'Cooks to the Galley' in three large trays; one tray, for example, would have roast potatoes, with a joint of roast beef in its centre, called later a 'strait rush'; there would be a dish for vegetables, and the other dish would be perhaps steamed plum, fig duff or date pudding. There would be an extra pot of custard supplied, the pot called a 'Fanny' from the time a girl called Fanny Adams went missing in a corned beef factory in Victorian days. This was from the days when the corned beef was issued in large 5 lb. tins, and Jack, seeing how well made they were, would keep them and utilise them as utensils, or so the story goes.

Also in the scullery was a long trough with tip-up basins in it for each set of hot and cold water taps, so that when you finished you tipped the water away, so dispensing with plugs. This was to be the same on all ships later, before they were modernised with bowls and plugs. You always found that some one had lost the plug or nicked it, why I'll never know.

Entering through the double doors of the mess proper you came into the main accommodation area. In the first section were two mess wooden tables with stools on each side, and a smaller table at the far end by its exclusive self for the Leading and Petty Officer Boys' tables, who took turns in being in charge of the class in the absence of our two Petty Officer instructors. It was lucky for me that Michael was promoted in very quick time to PO Boy. The last and largest section in its oblong length was decked in with beautiful teak polished parquetry. No boots or shoes were allowed on it, which meant each time you went to your bed or kit-bag you took your shoes, or usually boots, off and ran with them in your hand. We became expert at taking them off and on quickly, a skill not wasted but which saved our lives later in the water.

In three rows were our beds which could only be described as steel rigid cots. On each bed was a thin but warm mattress, that was folded in three and placed at the head of the bed, as were the blankets, folded in three in a certain way and placed on top. Woe betide anyone who did not conform; punishment was dished out by the PO Boys in the form of a whack across the backside with a broom handle, for which my friendship with Michael gave me no immunity. Finally on top went our pyjamas.

Placed neatly in a line at the foot of our beds were our shoes, boots, football boots, gym shoes, and our off duty light canvas low-heeled brown shoes. Above the beds each had a shelf on which rested our 'ditty boxes', about a foot square, almost the same size as my first sextant box many years later. The sextant not being a micrometer one, you had to read the degrees, minutes and seconds etched into the brass base plate, which took time and perfect eyesight to read off. That time was also hard for me coming 'Up through the hawse pipe'. These small but nicely grained wooden boxes were for letters from home, etc., and had a small brass name plate on the front. They each had a key, and it was an offence to leave them unlocked to put temptation in someone's way.

Next to our 'ditty boxes' were cap boxes for the No. 1 best blue cap and white cap for summer or foreign service. Today there are no longer black hats.

At each end of the room was a huge coal fire that was regularly black leaded. In my time they had a half rectangular cushioned seat that enclosed each fire. In the winter we were able to sit round and spin a yarn, and at night we could snuggle down in the warmth of our blankets and watch the firelight glow as we dropped off to sleep. The Royal Marine sentry on his patrol would come in later and damp down the fires for safety reasons, but by then after a very tiring day of 'double here, double there, double everywhere,' we were sound asleep.

Our day began at 0600 hours with the blast on a bugle from a Royal Marine at the head of the covered ways, which acted like sound boxes, a deafening sound that seemed to say, 'Charlie, Charlie, get out of bed, rise and shine,' so we marked our calendar's days off as Charlies. Now inside our mess came the equally deafening sound of a raucous Royal

My initial class, Collingwood division, lost on HMS Hood *and* HMS *Royal Oak.*

9

Marine Corporal shouting in his broken gravelly parade voice, 'Take your hands off your cocks and grab your socks.' It was wrong of course, to address youngsters in this manner, and he could have been in serious trouble as this new Navy emerged, where bullying, sarcasm and above all obscene language were treated seriously. However, the old Corporal meant no harm; it was the way he had always called his equally hard-bitten Platoon in the past.

We all understood this phrase and did not object to it; after all, it was where our hands usually were. We sprang out, grabbed our toothbrushes and rushed to wash. One time we had been sluggish getting out, so he doubled us up and down Laundry Hill in our pyjamas, missing breakfast, seamanship, Gunnery, and evoking the wrath of all concerned, the school teacher putting in a complaint. After a wash it was to our cocoa and biscuits. The biscuits came in two different kinds: round, soft and slightly sweet; the other square and hard. At first when we first heard of this cocoa and biscuits we had visions of the kind at home. What a shock that was. I being one of the smallest was last at the tray to find all the round ones gone and only the hard ones left. Furthermore the cocoa had lumps of fat floating on top. This was naval issue and later in the cold sea watches, made properly with sugar and milk, was called 'kye' and enjoyed by officers and men alike.

As I now nibbled one of the hard ship's biscuits, a wave of homesickness swept over me as I remembered my old dog Birky.

The meal completed, we attacked everything in sight with metal polish, including our battered tin plates and mugs, knives and forks, and the dustbin became the only one that you could see your face in. Now it was breakfast time and we awaited our instructors, standing either side of our clean scrubbed wooden mess tables, looking down on our plates where lay two large fat kippers, with a large chunk of black bread. In spite of its unusual appearance, this bread, fresh from the ship's bakery, was delicious. Beside it was a large battered tin mug of tea, sometimes coffee, said by us that the cook had waved an empty sugar bag over it.

The Navy attached great importance to our teeth, from the past

With my Airedale, Birky.

happenings far out to sea with no dentist; the classic occurrence of a seaman with toothache could not be worse. The food was well cooked and plentiful, even if it was not always piping hot and did come with a faint smell of metal polish. That would not have been noticed by adults, but we were young and healthy, our smell of things sensitive, and of course we did not smoke. My letters home said, 'Please send a food parcel, we are being starved to death.' The food was the best by Royal Appointment, but the galley was some distance from the messes, half way up covered ways, so the food was not always hot. The training ship had been built in the days of sail.

The Petty Officer instructors were dedicated to training and teaching us for a better Royal Navy in the sometimes thankless job those also outside in the teaching profession go through. There were of course many ex-*Ganges* boys who had the aptitude and education to reach higher but who chose to remain teaching us, unlike the others who rose in the ranks, such as Admiral Flint, Captain Dunlop, Commander E.R. Monaghan, to mention only a few.

Commander E.R. Monaghan had been a PO Boy at *Ganges*, and on the *Repulse* made history by being the youngest, at nineteen, to be rated up to acting Petty Officer. This was unknown, and unbelievable at my Uncle Andy's and Bagsy Baker's time in the service. Bagsy, with his dull pale features – he never left the fo'c'sle locker – came out to venture the elements to see this phenomenon.

Monaghan earned his respect right from the start from us, as one day a seaman painting what could be roughly described the main-mast top gallant yard, but which was now a signalling yard to give its position in the ship, had got stuck. As he had leant backwards to paint an awkward spot on the yardarm, he had got cramp, and couldn't regain his position. He was now hanging with his legs, the foot-rope trapped behind his knees, and slipping. Monaghan quickly went out on the yard, dropped a loop of line over him and pulled him up just in time to prevent him falling to his death.

Another time the fast Captain's barge hit some debris and began to sink, but Monaghan brought it alongside gunwales under, again just in time for the ship's crane to hook on and hoist.

This may not seem much, but at the time, as a young ordinary seaman, it impressed me. A final anecdote about Monaghan: as the Officer in charge of seriously wounded men, at the time when the sloop *Amethyst* went into action on the river Yangste, after being fired on by the Chinese at about the time of the Korean conflict, Monaghan braved the shell fire and took his wounded off in a boat for treatment otherwise they might have died of their injuries. So I've a great respect for Commander Monaghan, then as now. However, back to *Ganges*.

We attacked everything in sight to clean. We now turned to, polishing our teak-decked parquetry, as two of us went up each passage-way between the beds rubbing in Ronuck, 'Pusser's floor polish', as the others followed up with old pieces of serge, using a piece as a kneeler, appearing like so many moles digging and scrambling backwards on their hindquarters.

Now at last came breakfast. We stood silent and quiet behind our tables, awaiting the instructor's order, 'Say grace', after which we chanted, 'For what we are about to receive thank God.' Then came his 'Carry on, you've got three minutes,' meaning not literally three minutes but don't take all day. It was merely an expression, and I understood this more than the others as my hero of the time was Richard Henry Dana and his book, *Two Years before the Mast*. As they rounded the Cape Horn in a sudden squall and snow blizzard, carrying too much sail, the Mate went for'd and rapped three times loudly on the fo'c'sle deck scuttle (hatch) with, 'Do you hear, you've got three minutes, come as you are,' the 'come as you are' stressing the danger.

The Royal Navy was so impressed by his book in 1836 that much of it was to form the Naval Seamanship Manual. After all it was not so strange as the Navy developed from the Merchant Navy. The British Indian Steam Company and before that Sail Company were the first to dress their officers and men in uniform. So they eventually became the Royal Navy.

In the beginning, as we were training to think fast and obey orders, the three minutes usually meant three minutes, as we no sooner seemed to have sat down than we were told to rise and fall in outside at the rush – and it was a rush as the instructor's rope's end hurried up the ones who were slow, as we tried to eat what was left on our plates.

The rope's end was really a gesture from the bad old days and no one was ever hit with severity; later it was eased off, I learned an important part of leadership: it's better to be firm in the beginning, then when you ease off you can be firm again; it's impossible the other way round, or nearly impossible.

Now we ditched plates in the scullery for the duty 'Cooks of the Mess', and fell in outside, waiting to be doubled off for instructions. Those going to the heads made a wise decision, as once before on parade, a boy with his hand up, 'Please, sir, can I go to the heads?' was refused with the dire consequence that he now stood with his rifle in a pool of water, but with relief on his face.

Serious offences like running away, and smoking, were punished by six cuts across the backside with a cane, administered by the Master at Arms, the 'Jaunty'. His arm wielding the cane had to be no more further back than at right angles to the shoulder, and the process was overseen by the surgeon, the Padre and the Commanding Officer. The trousers at the seat were reinforced by a pair of sports shorts, and sometimes with newspapers, so the actual pain inflicted was minimal, but the whole performance leading up to it was far worse. Across the bare buttocks, maybe, but not in my time.

Another punishment was the 'Shotley routine' when the whole class was made to suffer. This entailed being called at 0530 in the morning and doubled round the parade ground, and finished off with fifteen minutes up and down the dreaded Laundry Hill. Next was 'Running the Gauntlet'. This was inflicted for minor offences committed in the mess. I remember being a victim of this, when the mess lined up on both sides and you had to run from one end to the other, being beaten by the others with rubber gym shoes. The blows on myself I remember were very light, and again it was the performance leading up to it that was worst, or, when I now reflect on it looking at that early photo of myself, who could have hurt such an innocent looking waif?

Here is a good example of 'Shotley routine'. It was the time someone gave his boots a final polish with someone else's pyjamas and wouldn't own up. We had to double to the armory that lay at the other end of the parade ground and were already tiring after doubling the length of the covered way. Our doubling was in fact always twice as much in distance, as the (walking) instructor would shout as we got too far ahead of him, 'About turn!' and of course, when we became abreast of him, 'About turn!' again, so that by the time we arrived at the dreaded Laundry Hill the smaller boys like myself were nearly done for.

Michael, our PO Boy and leading, hearing my breath rasping as I doubled from behind him, but more like a shuffle as we had all come down to that, tried to slow the pace down and this was a great help. We had of course doubled up and down Laundry Hill before, but not with rifles. These were held by the palm of the left hand, fingers all round the brass butt plate, elbow close into the side, and the forearm making an exact ninety-degree angle to the body, as the rifle lay angled on the left shoulder. The trick was to stop the rifle banging up and down on

14

the shoulder bone, that could be painful, by applying to the outside little finger a torque, so bearing down on the butt and keeping it in place. We were all aware the value of property now, even a boy's pyjamas!

Now, having got our second wind and feeling better, we were able to swing into our old doubling routine, 'stamping it down' in unison with our tackitty boots, the beat helping us along, as we now began to synchronise with each other. The sweat streaming off us showed up in dark patches under the armpits and in the crutches of our canvas duck suits.

At last came the order, to everyone's relief, 'Change Arms', which meant placing the rifle on the other shoulder. This was done by grasping the rifle by the small of the butt by the right hand, and bringing the rifle across the body to place it on the right shoulder, at the same time shifting one's grasp of the left hand from the butt plate to the small of the butt and withdrawing the right hand from the small of the butt to the right butt plate. The rifle was now in the same position as it had been on the left, at the slope on the right shoulder. Easier said than typed. It was done to time by numbers, making a pause of two marching paces between each movement. We were calling out together, 'Hup two three, over two three, down.' On the last movement we cut our disengaged hands smartly to the side.

Next, a short time later, to even greater relief, came the order, 'March!' – only just in time as I along with some of the other smaller boys in a daze stumbled from the ranks.

It was not some sadistic operation that the smaller kids suffered, but the inability to judge us all as we varied so much in physique, real genetical and age. After this was seen to happen to the smaller ones, we were never again put to this limit. We doubled to instructions, we doubled from instructions, the only time we marched was at Sunday divisions, but as time went on we became hardened to it. We thought of the day we joined when we had strolled up from the pier, happy like a sight seeing tour pointing out places of interest, and so happy to have left that nightmare of a train journey. Oh, how we wished we were

HMS Ganges.

back on it and on our way home. That was too late now; we belonged body and soul to the Royal Navy for twelve years, and even so we still had to wait till we were eighteen years old.

After our ordeal we showered, changed out of our sweaty gear, and were now dressed in 'night clothing', our warm, dark blue serge suits, without the blue jean collars, and wearing our light brown low heeled canvas shoes in comfort. I'd joined our select band of 'draggers' union' and we were waiting for 'Pipe down' or lights out when we met up behind the bag racks. The bag racks were at the far end of the mess, and took our kitbags, almost the same height as ourselves and just as heavy. Our names were stamped in black across the bottom and these names faced outboard. After sweating to get the damned thing out to change into sports gear, for instance, with that ominous, 'Three minutes,' ringing in your ears, you would find what you wanted was at the bottom of the kit bag. Then you had to pack everything hurriedly back in, then lift the heavy bag back in place, screwing it one way then the other to get it in, making sure the name was uppermost.

Now, in our pyjamas after 'Pipe down', four of us collected behind the bag racks and one lit the single cigarette by opening and closing the fuse box breaker slightly so causing a flash sufficient to light. This was a dangerous practice, as dangerous as that dreaded whisper, 'Lobs a jock', meaning that one of our Royal Marines was around. They were all up to our tricks, which meant six cuts across the bottom.

Now, gathered in a circle, someone muttered 'One all round,' a phrase we had heard submariners used for something. Taking that first drag after so long without, I nearly passed out.

It was Sunday afternoon when we were allowed leave, and Michael and I were very fit after the amount of doubling we did. Being still smaller than him, I paced behind him as usual and in our loping strides we soon arrived at Flatford, the next village from Shotley which we had just left. This was the village where John Constable RA came from and from where he captured the surrounding beautiful countryside, but all this was lost on Michael and me as we raided the only fag machine for miles. We became tobacco barons as one fag was enough for us to last for weeks so we sold the rest at a profit On one trip we were searched and made to eat the lot; after being violently sick I let my membership of the 'draggers' union' lapse.

It was about this time that my father visited me, on his way back to Glasgow from a business trip. This of course was during working hours and not in visiting time which was rare in *Ganges*, but perhaps because of his RNR time in the 1914–18 war this was allowed. Knowing the almost impossible attempt to stop me smoking, he asked the Master at Arms, who replied, 'If they haven't smoked before, Sir, they don't learn here.' Little did they know that I was already cured of smoking.

The first place I took him was the dreaded Laundry Hill, just in time to see some class doubling up and down, and given a warning frown from the instructor we left. However, my father was not impressed, so later on, after a tour of the mess and approaching four o'clock in the afternoon, and out of sight of the parade ground, I took him to see the 'Janker boys'. These were being punished for minor offences and were in a long line, one behind the other, squatted down on their haunches with wooden poles stretched above their heads. This was a very painful process if they were kept there too long but, now added to this, was the order, 'Rear man to the front.'

This meant that the rear man had to hop twice as fast to get to the front of the line, and now they came past like a crowd of little red-faced frogs, croaking as they hopped to the order. When I first saw this, after going to the Mail Office, I had burst out laughing, only to hear that dreaded phrase, 'Come here that boy,' so I knew how painful that exercise could be. However my father was not impressed and did not demand that he should take me home. Instead he said, 'Ian, at least by the time you are finished here you'll be a hundred per cent fit.'

I knew he meant no harm; it was just his sense of humour, but I was on the point of tears. He took me to Ipswich for a meal, however, and so I had rather the anticlimax of having to say goodbye twice. Dad said his goodbye quickly as he had done at Glasgow railway station, as he knew how emotional I could become, leaving me as I got on the bus back to Shotley village. He drove off for the long journey back to Glasgow, and I in spirit with him. It had been agreed when we had left that I should be back at 'Pipe down' or lights out at 2200 hours. I arrived back just before this time. Michael took one look at my face and withdrew silently. I turned in and buried myself under the blankets.

I though of the time I'd said, 'Dad, take me home, away from this terrible place,' and his understanding smile as he said, 'Keep your chin up, it won't do you any harm, only good,' as he remembered his time at boarding school, much younger than myself. There he had suffered the 'fagging' system, the younger boys acting as slaves to the older ones, and constant bullying and physical abuse, but nothing compared to what twelve-year-old children midshipmen at Dartmouth and on ships had had to put up with and it was not so long before. It happened in Admiral Sir John Hayes' time and was described in his book *Face the Music*. Before that it was the same and in the book *A Midshipman's Hell*, there was a naval officer called Morgan of unbelievable cruelty. The book was banned.

Compared to that, we had it easy at *Ganges*. There was no physical or sexual abuse, bullying, or being made to do anything of an immoral nature. If at times the physical punishments were hard, they were not more than athletes did every day or, for that matter, keep-fit fanatics like myself today volunteer for. As my Uncle Andy, a three-badge AB would have said, 'We had got jam on it.'

Chapter Two

THE DEVIL'S ELBOW

The name 'futtock shrouds', as you can see in the photograph of the mast opposite, was probably a corruption through time meaning foot-up steps or shrouds, as that was what they were, coming out from an angle of about forty-five degrees from the mast and going up to the main top mast platform. Seamen swarming up to the higher yards could go up together over these futtock shrouds whereas, if they tried to go through the 'lubbers hole', an opening in the platform, they would all bunch up and cause a traffic jam. This was in the days of sail and the futtock shrouds were only used for working aloft and not for setting sail.

The mast at HMS *Ganges* had been installed in 1905 and was the highest mast in the Royal Navy, just under 200 feet, and dwarfing HMS *Victory*'s main mast at Portsmouth. Now, as I look at the photograph, I remember that time of terror being stuck at those futtock shrouds, also known as the Devil's Elbow. The other main shrouds slope the other way from below the platform down each side of the mast to the ship's side, in this case the parade ground.

The shrouds comprise six steel cables, and crossing them at intervals at right angles to them are the ratlines, thin cordage, secured at each end to the steel shrouds by clove hitches, so that they could be tightened or renewed. Unlike the steel shrouds that could be tightened up by bottle screws, the ratlines were made of tarred hemp and therefore could become slack; a wobbly step could become dangerous, as could a broken ratline, so the shrouds and not the ratlines were grasped when

The Devil's Elbow.

climbing, the hands moving upwards alternatively, so that, at any one time, one hand always had a grasp.

If you can imagine scaling half way up a tower block, and then leaning out and backwards at about forty-five degrees, without a line holding you from the overhang, and also without mountain climbing gear, crampons, pin hooks, and the like, then you have a good idea of how we fifteen and sixteen-year-old lads felt the first time, most of whom, like myself, had only climbed building sites and the garden tree. We were all right on the mast till we looked down. In one sense it was easier to climb than the way a steeplejack climbs, straight up; as the shrouds were at an angle of 45 degrees, your body was almost upright when climbing as far as the Devil's Elbow, allowing the body to lean back to the full extent of the arms, and looking up, also allowed the knees to come up without being restricted by the legs, owing to hugging the rigging in fear as we did at first.

Now we were fell in four deep at the base of the mast below the safety nets that were supported by steel supports. These were no guarantee of safety, as boys who had fallen had been known to hit them, bounce off on to the adjoining roofs, and be killed. At the order, 'First four, man the rigging,' we stood with one foot up on the rigging, both hands grasping up as far as they could, then at 'Way aloft,' up we went slowly and carefully.

I made my way up gaining confidence by having the others either side of me, thinking, it's not so bad as I'd thought, till I started to climb out backwards, with nothing between except the 'Devil and the deep blue sea',* and looking down, the hard parade ground began slowly to spin, followed by that dreadful vertiginous feeling of falling, falling, falling. Suddenly out of nowhere the instructor was beside me; he must have been watching and immediately saw the signs and swarmed up, no doubt saving me from death or terrible injury. Now he was stretched spread-eagled behind me so that whatever happened it was impossible for me to fall.

I heard his quiet voice saying, 'We all get scared up at this height, and it's a good thing; it makes sure you don't make a mistake. Use it as a stimulus to think and act fast in dangerous situations; this is a time when you're at your best, when all systems are at go.' Now, following his instructions, I reached up as far as I could with my right hand, at the same time stepping up with my right foot, and so on, till at last I found the small raised hand rail that went round the main top mast platform, and hauled myself over it with no trouble now as I would never look down at a height again.

Then began my climb towards what would have been the main T'Gallant yard. Now I heard faintly below me, 'Up you go, Ian,' and smiled to myself at this conquest, remembering my plea at the Devil's

---

*From a ship's construction manual: the devil plate around the ship's side takes the guard rails and plate for the deck plating, so that if you're between that and the sea you're overboard, as I was later in my life on the aircraft carrier *Implacable*.

Elbow, 'Sir, I'm a bit off colour this morning, please, if I can just this once go through the "Lubber's Hole" I'll have a shot at it tomorrow.' Most importantly I had learned something that was again to save my life. Now, with this new found confidence in myself the mast had no terrors for me and I often went over it in my spare time.

It was the 'Dog watches,' six till eight at sea, but now our leisure time, when we dressed in what was called 'night clothing', our thick blue serge suits and light brown low heeled canvas shoes. It was a time when I liked to do a bit of day dreaming away from the crowd. As usual you could not do anything without someone wanting to know where you were going, a compliment in a way as it showed they thought of you, although I did not think so at the time. I told them, casually, 'I'm just going for a run over the mast.'

Now they all looked at each other as if I'd taken leave of my senses. I climbed easily but carefully, reaching the lower main T'Gallant yard, the highest point on the mast except for the 'Jacob's ladder' that would have led to the upper T'Gallant yard if it had been carried and the Main Royal yardarms. This led to the weather protection cap called the Button, which some daring types stood on, the very thought giving me that dreadful vertiginous feeling.

Spread out in front of me was Harwich and the railway station. A short while ago we had wished so fervently that we were on the train home, but now we had settled in and were happy, for some of us the first time in our lives. To the right and directly below was Shotley village, and again to the right but in the distance was the beautiful village of Flatford. I could now see John Constable's beautiful paintings of the surrounding countryside from a different perspective.

Further away in the smoky haze was Ipswich though not visible at that time, and in a complete 180 degree turn was Felixstowe, the beaches visible where we had our Saturday afternoon banyan parties. They got their name from the tropical tree under which seamen of old sheltered. The instructors would draw stores of tea, sugar and milk, and a large messkettle of fresh water, together with a couple of home-made cherry cakes made by their wives and paid for out of their own pockets.

We took two large dipping lug cutters, twenty-five in each boat. These open sail boats had been used by the Cornish fishermen for over a century with success, and also by the smugglers for their fast sailing qualities. They were built by my mother's family in Brixham, Devon, 'the Mitchell boat building family', nearly five hundred years ago, and were then adopted by the RN. They had a large dipping lug foresail, and providing a large crew was available to handle the foresail they were used to give young officers and men instructions in the art of sailing, the only type of boat remaining in which competitive sail drill could be carried out satisfactorily.

Now, tiring of the magnificent view of John Constable's countryside from my young eaglets' eyrie eye view, I climbed carefully down to the main yard that would have taken the main sail. This was a heavy teak quadrangle twice the size of my girth, the angled sides of the quadrangle giving support in the old days, rather than being smooth sided, to the seamen lying across them while furling sail. Their feet would be in the foot ropes that were rove through penants that hung down from the handrail on top of the yard, which were called 'stirrups'.

Now, with my feet in these foot ropes I side-stepped carefully along to the end of the yard, pride of place for the upper yardsmen, candidates for officer in the Merchant and Royal Navies. Here I lay over the yard, day dreaming of my hero Richard Henry Dana from his book *Two Years before the Mast* written in 1836. To furl sail in those days was like brailing up a venetian blind, those on deck doing the hauling while those stretched along the yard bundled the sail up and secured it along the under part of the yard by passing rope stops underneath and securing it.

A strong cold evening breeze blew my thick blue serge collar up to the back of my head. It was coming off the sea, with its tang of seaweed combined with the tarred hemp of the rigging and the faint scent of the huge teak yard held by a massive chain cable to the mast. All helped to create the daydream of being at sea, rounding the Horn in a howling blizzard, now as I became Dana fisting and beating the sail trying to furl it, as the blizzard tried to sweep all of them off the yard.

24

'. . . Our watch was so reduced by sickness, that with the one man at the wheel, we had only the third mate and three besides myself to go aloft, so that at most we could only attempt to furl one yard-arm at a time. We manned the weather yard-arm, and set to work to make a furl of it.

Our lower masts being short, and our yards very square, the sail had a head of nearly fifty feet, and a short leach, made still shorter by the deep reef which was in it which brought the clew away out on the quarters of the yard, and made a bunt nearly as square as the mizzen royal yard, besides this difficulty, the yard over which we lay was cased in with ice, the gaskets and rope of the foot, and leach of the sail as stiff and hard as a piece of leather hose, and the sail itself about as pliable as though it had been of sheets of sheathing copper.

It blew a perfect hurricane, with alternate blasts of snow, hail and rain. We had to fist the sail with bare hands. No one could trust himself to mittens, for if he slipped he was a gone man. All the boats were hoisted in on deck, and there was nothing to be lowered for him.

We had need of every finger God had given us.

I suddenly awoke from my daydreams, to see it was now getting dark, approaching sunset, as another chill wind blew up my collar, and felt fear as my hands were cold and stiff through holding the steel hand rail, my legs stiff in the foot rope stirrups. It was a dangerous predicament. Now I saw Michael and some others of the class below like midgets, their white discs of faces looking up anxiously at this solitary little figure silhouetted in the dying embers of the sun about a hundred feet up, lying across the mainmast yard-arm. Now with concern in their voices, they shouted up, 'Ian, come down, you daft little git, before you break your neck.'

I carefully side-stepped my way along after beating some life into my hands on the yard, as Dana had done, my legs still stiff on the foot ropes, but the main thing was that my hands could still grip. I wisely

1. Flying jib; 2. Outer jib; 3. Inner jib; 4. Fore topmast staysail; 5. Foresail; 6. Lower fore topsail; 7. Upper topsail; 8. Lower fore topgallant sail; 9. Upper fore top-gallant; 10. Fore Royal; 11. Mainsail; 12. Lower main top sail; 13. Upper main topsail. 14. Lower maintopgallant sail; 15. Upper main top-gallant sail; 16. Main royal; 18. Cross-jack; 19. Lower mizzen topsail; 20. Upper mizzen top-sail. 21. Mizzen top-gallant sail; 22. Upper mizzen top-gallant sail; 23. The mizzen royal.

decided to give my usual challenge to the Devil's Elbow a miss, and climbed carefully down through the 'Lubber's Hole,' reaching the bottom cold and stiff to find Michael waiting for me. 'Don't you know that f— mast is dangerous? It becomes dangerous when you forget it's dangerous; don't be so f— wet next time.'

This episode added to my store of knowledge.

Chapter Three

THE SWIMMING POOL

We quickly untied our boots and unlaced our green gunnery school gaiters, carrying them both in our hands as we rushed across the polished deck, dumping them on our beds as we passed on our way to the bag racks that were at the end of the mess, with that ominous, 'You've got three minutes,' ringing in our ears.

Now we struggled to pull the unwieldy kit bags, as big and heavy as some of the smaller boys. This was done by screwing and twisting the bag from its tight fit in the racks. Then, when you had eventually got it out, only to find your sports gear was at the bottom, you had then quickly to restow everything, every so often dumping the bag up and down to shake the contents down.

The same drill was carried out to get the damned thing in again, and woe betied anyone who left his name, blazoned across in large black letters on the bottom, skew-whiff.

Dressed now in sports shirts, shorts, stockings and gym shoes, we doubled towards the swimming pool, Michael our PO Boy in charge. We now discovered the importance in doubling of the cadence or the rhythmical beat of our tackitty boots; now the silent rubber gym shoes made the doubling twice as hard.

We arrived breathless and out of step, to be met by two physical training instructors, Petty Officers with bulging biceps, their appearance and deportment as if they would leap over the top of us in one spring, having springs attached to their feet and pillows stuffed up their chests. The words blazoned across their white sport shirts in black: 'PTI' was superfluous. Now we undressed naked except for a cotton jock strap that covered the front giving protection, for later when we would have to jump off the high diving board, but there was no protection for our bare buttocks.

We became very vulnerable to the orders, 'When you're told to move, your feet don't touch the deck,' 'Move!' 'Wack, oh!' and from a rubber gym shoe this could be painful.

We lined up with swimmers on the left, non swimmers on the right, standing at the edge of the swimming pool. The non swimmers were now given a gentle push and told to swim; this was a big improvement from the old days when they were chucked in from boats moored off the pier head into the cold sea water and strong tides.

Some, to their amazement, found they could swim; others, seeing there was no help being given to those obviously drowning (of course they were led to believe this) also struck out swimming for the first time. The few who were in difficulties were put into life belts on the end of a long pole and then gradually weaned off them. It was harsh treatment, but then they were not being taught swimming for recreational purposes, but for a future matter of life and death on board ship.

So in about the space of two days all fifty of us could swim. Next came the jump from the high diving board, when the jock strap was not for modesty but for protection. This procedure was also for a good reason, as they had found in the past Navy that many young seamen's lives were needlessly lost as they were too scared to jump from the sometimes very high ramparts of a battleship. As the old Admiral, retired, at the Bath Street Recruiting Office Glasgow had said, 'There will be many things you will find puzzling, but remember there's a reason for everything in the Royal Navy.' It was good advice, and I was always able to show others who were disgruntled the reason why. This also helped of course to take the heat out of my own occasional feelings of injustice.

I myself had learned to swim when staying with my grandmother at Rosyth. Her family had, like so many, come up from Plymouth for the dockyard. With the rest of the gang of ten-year-olds I had waded out to this old wreck; the tide came in and I was the only one trapped owing to remaining too long day-dreaming. My Airedale dog Birky came out to me doing the dog paddle so I followed him doing the same and found I could swim. For this, the Navy at *Ganges* passed me as a swimmer, but in later years, swimming from *Repulse* in the thick oil, many passed concerned at my slow progress, shouting, 'All right, Ian?'

Chapter Four

BOAT AND SAIL DRILLS

In the beginning as 'Nozzers', new entrants, we had been taught boat pulling by numbers in a mock-up of a cutter on dry land. This monotonous, soul-destroying drill was done by numbers. Now the real thing in a boat was not much of an improvement, except the feeling of being afloat. The instructor moving up and down the boat amidships used the tiller to correct mistakes, such as 'Bong!' on top of the head, 'Sit upright!', 'Bong' over the knuckles, 'Hands to be width of the shoulders apart!', 'Bong' over the knees, 'Feet to be at an angle of 45 degrees apart!', and so on.

Now the torture began: on the order 1, lean as far forward aft in the boat as possible, without dipping the blade of the oar in the water; then on the command 2, dip the blade of the oar into the water, at the same time pulling back with the arms straight and thrusting with the legs, the feet in the stretchers back until the body is back and past the upright, and the head nearly touching the boy behind. Hold it there in this back-breaking position, until the order 3, when the body springs back to the upright position.

Then, to our dismay, 'As you were. This time everyone will catapult himself upright as one man,' and now the whole process is repeated all over again. After about an hour of this we go on to sail drill, as we now 'toss oars,' jerking them upright, and then boat them either side of the boat. Later we stand either side of the boat, about twelve each side as we are numbered twenty-five to a crew for each boat. We stand with our arms outstretched like firemen waiting to receive someone who has jumped.

Then comes the order, 'Out pin.' This was a pin that went through the clamp on the towing thwart, a specially strengthened thwart that retained the mast in its 'tabernacle', a kind of slot that is bolted to the keel that took the heel of the mast. The mast falls down into our waiting arms, we boat it and out oars then, after half an hour, boat our oars up mast and sails.

After about a week of these drills, so that we could do them in our sleep, they were dispensed with. It was almost a pleasure to go sailing. They usually picked a moderate to fresh breeze, with short choppy waves. We looked on with apprehension, thinking it was the roughest day we had ever seen, but it was good sport sailing with reefed main and fore sail, the gunwales right over as they heeled to the wind, the sea slopping in sometimes as we bailed out. To add to the stability and bring the centre of gravity down we had to sit on the bottom boards, which also gave less wind resistance. It was uncomfortable sitting with a wet backside in our canvas duck suits, but nevertheless we enjoyed ourselves and were allowed to take turns taking the tiller.

We tacked in the area of Harwich, Felixstowe and the pier head, and four hours went past quickly, as before ten minutes boat and sail drill had gone like four hours. Now, approaching the pier, we downed sails smartly, out pin and caught the mast expertly and boated it, then out oars to pull the last hundred yards to the pier head. The boats were hoisted, the sails stowed in their cover and the gear neatly secured each side of the boat, leaving the boat's plug out for the boat to drain. This was always the last thing done, just as the first thing done was to make sure it was in.

Now, tired but looking forward to our supper, we were together again as a fifty numbered class, as we doubled up the steps 'Faith, Hope, and Charity', the way we had come the day we had joined, when I had put my daft polite question. Now, as Michael tried to imitate with, 'Do you tink it will be possible to use those boats tied up at the pier,' the class laughed, and I laughed with them.

We arrived back in the mess tired but happy, but I noticed that some, when they felt in the mood to go boating, lay down somewhere quiet till the mood had passed. Now we grabbed soap, toothpaste and towels, and marched for a change, as now it was in our own time, to the showers. Under the luxurious hot showers we soaped ourselves down with strong smelling 'pusser's' carbolic soap, then the short arm inspection followed by a cold water hose down, completed it. We could not have had more care taken of our bodies if we had been prize race horses, from our teeth and ears, down to our John Thomases, toenails and feet. All that, with the amount of doubling we did, made us begin to feel like horses. The 'short arm inspection' was with raised arms above the head, when our lower parts were examined for hygenic reasons, back and front, but only at certain intervals was this done.

Gradually and imperceptibly the atmosphere in the mess had changed. Gone was the strictness of before and the silence during meal times. We rarely saw our instructors at these meal times which were conducted more and more by our leading boys and PO Boys, and we were now a happy crowd, knowing each other and our failings. Also, we wore blue jean collars with our duck canvas suits, this to show the others in the establishment that we were hard core veterans about to be drafted to sea.

Our doubling started with us swinging into our old routine, 'stamping it down', but was entirely false as we moved just above a walking pace. This was known as the 'Shotley shuffle' and a blind eye was turned by our PO Boys and instructors. Spontaneous laughter would often break out as we were happy. We looked forward to our time in the RN when, having passed Educational Test Part 1, this would take us to Petty Officers and beyond.

It was the last week of our stint in Shotley, and we felt regret and a deep foreboding, more so than we had felt leaving home, as we were now about to face the real world, a dangerous time for us as for all species of the young, as war was about to be declared. This had been our home, and at times, looking back, had given us some of the happiest times of our lives. For some like Michael that was order, discipline

32

and regular meals. The comradeship we had for each other at times exceeded the friendship with my own brothers at home, so on the whole we were happy to be in the RN. Little did we know what death and destruction and horror awaited us.

At the banyan parties, beaching the boats on Felixstowe beach of sand and shingle, little used perhaps because of this, we lit our camp fire to make our tea and heat up our Cornish pasties, swam, sunbathed and played rounders and we were happy. The instructors joined in with us and were completely different from the time we were first under training, showing us the good leadership that we were to copy years later, in being approachable, friendly, fair in all things, without favourites, with no bad language or bullying; but above all, when the occasion arose showing firm discipline and firm leadership. It was important to remember that after being firm in discipline it was easy to be firm again after relaxing this and coming down to an easy relationship, but it was almost impossible the other way round; those that played 'popular Jack' soon came a cropper.

A bare and flat country surrounded the barrack parade ground square, and when the wind blew across it, it became twice as cold, and rifle drill an absolute agony. We had the pleasure of watching the other new entrant classes doing that dreadful torture of rifle drill by numbers, the immaculate instructor out front first demonstrating, then having the class do it. Because it was too dangerous to wear gloves as a rifle could slip and injure someone, the hand seemed to be frozen to the brass butt of the rifle, and every so often the order would be, 'Right, you've got three minutes; warm your hands up.'

This was done at the slope, when the rifle was held on the left shoulder by the left arm bent at the elbow forming an angle of 90 degrees. Warming the hands up was done by banging the disengaged hand on the small of the butt, that portion just above the butt, then holding it by the small of the butt with the hand warmed up allowing the other hand to be warmed. We were issued with thick blue woollen gloves but only wore them on leave. So, caught in the open without gloves in Arctic conditions, this was the best way to warm the hands up to prevent frostbite creeping up on you: painful but effective. In *Two Years before the Mast*, seamen never wore gloves, even when furling sails that were coated in ice, and warmed up their hands by banging them on the yard.

Now the great evening arrived. Tomorrow we would be on our way to join different ships in the Fleet, some to *Repulse*, some to the *Royal Oak*, some to the *Hood*, some to aircraft carriers. Boys were sent generally to the 'big ships' or capital ships, approximately about two hundred to each ship. What a waste of the corn feed of our future Navy, as most of the capital ships were sunk in the first two years of the war, that were anything but a phony war for the Devonport ships. What a waste of young lives and all that training.

Standing silent and obedient behind our clean scrubbed wooden mess tables, heads down looking at our battered tin mess plates and mugs, that were always to smell of Bluebell metal polish, we awaited the order from our instructor to say, 'Grace, carry on. You've got three minutes.' I glanced towards Michael at his small select table of the PO Boys and met his steady gaze as we chanted together, 'For what we are about to receive, thank God.'

This was our last supper together at HMS *Ganges*.

Chapter Five

HMS CORNWALL

A few short stories to show how we lived as seamen at that time.

We arrived on the station platform at Harwich, the time I'd arrived from that long nightmare of a train journey from Glasgow forgotten. Trotting up to us was an old weather-beaten railway porter, who said, 'Right you are, lads, there be a compartment reserved for you up for'd.'

The temptation to salute, say sir, and move off at the double, was the effect Shotley had had on us. We were on draft for HMS *Cornwall*, a light County class cruiser, for the Mediterranean Spring Cruise. It was a boys' sea training ship, manned by boys, except for a steaming crew of professional seamen and officers.

Now on board, we were captivated by the feel of the ship moving under our feet, as she gently rolled alongside Devonport dockyard, with the sound and smell of hot steam, that hushing sound of the powerful intakes pumping fresh air into the ship, and the throb of engines. Next came slinging our hammocks, which was not an immediate success, but we did not mind as the novelty was great.

We soon arrived at Gibraltar, the first leg of the cruise, and were at anchor awaiting a berth alongside the mole. The North African mountains lay opposite, distant in a blue haze. As I was the ship's office stores messenger, and had not a great deal to do running messages, I spent a great deal of my time looking out of the office side scuttle (porthole), standing on a chair as I was still only 5 ft 3 ins. It would be a while before I shot up to 5 ft 9 ins. The sounds and scents that wafted through to me were fascinating and new as this was the first time I'd been outside UK.

I strained my eyes, looking perhaps for the apes or wild animals would show themselves, my mind still fresh with Tarzan, the Apeman, and the mystery of the *Marie Celeste* that was found abandoned in the Sargasso Sea, or so my school story book said. Perhaps, as I'd always imagined, a huge man-eating octopus had come on board and had eaten the crew!

Suddenly, looking down, I nearly fell off my chair in horror, shouting out, 'There's a huge man-eating octopus under the ship!'

There was a dreadful silence in the office; the buzz of talk and the chatter of typewriters ceased. Now, still standing on my chair, my face red with embarrassment, I stuttered, 'Oh, I'm sorry, sir.' It turned out that what I'd seen was part of the starboard propellor showing in the clear Mediterranean sea. Next day I was back, demoted 'part of ship duties'. I'd lost my quiet number.

In the morning we dreaded the order, 'Boys off boots or shoes!' We placed our footwear in the passageway, rolled our trousers up to the knees, grabbed long handled deck scrubbers, and got into line with the others. We scrubbed to the order, 'Scrub for'd; let's see these handles bend; put some weight on them or else.' Now we sounded like an old fashioned steam train, 'Shush shush shush,' till we got to the end for'd; then, 'about turn, scrub aft;' this went on till hearing, very relieved, 'Cooks to the galley.' The cold sea water was said by those Ordinary Seamen and ABs who were allowed to wear sea boots to be good for the feet.

Still burning with humiliation after that last episode, and even though I was suffering like the rest from my yellow fever jab, I went full out to curry favour from the Petty Officer Captain of the top, by working hard at everything he gave me. This so impressed him that I landed another quiet number, Flat sweeper. This was a job where you were more or less your own boss, and trusted to be left on your own to do it. The flat like all flats and messdecks had yellow corkazine kept in place by steel strips, but I must explain first that flats on board ship are literally flat open spaces. I'd noticed that no one had ever thought of polishing these steel strips, so I polished mine till they shone like silver, and it paid off.

The Commander always had his 'doggie,' a midshipman who trailed behind him at a respectful distance ready to bolt off somewhere on a life and death message. Although he was the same age as myself he chose to look down his la-di-da nose, but youth calls to youth and we became friends in the end. One day I was told to report to the Commander's Office and was told I was now one of the Commander's doggies, and found myself sitting outside his office on a stool along with the snotty. We had something in common: he had joined as a twelve-year-old and I at fifteen, but he had had a harder life, almost shocking in its brutality, than I'd ever known. Midshipmen were called 'snotties' because of the brass buttons on their sleeves to prevent them wiping their noses.

Now the Commander poked his head out of his office door, in his usual harassed way, trying to do a dozen jobs at once running a boys' sea-going training ship, with his usual expression, 'Ah, there you are; tell the quartermaster to pipe "Away first picket boats crew," and take this parcel with you ashore to the address on it.'

We had left Gibraltar and then St Tropez, the scent of the tree-lined boulevard's orange blossoms and the quiet beauty of this little French town on the Riviera making a great 'run ashore' for Michael and me. Now we were at Menton, a bit further down the coast, and the infamous haunt of the gambling fraternity. I would be the first one ashore, as we were at anchor awaiting a berth, and when I returned would be besieged by those eager to find out what it was like. Most of them like myself were out of UK for the first time and we found everything fascinating.

The gharry driver was waiting on the quay. It had been commissioned by the ship for official duties and was a horse-drawn affair. The driver sat up in a high seat, and I sat in the open carriage that had a folded back tarpaulin cover like that on an old-fashioned MG. In his fractured English and my unintelligible school French we got by. I showed him the address and, with great show and a crack of his long whip, off we galloped, but only for a short time. When we reached the steep snake winding terraces of Menton, as we climbed, the old horse, I was pleased to see, was allowed to take its time.

The driver was enjoying this sightseeing trip as much as myself, perhaps seeing it afresh through my first time experience and youthful eyes. He explained points of interest, including where the gamblers leaped after they had lost everything. At last we reached the little red-tiled villa with green shuttered windows, perched on the side of the hill almost buried in flowers. I delivered my parcel to a very attractive lady who I presumed was the Commander's wife. She hurriedly took from me a glass of something someone had given me and replaced it with a glass of lemonade.

To the sound of happy laughter, and the clink of ice into glasses I answered their questions as politely as I could, and then stole out to the garden. The scent of the flowers and red tiled roofs of the other villas was pleasantly stimulating after the harsh surrounds of a steel County Class Cruiser like HMS *Cornwall*, which I could see far below like a toy shimmering on a burnished steel sea in Menton harbour.

I was suddenly alert and sprang instantly to attention, my cap tucked under my left arm in the regulation manner, as a voice said 'Ah, there you are, Hay!' Our Commander breezed in to my prompt reply, 'Sir!' The Commander was attired in an old but well cut tweed sports jacket, flannel trousers, scuffed shoes and a soft hat. After his usual smart brass-buttoned three-gold-banded sleeves and gold scrambled oak leaves on his hat brim, he looked scruffy to me. On the lower deck it was said you could always recognise an officer on shore in civvies, as they looked like tramps, but then, few people could keep up two different wardrobes.

The Commander then gave his customary eagle-eyed inspection of me from top to toe and, in his curt way, said, 'Had your lemonade, then off you go.' I returned to the ship by the gharry that had waited for me, the old driver taking his time for me to make the most of this sightseeing trip, he enjoying it as well.

Chapter Six

THE GREYHOUND INN

The top bar of the Greyhound Inn in Brighton was old even in Charles Dickens' time. I was awaiting an old shipmate and sat in a corner by the bow window where one could imagine oneself on the bridge. The sound of the storm of the sea just below contrasted with the warmth and sight of the log fire, as I sipped my double whisky recalling the storms I'd been through. Every so often the old inn would give a slight shudder in the defiant howl and scream of the wind, and there would follow a deep boom as a 'big one' hit the beach below, which would recede with a sucking rattling sound over Brighton's pebbly beach. A rapid staccato of rain blasting the windows would again emphasise the cosiness of the inn.

The gale was steadily increasing from force 7, to the sound of the seabirds' raucous shrieks of joy, as they wheeled and darted in and out of the cold grey sea wrack, to the scent of seaweed and clean ozone air. For some reason I never could smell this far out to sea, where the air appeared only flat and acrid. I now observed the sheer walls of water with their brilliant white topped coiffures, their hair strands like cirrus streaked foam trails behind them, advancing like an invading army in their serried ranks, one after the other into the attack, tumbling and collapsing on themselves in the greedy inward curl that in the past had been known to rip the upperdeck structure of sailing ships. Then in a roar of spent force they made ready for the next one.

There was of course the most dangerous wave, about every sixth one, if you made a rough count, which came stretching its neck up above all the others, seemingly looking all around for a victim. On board ship, hove to in a storm, the vessel's head had to be to the prevailing weather, at reduced speed at just the right revolutions; too much and the bows began pounding; too little and the bows would pay off, bringing the ship broadside on to the pounding, screaming wind and weather, a dangerous position to be in, with crew members maybe suffering injury apart from potential damage to the vessel.

I remember once as a junior navigating officer on a Bay Class frigate the bows falling off to leeward, and struggling up the steep list on the bridge deck towards the battery of telephones to ring down to the engine-room for increased revs, shouting above the screaming and howling wind, to make myself heard. The engine room officer, Shamus, my opposite number in watches, had however in anticipation already put the extra revs on, so the vessel gradually came back to its hove to position. I was thankful for this and that the 'Old Man' did not appear on the bridge, in spite of the sounds of broken crockery coming up from the pantry and the Doc's (cook) bad language in the galley. Captain Morgan, RNR believed in giving his junior officers confidence in themselves. The Bay Class frigates with their broad beams giving a good stability, but with a dumpy look, were called the ugly ducklings of the fleet, compared to their graceful older sisters the V & W Class destroyers on which I had once served as an acting temporary Leading Seaman. I had been in No. 1 mess in the bows of HMS *Vansittart*, a bad place even if you were not inclined to be seasick. These old 1914–18 destroyers that leaked like a sieve were wonderful seaboats, as Admiral Hill Norton points out in his book *The UB War*. With their narrow beam they were known as the 'Greyhounds of the Sea' and in the Battle of the Atlantic outdid the U-Boats in the length of time they could spend at sea.

I took another sip from my double whisky in the cosy Greyhound Inn, recalling these times. Suddenly my mind was wrenched to a memory I'd always repressed in the past, as another heavy roller hit the beach in a thunderous roar. I thought of a time in a small, sandy cove near the Johore Causeway, Singapore. I had just left Michael on the boat secured at Princess Pier Singapore, with much misgivings on his part, so that I could visit the well of an Eurasian at his country residence called the Teak House. How all this came about will be told in another chapter. There lay the two sunken ships with over half our ship's company entombed inside, their steel hulls now burnished shining clean by the strong South China Sea's currents, the drifting sea tumbleweed weeping past. HMS *Prince of Wales* and the battle cruiser HMS *Repulse*.

I remembered the thunderous boom every so often on the small sandy cove together with the soft scratchy papery sound of the tall palm fronds in the gentle South China Sea breezes; the jungle symphony of the crickets' orchestra with their high and low music, and seemingly at just the right moment the little bullfrogs would join in with their croaks.

The fragrant scent of the undergrowth was like an aphrodisiac to me, but to be lulled into this could be fatal; death and destruction were close at hand. I was approaching the Teak House with caution, each foot put down carefully clear of any broken foliage. I suddenly froze to a statue of immobility, almost like one of those hunting dog prints with his body stiff, pointing; one foot in Michael's case was half raised clear of the ground, caught in that instant of time.

The little bullfrog's conductor seemingly swept his baton down in a dramatic flourish for silence, and there was a shattering hush in my ears and taut nerves as I listened so hard that I could not hear the noises of nature. My heart no longer seemed to beat but fluttered up into my mouth like a frightened mouse running frantically round its treadmill.

Now in this dense tropical undergrowth of Singapore the perspiration dripped from me in torrents; I felt alert but relaxed. With the heavy automatic machine gun in my grasp I knew that all my systems were at go.

Chapter Seven

HMS DORSETSHIRE

Another short story to show how we lived as seamen before the war.

That deep unsettling reverie from that dreadful past was suddenly swept away by a familiar voice, 'Ah, there you are, Ian' as he breezed in; not so much of a breeze, more of an intermittant light air helped by his walking cane. After taking a long sip from the double pink gin that I'd already ordered in readiness for his arrival, he began his 'preliminary cast loose drill,' to use a 15-inch gun turret's gunnery expression. The RN had gone to the dogs, it was never like this in our time, and the Government should be kicked out; and here he spluttered, nearly choking on his drink, and said, 'There's talk of sending our Wrens to sea, it'll never work.' In later years he was proved to be correct? Or wrong? Time will tell.

He began his yarn by comparing our old ship the *Cornwall* in which we had both sailed just before war broke out, with the *Dorsetshire* on which he had sailed as a young upper yardsman as candidate for officer long before the Second World War. It was not a boys' sea training ship but a fully operational one, and in the war took part with *Repulse* in the sinking of the *Bismarck*, the most powerful battleship afloat, by one torpedo to starboard and two to port as a *coup de grâce*. Germany never dared to engage the Royal Navy with her heavy units again.

Now he began to relate his time aboard *Dorsetshire*. Act I was about to unfold like a Greek tragedy, as the County Class cruiser rolled gently in a flat calm sea of mirrored beauty, reflecting the shining moonlight as burnished steel. They were passing the Peleponnese in the Mediterranean, home of the Spartan army which fought so bravely and savagely against overwhelming odds, when suddenly a dark cloud swept across the moon, an evil thought from time immemorial. Selene was the moon Goddess, daughter of Zeus, who from his kingdom on Mount Olympus sent bolts of lightning, in anger at the treacherous act that was about to happen.

Stretching out as far as the eye could see were miles and miles of empty ocean, giving one the feeling of loneliness in this empty expanse where the sea meets the horizon in an endless circle. The moonbeams were catching the tops of the glassy swells, bursting into billions of sparkling jewels, that were even more highlighted by the black troughs of the swells in a sea of burnished steel.

The vessel rolled and pitched to a hiss as the bows sank and rose, throwing out streams of bright phosphorescent light each side of the bows from the many millions of plankton creatures that rose to the surface about midnight. It was now 2345, a quarter to the bewitching hour of midnight, and on the ship's address system came the quartermaster's drowsy husky whisper, so as not to disturb the others off watch and sleeping, 'All the middle watch, all the middle watch, middle watch men Heave Ho, lash up and stow,' said from time immemorial in the RN. No bos'n's pipes were allowed in the silent hours, from 2230 at 'Pipe down' to breakfast time, 0700.

Below on the sweltering muggy messdecks slept the crew, almost naked. Pyjamas were never worn by seamen, since from boys training on *Ganges*. Hammock nettles are the cod line strands, twelve in number, that secure the hammock at each end to ropes that were tied at each end to the hammock bars or sometimes hooks high up on the deck head beams. Two hundred on *Repulse* were all slung up like bats in the belfry, and the conditions were enough to send you to it. Chits said, on some hammock nettles, 'Please call; middle watch man,' and these men were now gently shaken by the feet so as not to startle them. No officer or man was allowed to be shaken anywhere else but in this way.

About two feet up from the clean scrubbed orange deck corkazine were the 'police lights'. These were spaced at intervals and shuttered to throw the light down and not upwards to disturb those in their hammocks above the faint gleam of the scrubbed white mess tables.

The hammocks are in rows fore and aft and the ship swings gently below them, as they sleep head to feet sardine fashion, each hammock so close to its neighbour that they might all be sleeping in a giant double bed. To get in or out of your hammock, you have to prize apart the hammocks either side to make a space to squeeze in or out. The hammock stretchers, the wooden battons that keep the end of the hammock open, are only allowed twelve inches. It was said as a joke that if someone coughed we would all suffer broken ribs, but that was the way most seamen lived at that time. In the heat conditions were appalling, with less room than the slave runners gave their slaves, of whom a great many died.

Now, after the 'Heave ho, lash up and stow' call, the faint glimmer of the police lights shows dozens of youthful legs swinging down from above from their hammocks. They hit the deck to stumble to the roll and pitch; sleepily they dress, taking their clothes from where they have stowed them in the nettles at the end of their hammocks.

It is now five minutes to midnight, and again comes that drowsy whisper, 'All the middle watch, all the middle watch, seaboat's crew and lowerers of the first part of port watch to muster.' This has no sooner been said than suddenly from above in the hammocks a mad scramble takes place of late arrivals as bodies tumble down to dress in haste. They have five minutes to make the muster but they always do; these young ODs have got this down to a fine art, as the penalty and discipline is severe for late-comers.

The seaboat's crew are now mustered abreast the seaboat by the leading seaman of the watch, who details off two hands for either side of the bridge wings as lookouts, and one for lifebuoy sentry aft. This is the whole object of the seaboat's crew, 'Man overboard' being more common than you would think. Down aft amidships is a push button 'man overboard' alarm, and on both sides are lifebelts in their racks.

Those not required till the next hour when they relieve those on watch are allowed to stow themselves away in sheltered corners like by the warm funnel and engine hatches, and in wet weather usually in that part of the passageway near the door leading out to the seaboat's deck. In *Two Years before the Mast*, it was common practice in the days of sail in fine weather for the watch on deck, after setting the sails in the night watches, to be able to stow themselves in sheltered places on deck, so the tradition still flourishes.

The leading hand of the watch keeps his watch in the vicinity of the seaboat, and the whole operation is overseen by the Petty Officer of the watch who has a 'roving patrol', but keeps his watch with the Officer of the Watch on the bridge. Now comes a shout down from the wings of the bridge from an alert young Sub Lieutenant: 'For exercise, away seaboat's crew,' which catches everybody out unexpectedly, as most OOWs exercise seaboat's crew either at the beginning or the end of the watch, which is no exercise at all. The crew realise this but, although grumbling (the only privilege a seaman has), knew he is a good officer.

Now comes the mad scramble into the boat, with the leading hand aft as coxswain holding his arm upright with, 'All ready in the boat, sir.' It is not, in fact, as the lifelines hanging down from the jackstay secured between the boat's davits for the crew's safety on being lowered, are, as they described them in a common expression, 'a bunch of bastards'; that means they are twisted up around themselves, but out of sight in the bottom of the boat. The Sub, looking at his stop-watch, says 'That last exercise was very well carried out, keep it up; leading seaman, fall the crew out.'

The leading seaman of the watch usually kept his watch sitting on the brass stag horn in the shape of a cross: by taking a couple of turns diagonally across this bollard the boat could be lowered. He is making sure the others are wakened to relieve those on watch when their stint is up. He is now, as he is used to doing, spinning a yarn with a young ordinary seaman from his mess, unofficially his friend.

The young seaman was about to take his exam for leading seaman so it was natural for the leading seaman to pass on all he knew, and of course the consequences were that they became firm friends, but this time he is by his usual place at the seaboat's bollard and spinning a yarn to an ordinary seaman and it was not his friend Blondy. The heavy balmy heat at night, together with the beauty of the moonlight catching the topes of the low swell, and the slow roll and pitch of the vessel, tended to lull the senses into an hypnotic trance for those above, but below in the depths of the murky ocean some were fighting for their lives. This was a world of hate and bloody carnage and to show mercy is imbecility. It was a question of survival of the fittest, as a flying fish, fleeing desperately from something chasing it, bangs its tail down with a plop on the surface of the sea to gain those life-saving yards, only to go straight down the jaws of another predator that had calculated that in those seconds that would happen.

As a black cloud crosses the moon, the god of thunder, Zeus, roars in anger as he sees what is about to happen as a shape lying on the fo'c'sle discloses itself but out of sight of the bridge and makes also his three second calculation. His heart thumps, the safety catch is off, all systems are at go, he squeezes gently the third trigger pressure away, so gently that he is unaware of the precise second the rifle explodes thunderously giving the small kick in the shoulder. This predator is an expert, one of the very best.

The sound lingers on in the ears, zinging to the smell of cordite fumes and death as the predator breathes them in satisfaction. The leading seaman who before has been sitting on the bollard is pitched violently into the shocked arms of the ordinary seaman he was speaking to seconds earlier, now to his horror covered in gore.

All the rifles kept on board for landing parties, are locked in racks and are outside the wardroom, the officers' accommodation aft; a chain passing through all the trigger guards prevents removal. Here however they find the chain sawed through and one missing. They never found it and never would, it lying somewhere on the bottom of the Mediterranean Sea, nor for that matter the one who fired it. Several witnesses recalled that, in the weeks before at the Royal Marine shooting range, Recassly Malta, they had overheard a very emotional traumatic outburst from Blondy to his Leading Seaman friend. He appeared to be remonstrating with him, repeating over and over again, 'No, no, it was not like that, I did not mean ... it was, it was, listen to me.' As those deep body-wrenching gasping sobs came out in gasps, his voice had risen in despair and desperate turmoil as he felt he was not getting through convincingly, and he said, 'Right, you rotten bastard, this is what you'll get,' and in his clenched fist was a 0.303 rifle bullet.

No one found the rifle, no one saw who did it, so the witnesses' statements together, were only circumstantial evidence. At his court martial Blondy stood, not seeming to care one way or the other as to how it would go, but his good looks haggard as he pleaded not guilty. His Defence Officer objected to the Prosecuting Officer, as he put forward his theory that the rifle had been fired from the starboard side of the fo'c'sle out of sight and below the bridge, but in direct line to the starboard seaboat's lowering bollard where the leading seaman kept his watch.

The Defence Officer now held up the 0.303 bullet, showing the top in his clenched fist and saying to the witnesses, 'Is this what you saw that day on the Royal Marine shooting range in Malta?' The witnesses agreed, then he unclenched his fist to show not the top of 0.303 bullet but the top of a silver propelling pencil.

He was of course found not guilty, as who was to know if someone else might have been involved and had set him up knowing the circumstances, so Blondy tried to put his life together again, mourned the loss of his friend and eventually became a Leading Seaman. Then came 'Upper yardsman candidate for officer'. In the days of sail the Merchant Navy and Royal Navy in the days of sail put their youngest and best seamen in pride of place on the extremities of the upper yardarms, the most arduous and dangerous positions. The upper yardsmen had to be as good as or even better than the older, more experienced seamen, and today this position is still in existence as an expression for future officers from the Lower Deck. Blondy mourned the loss of his friend the Leading Seaman and became one himself, later becoming an upper yardsman and eventually an officer.

The old Admiral took a long reflective sip. I waited, as he said, 'Blondy was gunshy; remember when you were a boy on HMS *Cornwall* under gunnery training how you all shuffled backwards after the fall of shot hooter announced the fuse set. Remember gun firing, the steel deck bouncing away under your feet, the flash of flame and thick brown cordite smoke and the clang of the heavy brass empty cartridge cylinder ejected from the breech. You were brought up short from your retreating shuffle to the rear by a stinging whack across the seat of your tight duck suit trousers from the GI's whistle chain, and the roared order, "Stand still, take your fingers out of your ears." '

The crack in your head of sound from the 4-inch HA (high angled) made even the 15-inch guns seem pleasant in comparison, as we were made to stand under the barrels of 'A' turret outside on *Repulse* and watch the shell leave the muzzle. It appeared like the flurry of three balls and the sound was a deep roar compared to the short, sharp, loud crack of the 4-inch guns. However, for some it took longer than others to get over and get used to, and Blondy was one of them.

After four hours on the rifle ranges, their nerves shot to pieces while being taught, and not knowing Blondy's 'Gun-shy' ailment, this misunderstanding arose.

At the rifle range of the Royal Marines at Recasslie, Malta, Blondy had been flat on his stomach, legs stretched apart, left elbow in the ground acting as a fulcrum to the left arm supporting the rifle, the butt of the rifle tight into the right shoulder. As the right arm and right elbow completed the fulcrum support, the right forefinger curled around outside the trigger guard as a safety precaution, awaiting the order, 'Off safety catches.' On completion by pushing forward the catch, he gently curled his forefinger around the trigger, that had three pressures. Then taking aim through the backsight in line with the foresight, above or below the target depending on whether the rifle shot high or low (that's if it had not been previously 'lined up' in a vice) he fired till the shots hit the bulls-eye.

The next order was 'To your front, in your own time, five rounds, go on.' Blondy did all this correctly, even mastering the trick of breathing so shallowly as not to be breathing at all, as he gently squeezed the trigger like an orange. Some people filed the trigger down to make it more sensitive. The first and second pressures were perfect, but when he came to the third the fear and anticipation of the explosion that was to follow tensed him like a snooker player under pressure and off course he just missed hitting the bulls-eye.

The Leading Seaman, his friend and instructor, not realising Blondy was too proud to admit he was gun-shy even at the court martial accused of shooting him dead, said something like, 'Well, that's that, we're finished,' and the result of Blondy's anger was overheard by the witnesses. One of those witnesses was a marksman, who was never found, but who was a rival to the Leading Seaman's friendship. Therefore Blondy was not guilty of murder.

I rose to refill our glasses, and suddenly remembered that my old friend had begun life in the RN as an upper yardsman candidate for officer and had represented the RN as a marksman at Bisley.

Chapter Eight

JOINING HMS *REPULSE*

We had now finished our sea training on HMS *Cornwall* and joined HMS *Revenge*, an old battleship. This was an operational ship, unlike the *Cornwall* run by boys. Michael and I kept our fingers crossed that we would still be together. The photograph of me on p. 139 is at this time.

Now we were again on draft to *Repulse*. We had no qualms about joining another ship and never had as, unlike the Army and the Royal Air Force where different regiments had different ways, everything was done in the same way on all ships. Sometimes tradition was responsible, and if it had proved to be the best way it was continued. There were of course some minor differences; we said: different long splices, different ships; nevertheless they were all long splices and, because of this, everyone quickly adapted to a new ship.

On the ship's notice board was a short list about six of us on draft to *Repulse*, including our names, much to our disappointment in not going with our mates since *Ganges*. They were to be drafted to *Hood*, *Rodney*, *Renown*, *Royal Oak* and *Ark Royal*. We of course had no idea that *Repulse* was chosen for the Royal Cruise or of the tragedy that would befall the others on HMS *Hood*, HMS *Royal Oak*, HMS *Ark Royal*, and of course ourselves on *Repulse* and *Prince of Wales*, only to mention a few of the 'Guz' ships from Devonport Division all manned by boys, so that by the end of the war few survived from that *Ganges* time.

We arrived on board *Repulse* at Portsmouth dockyard, in the outside berth in pride of place next to HMS *Victory*, that looked very impressive but was only a quarter the size of *Repulse*.

Although the *Victory* in No. 1 Dock looked impressive, we on *Repulse* looked anything but, with coils and coils of electric cable snaking about all over the filthy decks, swarms of dockyard maties, the deafening noise of rivetting, welding and hammering, with huge patches of painted red lead disfiguring everywhere. We looked at all this in dismay, especially the newly replaced teak decking. The tar between the seams had spread out all over the place. Whoever had done it believed in the saying, 'Don't spare the ship for a ha'porth of tar.' It meant that we would be down on our knees for weeks with scrapers, holystones, wire scrubbers, lime, sand and deck scrubbers.

I was given the job of chipping and painting an old deck ventilator and wire scrubbing any loose chips away. My *Cornwall* experience came in handy. A good job is well worth doing, so that when it had had a coat of red lead, then been painted with flattening to be ready for its final coat of enamel, it looked as good as the new deck ventilator alongside it put in by a dockie.

At both watches of the hands next morning, fell in on the fo'c'sle, my painting job had paid off, as our Captain of the FX, 'Shorty' Brown, Petty Officer (who after the war was the Station master of North Road Station, Plymouth) detailed me off like this.

The Chief Buffer read out from his list, shouting out, 'Six hands required for stores party, two each part of ship' which meant, two hands from the quarter deck, two from the top, and two from FX. Michael and I were detailed off from the fo'c'sle, so we doubled out to the front, trying not to show how pleased we were, and took our position with the others to double away and man the stores lorry.

The huge store blocks of Portsmouth Dockyard, that go back to Tudor times, possessed everything from a pin to a 15-inch gun barrel. This time we were at the furniture store house block, to get furnishings for the Royal Apartments that had just been put on abaft the hangars and catapult decks. There were rolls of carpet and the Queen's bed

51

with a plain wooden headboard, a figure of her head embossed on it; its simplicity amazed us.

Items that I was to discover much later were the wooden staves that moved our one-ton 15-inch shells about on deck, to manage them under the grab hoist when ammunitioning ship. They are exactly the same ones as used in Admiral Nelson's day. See the photograph on page 53 showing us de-ammunitioning the ship before docking for emergency repairs, the bow anchor having banged a hole during heavy weather and the cable having slackened, and below it, the same equipment on board HMS *Victory* being used for elevating the guns.

It was 'Stand easy' or tea break, and in the next dry dock to *Repulse* was the *Victory*, that we could see from the store house, so we strolled across to it and asked the OOW permission to come on board. It being granted, we had a good look round, bearing in mind we only had ten to fifteen minutes of our standeasy. The broad side messes had not changed so much; they were the same as ours on board, except about half the length, but secured in exactly the same way, the outboard end attached, but the inboard end secured by a hook and a strop to the deck head, so as to be able to be hoisted up clear for the gun to fire or, as in our case, so that we could scrub out underneath on the deck.

Our pleasant week of store ship completed, we had to shift ship without engines, and we gained great respect for the old dockyard foreman, as he stood on the fo'c'sle with his whistle between his teeth, one foot on the six-inch steel hawser, it flattening itself and smoking round the bitts, knowing by the feel just how much tension the wire could take before breaking. Some when they snap just drop down, others flip around causing dreadful injury; on one ship the cable party lost their legs. After this kind of strain on the hawser, it is so kinked up to be useless, but this is better than causing thousands of pounds worth of damage to the ship.

In the meantime we were fell in in single line abaft the bitts, the ship's securing bollards. It made funny noises and smoked as it flattened itself round the bitts, to our great concern. The First Lieutenant passed with a sympathetic glance, and we were almost

Coincidental depictions of gun crews on HMS Repulse *and* HMS Victory.

tempted to ask if we could move back a bit; however I noticed the old dockyard foreman was watching us as closely as he watched his wire.

Later on, as seamen having to coil up a small hawser, say a two-inch back spring, the coils just refusing to coil down, we flung them down in exasperation, and the only thing left to do with this part of the wire that is kinked is to chop it off. When a wire rope is in this state it is known to be 'a bunch of bastards'.

Our next task on *Repulse* was the beautiful expensive new teak deck, that was now covered in filth, paint, and the caulking of the deck seams. Dockyard mateys had to pay in the seams with oakum, then fill them with hot pitch, as done from time immemorial from the days of sail. We looked at it in complete despair, thinking of the many long hours we'd be down on our knees with scrapers, holystones, wire scrubbers, lime, sand, and deck scrubbers.

Now the mast and superstructure and turrets had been painted, and the beautiful teak deck showed in all its splendour, including the beautiful small teak ladders, and brass rails, with the other bits of brass glittering here and there. With the largest bow flare in the Navy, she did begin to look like the yacht the press described. She had been built on the Clyde by men who were world craftsmen in building ships, though other nations were soon to copy them, in particular Japan and Germany.

Now we tackled that very steeply inwardly inclined bow. It was almost like the futtock shrouds on the mast at *Ganges*, and it meant awkward painting, having to be leaning backwards, and the bowsing in line that kept the stages in had to be tightened or eased away, depending on the level reached, but we enjoyed ourselves. It was done in the old tradition of 'Coal ship'; everyone was over the side in all their old gear, including the officers, and there was much singing and laughter.

Below us on the seaward side the First Lieutenant, the Commander and the Chief Bos'n's Mate ('The Buffer') went round in the pinnace to make sure there were no 'holidays' (spaces missed not apparent to those so close up painting), and also to make sure the expensive paint

H.M.S. REPULSE

COPYRIGHT SPENCER, PLYMOUTH.

Ready for Royal World Cruise.

was put on carefully, to stop the high spirits of the boys, and the ODs' skylarking getting out of hand. For example, when you had finished a 'Fleet', the section you had been painting, you shouted 'Up Top!' until the reply to your shout came: 'Lower.' The stages were secured by rope lanyards at each end. Those above skylarking would shout out, 'Stand by,' as, now standing on both stage lanyards, they would take a few turns off from around the guardrail stanchion or whatever they were secured to, and then turn up and secure them again. The consequence was that when they stood off the stage lanyards you shot downwards at a terrific speed, and *Repulse*'s bow was forty feet from the water line. It gave you quite a shock to the glee of those 'Top sides', as you dropped to be suddenly brought up to a sudden halt.

It took us less than a week to have the decks looking as if you could eat your meals off them. Our ship's company was 1,400, plus two hundred boy seamen as I was at that time, and about thirty midshipmen all under training. The vast number of the ship's company were eighteen to nineteen-year-old ordinary seamen. Not only the deck but the whole ship was made fit for a Royal Party. Here I'm again jumping ahead, as we commenced 'Suggeing', washing down aloft, in preparation for painting; here we enjoyed ourselves, hundreds of feet up from the deck, the figures below walking about like midgets, but without the security of the rigging to cling to like the *Ganges* mast.

We were slung on stages over the side of the Anti-Aircraft director and lookout's position, but of course tended by lifelines. It looked so easy to jump outwards, and it appeared you would be in the sea. The total breadth of *Repulse* was about a hundred feet, so that meant you would have to jump about fifty feet. This is what happened to the twelve boy lookouts at 'Abandon ship'. This is that square box-like structure on the foremast.

The Turret 'Y' and the surrounding screens on the quarter deck were painted in 50/50 enamel blue paint, then polished with Mansion Polish.

The two foot high and twelve foot long brass plate with HMS *Repulse* in embossed lettering on it was on the after quarterdeck screen; at the foot of the gangway was a teak stained stand that supported the lifebelt with again in small brass letters the ship's name. Finally a Royal Marine stood with his rifle.

In the dog watches, the evenings, we would gather on the fo'c'sle, about a thousand of us, with our Royal Marine band and, led by 'Jimmy the One', the First Lieutenant, we would sing 'Shenandoah' and 'Uncle Tom Cobley and all'. We were happy and looked forward to our time in the RN. Most of the ship's company were from Devon and Cornwall, the rest from the North.

Repulse was finally painted from truck to stem to stern. The teak deck, in its new splendour of yellow teak, would soon change to white with its many scrubbings. The ornamental brasswork sparkled everywhere. We were dressed in our No. 1 best suits that were tailor made and clung to our youthful slim shapes; our blue jean collars, 'dhobied' to a light blue Mediterranean colour, fluttered in the breeze and our bell-bottom trousers covered the toes of our shoes. We were fell in for 'cheer ship,' a practice run for when His Majesty would arrive.

'Three cheers for his Majesty!' came through on the loud hailer. Our caps were then seized by the right hand moving across the body to the left side of the cap brim on the command 'One', then on the command 'two', we raised the cap from the head, the white disc of the hat showing outboard. Then on the command, 'three' we circled the cap, shouting 'Hurrah!'

From shore sides the long lines manning the ship's side and the white caps and hurrahs were impressive, but for us the sheer monotony doing it by numbers till we got it right nearly made us feel like jumping in the 'Ogwa'.

The red carpet that would greet the Royal party as they stepped off the Portsmouth dockyard station train was stretched out at our gangway, and above in huge three-foot brass lettering ten feet long on the quarterdeck screen would spell out HMS *Repulse*. That no doubt in a short time would shine dully beneath the South China Seas, along with the hundred per cent enamelled paint work. War had been declared and the Royal cruise was cancelled.

Michael, Walter and the rest of our boy seamen and ODs who had born the brunt of the cleaning took fiendish joy in covering the paint work, brass work and the beautiful teak decks with camouflage paint. The bosun's pipe shrilled out 'Special sea duty men, to your stations; cable party muster on the fo'c'sle; close A, B and C doors; down deadlights [the steel plates that came down over the side scuttles].' We headed north on Arctic patrol a month before war was declared so whatever anyone might say, the RN was ready.

Chapter Nine

MY UNCLE ANDY IN THE 1930S

In the 1930s, my Uncle Andy was in the Royal Navy which was going through a difficult period. My aunt along with thousands of other RN wives and families was on the poverty line: 'She took in washing,' was the saying then. The result was the infamous Invergordon Mutiny, which lost the respect of the nation after so many hundreds of years. Even more devastating was the loss of world confidence by going off the 'Gold standard'. Winston Churchill was First Lord responsible.

Now discipline was slack; there was not the care, or the pride in the uniform. A good description of this was the old seaman on a Player's cigarette packet; the black silk scarf, its origin to help keep the sweat from the eyes in the sailing battleships of yesterday, tied loosely and haphazardly; even more carelessly then was the bow of the cap ribbon. See how neat it was on myself on the frontispiece, it was tied individually by the ABs for us boys, and then sewn neatly in place, but the jumper in Andy's time was loose and ill fitting, as were the trousers slack, ill fitting and shapeless.

In contrast our trousers were tailor-made to measure, the jumper and trousers fitting our youthful forms snugly, tapering to bell bottoms, a pleasant sight to the public as our bell bottoms flapped and our blue jean collars, Mediterranean coloured, ruffled in the breeze. We wore light black court shoes sometimes as in the old days, traditionally with a buckle. Some people sewed small coins into the end seam of the trousers for effect. We boy seamen, the new generation shortly before

My Uncle Andy.

the war broke out, were the regeneration of what the RN had been before the Invergordon Mutiny. Sadly most were to be lost before that war was to end.

Now the Bos'n's Pipe shrilled out, followed by the quartermaster's call, 'Boy seaman Hay 1st class, lay aft at the double,' and on the quarterdeck was my Uncle Andy.

My uncle was now a three-badge Able Seaman, and destined to remain as one for the rest of his service time, for taking part in the Invergordon Mutiny. 'Mutiny' was the wrong word, as it was no more than a protest at the wretched conditions imposed not on themselves but on their families, no more than today's legal shop floor representative. But they had sworn loyalty to the Crown and, above all else, their Country. Andy was well known in the Fleet, from the lower deck to the ward room, and because of this had now been given permission to see me during working hours, otherwise it would have meant requests and endless explanations.

His first words to me were, 'Ian, you really look smiget,' whatever that meant. I took it to be a compliment; it was an old expression before our time. In comparison, it was hard to recall how he had once looked as a young Petty Officer, and to use a present day phrase, he looked like a 'walking scran bag'. This was the place on board ship where any gear left sculling about was placed, and only redeemed by giving an inch of soap. So the mess decks were kept tidy.

He now stared in unbelief at our mess, although the layout was the same both in his day and indeed, in Nelson's. The broad side messes were little changed except that in earlier days the muzzle-loading cannons were between the messes. What startled him were the mess shelves stocked with food for snacks, cheese, bread and butter, cocoa, coffee and tea, and also the full set of china crockery, knives, forks and spoons and the menu: for example, breakfast – coffee or tea, fresh rolls, grapefruit, bacon, eggs and tomatoes. In my uncle's day all he had was a tin dip, about the size of Christmas pudding bowl. (In *Ganges* these had been used for our sweet, and I expect they were left over issue from earlier times in the RN.) For my uncle, this was washed out after soup and the dinner eaten out of it, washed again for the sweet and for tea. He had had to supply his own knife and fork, mostly making do for everything with just the knife. Our mess stools were covered in soft white rubber foam seating.

One thing still remaining in our present time, as in his day and as in Admiral Nelson's, was a small wooden cask, brass bound, at the head of the mess. From time immemorial this was the seat of the leading seaman in charge of the mess. In the days of sail it held the mess's rum issue, a pint of rum per man per day, until Admiral Vernon put a stop to this. Because he wore a green grogram coat, rum became known as grog.

Uncle Andy moved about examining this and that, with his habitual expression, 'Ian, you've got jam on it!' I remembered the time as a very small child, when Uncle Andy was on leave after the mutiny, and now disrated from PO to AB and my aunt needed every penny they could scrape together. After my father had criticised the way he had painted our garage, he said, 'What do you want, jam on it?' It had puzzled me then!

The next thing that interested him was the poster in all mess decks about unfair treatment. Yes, he had known about it when this had come about after the Mutiny, but here was the importance: it was posted up so that everyone could read it. Earlier, there had been doubt as to whether Jack should be allowed to see it, and the notices were suppressed. A copy of this can be seen on page 63. The *Daily Mirror* was banned for us to read, so that we all wanted to read it and it was read more than the *Express*.

It was now noon and as the goffer stall was opened I adjourned for a 'goffer', a lemonade drink that at that time most of the young ABs who were not entitled to 'draw' (be issued with their two of water one of rum, a small teacupful – you can imagine the potency of the drink), drank instead. Later in the war Captain William Tennant 'cleared lower deck' to expound on the health aspect in the tropics, and for us to put in for our tots. Of course those under age boys and ordinary seamen could only drink this lemonade supplied by the NAAFI called goffers.

My Uncle Andy retired to the holy of holies, the fo'c'sle locker, where Bagsy was an old shipmate. There was a delegation now in conference, but mutiny was far from their minds, as they chalked up the odds on the coming race on a huge blackboard. This was gambling and in a sense forbidden, but if organised like tombola or, as it is now known ashore, bingo, it was permitted. This was all due to a loophole

S.—212. (Revised May, 1947.)

REPRESENTATIONS ABOUT CONDITIONS OF SERVICE AND COMPLAINTS OF UNFAIR TREATMENT,

PART I.

REPRESENTATIONS ABOUT CONDITIONS OF SERVICE.

Any Petty Officer, Non-Commissioned Officer or Man who wishes to make any representations affecting his welfare, or has any suggestions to make connected with the Service, may proceed in accordance with the following procedure.

PROCEDURE.

1. He must make his representation (through his Divisional Petty Officer or Non-Commissioned Officer) to his Divisional Officer.
2. Each person must make his own representation. Joint representations by two or more persons are not allowed.

(NOTE.—These instructions do not alter

(a) the procedure by which a man may bring a request before an Inspecting Officer at an Inspection :
(b) the custom by which a man is allowed to request, through his Divisional Officer, to see the Captain about a private matter :
(c) the custom by which complaints of an immediate kind may be taken before the officer of the Watch.)

DUTY OF PETTY OFFICERS, NON-COMMISSIONED OFFICERS AND LEADING RATINGS.

It is the duty of every Petty Officer, Non-Commissioned Officer or Leading Rating to keep himself informed of any cause of dissatisfaction among the men and to inform his Divisional Officer so that the matter may be investigated.

PART 2.

COMPLAINTS OF UNFAIR TREATMENT.

Any Petty Officer, Non-Commissioned Officer or Man who feels that he has been unfairly or unjustly treated in any way, may, after due consideration, make a complaint in accordance with the Rules.

THE RULES.

I. THE RULES FOR MAKING COMPLAINTS PROVIDE AS FOLLOWS:—

(1) The complainant must make a request in the ordinary way to see the Captain "in order to state a complaint."
(2) He may ask any officer in his ship to 'advise him and help him in stating his case at all stages, and this officer will explain the rules to him. If he does not choose anyone to help him, an officer will be detailed for this purpose.
(3) When he sees the Captain the complainant is to state his complaint verbally in accordance with the custom of the service.
(4) In making his statement the complainant should do no more than state the facts complained of and explain wherein the injustice or unfairness to him lies.
(5) The complaint must not contain any statement which the complainant knows to be untrue.
(6) The complaint must be made in respectful language, and must contain nothing which is insubordinate or contrary to discipline, except in so far as is necessary to state the facts.
(7) Each person must make his own complaint. Joint complaints by two or more persons are not allowed.

II. IF THE COMPLAINANT IS NOT SATISFIED WITH THE DECISION OF THE CAPTAIN, THE RULES PROVIDE (AS WILL BE EXPLAINED TO HIM BY THE ASSISTING OFFICER) FOR HIS THEN MAKING A WRITTEN COMPLAINT WHICH WILL, IF HE DESIRES IT, BE PASSED UPWARDS TO EACH SUPERIOR AUTHORITY UNTIL IT REACHES THE ADMIRALTY.

THE DECISION OF THE ADMIRALTY IS FINAL.

III. BREACHES OF RULES I. (5) OR (6) ARE PUNISHABLE OFFENCES.

IT MUST, HOWEVER, BE CLEARLY UNDERSTOOD THAT NO PETTY OFFICER, NON-COMMISSIONED OFFICER OR MAN WILL BE PENALISED IN ANY WAY FOR MAKING A COMPLAINT IF HE FOLLOWS THE RULES.

PART 3.

COMMUNICATIONS TO THE PRESS, ETC.

OTHER METHODS OF SEEKING REDRESS OR VENTILATING A GRIEVANCE THAN THOSE PROVIDED FOR IN THE QUEEN'S REGULATIONS AND ADMIRALTY INSTRUCTIONS SUCH AS WRITING TO NEWS-PAPERS OR OTHER PERIODICALS ON SUCH MATTERS, ARE FORBIDDEN. IN THIS CONNECTION ATTENTION IS DRAWN TO QUEEN'S REGULATIONS AND ADMIRALTY INSTRUCTIONS ART. 2406 WHICH FORBIDS ALL COMMUNICATIONS TO THE PRESS ON ALL MATTERS RELATING TO THE NAVAL SERVICE OR ANYTHING OF A CONTROVERSIAL NATURE AFFECTING OTHER DEPARTMENTS OF THE PUBLIC SERVICE OR RELATING TO MATTERS OF PUBLIC POLICY, WITHOUT SPECIFIC ADMIRALTY AUTHORITY.

NOTE.—The regulations governing the method of making representations about conditions of service or complaints of unfair treatment are contained in Arts. 1850 and 1851 Queen's regulations and Admiralty instructions. This notice does not in any way supersede or replace either of these Articles but is issued for the purpose of making them more generally known.

that stated that in theory we were outside UK when at anchor or even tied up alongside; an example of this was the duty free cigarettes. A large proportion of the officers and men took part in this. Bagsy and his colleagues were the bookies and they took the money that made it worthwhile for everybody.

The Bos'n's pipe went and the call announced, 'Out Pipes'. This dated from long ago when for seamen the pipe was the favourite smoke. Another pipe was 'Clean out and stow away spitkids' but these were only used as large ashtrays; they were large, flat, round receptacles once used to spit in after the pipe smoking. Now 'Out pipes,' meant it was a five-minute warning for the pipe 'Both watches of the hands fall in.' This then was the commencement of work in the afternoon. My uncle parted with again, 'Ian, you've got jam on it. Don't forget your aunt wants to see you.'

I felt sorry for my uncle for being married to my aunt who was an awesome character. Knowing how 'Pusser built', stickler for anything Navy, she was, just before ringing her door bell, I undid my cuffs and rolled them back to show two Chinese silk dragons stitched on, the fashion then. I then put my hat flat back, so that when she came to the door she simply erupted with, 'Square yourself off, young man, you look like a Chinese quartermaster off watch. One of these days you'll be brought up with a round turn and two half hitches.'

When the war broke out she joined the Royal Marine Women's section as an ordinary Wren, but in no time after promotion became the equivalent of the Master at Arms. The story goes that when once invited to an 'at home' on one of our destroyers as chaperone to the young Wrens, on going up the gangway she told the startled young quartermaster, 'Get that after back spring tightened up!'

Chapter Ten

THE INVERGORDON MUTINY

There were only a few ships involved, the rest of the Fleet stayed loyal, but what was merely a protest turned into a full scale uprising on the ships at Invergordon. It was all through the inability of the Admiralty to direct Admiral Tomkinson on his Flagship *Warspite* who waited and waited for an answer to his desperate signals. Nor would they communicate with the delegation led by Able Seaman Leonard Wincott of HMS *Norfolk*, a County Class cruiser. He was aged only twenty-four, and his delegation were simply stating that they would take the ten per cent cut in wages if it was fair, and stressing they were loyal to King and Country. All this got out of hand with the Admiralty's panicstricken silence. They 'froze at the controls' when action and leadership were needed, then as usual tried unsuccessfully to cover it up. Also as usual, MI5 bungled it, implying that it was a TUC and Communist take-over bid. This was proved completely unfounded.

A few stokers (engine room mechanics) returning on board ship HMS *Rodney*, sang the Red Flag. Poor *Rodney* always got the blame, as it was again to do at Scapa Flow many years later concerning a sheep. Now however the ships involved were *Repulse*, *Hood*, *Dorsetshire*, *Rodney*, *Nelson*, *Norfolk* and the Flagship *Warspite*. The seamen's and officers' pay had been slashed by ten per cent by the Labour Government, the basic pay of an average Able Seaman being 1*s*. 10*d*. a day, plus increments of a penny for each good conduct badge: about threepence a week plus grog money, about the same for those who did not draw their tot of rum.

So all in all, they had been having a hard time supporting their families before; now it was almost impossible. The cut in pay was done to balance the budget (where have we heard that before?) which they had estimated at £33 million, only to discover it was £170 million. The delegation leaders with Wincott were Able Seaman O'Toole and Telegraphist Shields. They were now in the Fleet canteen at Invergordon behind locked doors with a large crowd from most of the ships present, about two thousand men, plus those returned from a football match and those who had attended the Highland Games nearby. The Fleet canteens the world over were always given a lot of leeway for Jack, who lived in close confinement more than any civil prisoner, needed to let off steam. The shore naval patrols always gave them a wide berth.

However, back now at Invergordon Fleet Canteen in 1931. The shore naval patrol normally would have steered clear, but now, with so many ships' companies involved, they decided to have a look. Lt. Elkins and his shore patrol, finding they could not get into the Fleet canteen, went around and got in through the Petty Officers' entrance. No Chief or Petty Officer was involved, or Leading rates. (Admiral Nelson, Chiefs and POs are the backbone of the RN.) Lt. Elkins and his shore patrol listened to speaker after speaker, in the seamen's canteen.

Now Lt. Elkins and his patrol listened to the speakers, all showing their three good-conduct badges of twelve years or, as some put it, twelve years of undetected crime. One large, drunk, three-badge AB got up with no cap and was immediately shouted down; this was to be a serious discussion. Lt. Elkins patrol were keeping out of sight in the POs' canteen but Lt. Elkins himself eventually came into the seamen's canteen. He was at last spotted to cat calls of, 'There's a spy in the camp.' Then things began to get rough, and glasses were being chucked about, as usual in these fracas from Gibraltar to the China Fleet Club, Hong Kong. One missed Lt. Elkins and hit a seaman behind him who was off *Repulse*.

The outcome, as at one at Flotta canteen many years later, was resolved by the duty Royal Marine's platoon, but in the meantime the seamen and the Marines also on shore leave formed a rugger scrum, and forced Lt. Elkin and his patrol outside where again the doors were locked. At last their meeting ended and the different Ship's Companies made their way back to the pier to await their liberty boats to take them back to their ships in a quiet and orderly fashion. Their leaders made sure that they did so and ensured that the seaman who had flung the glass that had just missed Lt. Elkins apologised to him.

Lt. Elkins arrived in *Warspite*'s wardroom to be met with loud laughter when he described how he'd been chucked out of the canteen, so at this time the uprising was not treated seriously. Now Admiral Tomkinson was receiving no reply to his many signals; he was a man of considerable resources, you don't rise from Midshipman to Admiral unless you have them.

The Admiral decided that one way out of this was to get his Fleet to sea, where the men were kept busy and would not be able to get together. This in fact had the opposite effect in that it brought about a coalescence of them; fused together they were even more determined.

Repulse was the first to be sent to sea, hoping that by her example the rest would follow. Now came the bugle call on the ship's Tannoy, echoing around the Fleet, followed by the Pipe, 'Special sea duty men to their stations, close "A", "B" and "C" doors, cable party muster on the fo'c'sle.' *Repulse* was soon slipped from her buoy.

She got underway for her 15-inch gun's turret's sub calibre shoot. This, to save tax payers' money, meant that small 2-lb guns were inserted into the barrels of the larger guns. By also firing small 2-lb shells they could carry on as they would have done with a full 15-inch shoot target practice. Furthermore the tug towing the target was in less danger of being hit by a 15-inch shell weighing a ton.

The others, *Dorsetshire*, *Rodney* and *Hood*, and others gathered on their fo'c'sles and jeered, 'You shower of West Country Scabs,' as *Repulse* passed them, and refused to sail. The *Dorsetshire* stokers refused to go below to 'Flash up' (raise steam), so the Captain sent the

Chief and Petty Officer stokers below to do it. The seamen on deck on the fo'c'sle also refused to let the cable party work.

On the Flagship, HMS *Warspite*, the Admiral, determined to go to sea, was meeting similar conditions as on the *Dorsetshire* but decided to go full ahead and break out by breaking cable. This does not mean literally breaking the cable, but is a term meaning unshackling the cable. This meant putting a senhouse slip on about three links from the end of the cable, in the cable locker, unshackling and now the weight of the cable, and the anchor on the sea bed is held by this slip below in the cable locker. Now all that was required was to buoy the cable and knock the slip off, so the cable ran out, buoyed for picking up later.

This process was however defeated. Jack sat down on the cable – in fact, about two hundred men. After much discreet signalling round the Fleet, Wincott and his delegation agreed to the compromise that providing a hardship fund was set up for those in most need, they would agree to the ten per cent cut in wages. This was how the first Royal Navy Welfare board came into being. Wincott was helped in this by a former shipmate who was now editor of the *Blue Jacket*, the Fleet's newspaper, the forerunner of today's *Navy News*.

HMS *Repulse* returned to her home base, Plymouth, in a deadly silence from the British public, and even more so in Devonport where the ship lay in the dockyard, in the crowded Fleet Club and the seamen's hotel in Morice Square, called 'The Free State' as so many men from Southern Ireland having spent their leave money, now stayed there. Many after completing their time settled in the area and most people are not aware of the great numbers of Irish who served in the Royal Navy, my life-long friend Michael O'Hern being a good example.

The crowded Fleet Club listened again to their mutiny leaders, and it was decided to go round the pubs and put their case. They felt confident as this was a strong Labour area, but to their surprise they met only silence. The public felt they had been let down, and it was to be a long time before that trust was renewed.

My eighteen-year-old boy has taken a keen interest in this

manuscript as, after all, it's about an eighteen-year-old ordinary seaman who didn't have a teenage life but was happy just to survive. He turned to me with, 'Ian, what happened afterwards, did they hang them?'

I replied, 'Of course not, they don't hang mutineers now.'

He replied, 'I meant the Admiralty.'

Chapter Eleven

ARCTIC PATROL

Somewhere on Arctic patrol we were on board the battle cruiser *Repulse*. Part of our duties as boys and ordinary seamen was to mop down every so often the insides of the turret from the condensation that formed through the warm air in the turret meeting the ice cold steel sides of the sub-zero temperatures outside. Now, in a white-out of snow flurries, sleet and gusting hail squalls and the wind howling in its low monotonous intermittent sounds, the deck hatch and conning hatch above in the deck head of the turret's control cabinet were both open to try and prevent this by air circulation. Now the ears would ping as she rose to another huge sea, and on the way down, 'thump' as the bows hit the bottom of the trough. There was a shuddering and creaking sound as the bows dug in from steel plates that were put into the 'bending stress' under tremendous pressure, as thousands of tons of foam-crested water in a roar poured over the bows then over aft; then another roar and howl as she rose, the howl silent before shut off when she was in the trough, now in a scream of defiance as the sea cascaded in white torrents from the bows to a sickening wild gyrating motion describing circles in the air.

This mopping operation had to be done, otherwise it was like living in a Chinese water-torture chamber or tropical rain forest, but in the Arctic, with its drip, drip, drip, on us night and day. To prevent this was not mainly for our benefit but for our two huge sleeping giants, sleeping peacefully side by side, ready to awaken in an instant to devastating roars. They must at all cost be kept clear of cold and damp.

Mack, Michael and myself, between 'A' and 'B' turrets' barbets.
Taken by Jan.

After a week being closed up at action stations, we were allowed in dribs and drabs to the mess decks for a hasty meal. Now we stood abaft the huge gun's breeches as big as barn doors in the space in the rear of the turret. In one corner was the turret control cabinet, that could control and fire the turret independently from the rest. The cabinet's crew were Lt. Cdr. Clark, 'Nobby' to us, and two midshipmen and Michael. There was a small range-finder attached to the turret operated by Leading Seaman Jan Horsford. This was 'A' turret on *Repulse* and in 'A' turret on the battle cruiser *Hood* they would be suffering similar conditions in similar gun positions. We were dressed in oilskins and sou'westers, and the three badge AB Bagsy Baker, Captain of the right gun, broke into song as he was wont to do in his deep bass voice with 'Fishermen of England'. The other ABs laughed though it was the last thing we felt like, but we managed to raise a smile; we knew it was Bagsy's way of subtly reminding us that he'd had it a lot worse, as a boy in the battle of Jutland when they started

71

HMS Repulse.

chucking 15-inch high explosive bricks about. Ships don't just sink; thousands of men are blown to eternity in minutes.

Bagsy I've already described. The Captain of the left gun was Taff Thomas, a large AB with distinct features as if carved from stone or coal. In fact the small blue marks were caused by chips from the coal face when he was a boy down the Welsh coal pits. Smudge was a sixteen-year-old boy fresh out of *Ganges* as left gun sightsetter who came from Mousehole in Cornwall; sixteen-year-old Cussworth was right gun sightsetter, from Yorkshire, and I was centre sightsetter in between the guns in my lonely position up for'd under the 'blast bags'. My back faced for'd looking aft unlike everyone else facing for'd, so from my position I could see all that happened in the turret. I had two range and deflection dials that could control the turret in elevation and depression. This information I supplied both to Smithy in front and to the person facing me who could control the whole turret if need be, a thin alert Southern Irish man who always reminded me as he peered into his periscope sights of an inquisitive fox terrier at a fox hole. Michael was the turret's cabinet crew along with a midshipman and Lt.-Cdr. Clark.

'Nobby', as he was known to us, was typical of the new breed of officer in the RN after the Invergordon Mutiny: approachable, friendly, fair in all things and above all firm in his leadership, he was large and friendly and like an old bear as he came out of his lair, the control cabinet. He joked with us, mainly the boys and ordinary seamen who knew we could get away with some things other couldn't, as he explained that the reason he walked about the turret in his stocking feet, was he had once been a door to door salesman in Manchester. Bagsy was shocked at our remarks to Nobby. 'You wouldn't shoot us, would you?' we said, pointing to the service revolver at Nobby's side. Nobby replied, 'It's empty and only for show.' Later his promotion and a 'Brass hat' came through, and he went to command a light cruiser. We were sorry to see him go.

No. 3 on the right gun rammer was another West Country man, Jan Tucker, with swarthy good looks and wearing gold earrings, unusual at that time before the fashion of today. The rammer was like a huge bicycle chain coiled down inside the gun loading cage. This could be described as a lift that came up from the shell room and magazine with, as we described it, the meat and veg, shell and cordite. The ammunition was then rammed in, the shell first then the cordite silk bags second.

On the left rammer was Scouse Hogarth, leader of our 100 Crazy Gang, a hard man refined down to muscle and bone from his visits to Pompey detention quarters and one of Bagsy's lieutenants.

The midshipman was friendly but a quiet reserved type who like myself didn't involve himself too much with the others. It was a case of my dreadful ailment, self consciousness, at that time in my life; but then, we were nobodies, as Bagsy reminded us, to be seen and not heard.

Now Bagsy finished his 'Fishermen of England' song, and *Repulse* played one of her spiteful tricks on us by pretending to roll to starboard but then giving a savage lurch to port, taking us all off guard. We went helter skelter down to the port side to bang up against the latrine bins. The smell had not been apparent before, but now with the clean fresh Arctic air, the smell of excrement, hydraulic fluid oil and grease was too much for Smudge, Cussworth, Michael and myself. Our arms around each other for support, we had a good spew, to the cheers from the others. This was followed by a bang as a big one hit the turret making it shake, and water came down through the turret's cabinet hatch and bubbled up through the deck hatch. We put the pumps on down in the working chamber and after mopping up were soon dry and snug again as we heard ABs Gibble and Parkinson's wheel spanners clanging, opening up valves to the powerful pumps.

Watching Commander Prince Charles on TV and the instant reaction from the seamen to him, I'd say he has all the qualities in an officer mentioned above. In my humble opinion he would be good to serve under.

The pipe 'Hands to change into comical rig' had been made a long time ago. This meant wearing any old clothes you fancied, as long as you wore a cap on the upper deck. Now we were all dressed like a crowd of tramps. Lt. Cdr. Clark, the turret officer, was wearing an old pullover, his old uniform jacket with the faded gold lace green on his sleeve hanging off and old flannel sports trousers. We were in our 'bundles from Britain'; someone had a jersey with sleeves down to the deck, I had on a balaclava and multicoloured pullover.

Those that wanted to grow beards had to meet the standards, and that meant a full square set, shaped by the barber to fit the face, no spaces, and above all no fancy Van Dycks, China or goatees. They had to request through their Divisional Officer to see the Commander to begin to grow one, and then, after a suitable interval, were seen again to see how it was progressing. If it was not up to scratch, they were given the order, 'Shave off'.

The turret cabinet hatch was in the roof or deck head of the turret, the hatch like the cabinet reinforced even more than the turret itself with four-inch thick armoured plate. The Turret Officer, when we were in cruising stations, would let us sit outside on top of the turret for a breath of fresh air.

Stowing our oilskins and sou'westers away, we changed into what had once been our *Ganges* issued overcoats. These were of good quality, and made under licence by Aquascutum of Regent Street, London, and other famous tailors. In the past they had been well looked after, hung up in a special corner set aside for them on coat hangers in the mess deck, our names stamped on the inside. They were now buttonless and stained with cocoa, paint, grease, and hydraulic fluid from the turret, tied at the waist and cuffs by cod line and everybody used anybody's that was handy.

There were never enough duffle coats to go around, except for the upper deck guns crews, so that going on watch lookout (in defence and cruising stations we did our share of lookout from the turrets), using old woollen socks for gloves, we stood shivering as the relief handed over his warm duffle coat for us now to wear. We had been expecting more coats from a clothing contractor at Greenock the last time we had been there, when we were awaiting another of 'the Winston

Specials'. However the contractor was an Arthur Daly type who dealt in things that fell off the backs of lorries and that included our duffle coats. He had made a pay day out of us, as land sharks had done for centuries, so now we were not only fighting a war for them but making a profit for them.

The lookout duties were one hour on, one hour off. The position outside on the wings of the bridge was a swivel seat attached to a fixed steel pedestal that had a bracket to fit the binoculars that were clamped in place. Underneath was a brass bearing plate from for'd marked 0 to aft 180 degrees, so that by adding the true ship's head to the bearing you were on you got the true bearing, which only the bridge needed to know.

Radar was in its infancy. Our eyes were the ship's radar, very important as the battle of the *Bismarck* and the battle of the Japanese suicidal aircraft were to prove to us later. We each had a sector to search, beginning at the top from left to right, and coming down slowly in stages of steps to the horizon. Then we used a trick we had learned, straining our eyes, pushing the binoculars in a quick up and down movement, above and below the horizon, to pick up something not seen before. Sometimes this might be the faint spider of ships' masts showing just above the horizon, in which case you sang out its bearing. That was followed by the alarm and an ear splitting bell, as we went to action stations, only to be told, 'False alarm'. Captain William Tennant never rebuked us, but encouraged us in this vigilance.

Sometimes we saw an Arctic skua, a true sea bird that goes deep sea, and stays on the sea only going ashore to mate. After two years on *Repulse* I was beginning to feel like one. The wind howls in all kinds of tunes, to flurries of sleet and snow and gusting squalls so that we had repeatedly to clean the glasses with the piece of chamois leather.

I would hear the Captain's voice say, 'You're doing well, Ordinary Seaman Hay; only ten minutes left of your watch.' He knew all our names. Standing beside him was Sub-Lt. J.O.C. Hayes.

In woollen jerseys, oilskins, sou'westers and sea boots it was plain to see that the Captain and his young Sub-Lieutenant were also suffering from lack of duffle coats. I suspect they in fact chose not to wear them as we had no duffle coats either. It was typical of them both to be out with us in a polar winter storm, in blinding bitter snow, to give us encouragement. The very thought of binoculars gave us headaches; as for Romeo and Juliet, the night was not long enough. For us four hours in a polar winter storm was eternity.

During our boys' training in HMS *Cornwall*, *Revenge*, and now HMS *Repulse* we were not allowed seaboots, but now it was war and they were on sale in the slop room for all. Of course they were soon sold out, but my uncle posted out seaboots and stockings. I was grateful to Andy for this out of his meagre AB's pension, but if my aunt found out he'd be in her report. I was now an OD of some distinction with red rubber-soled seaboots.

The TGI (turret gunnery instructor) in immaculate uniform, making us all look like tramps, stood in the narrow catwalk between the guns and in front of my position between them under the blast bags. The polished visor of his hat flashed as he turned to pad up and down with his alert cat-like tread. He watched and supervised the loading, an inch of white cuff showing from his shirt, his whistle chain, his badge of office, showing.

The huge breeches as big as barn doors were hot after broadside after broadside. The cages came up, the loading numbers stepped down on to their platforms on the gun loading cages and rammed the 1-ton high explosive shells rattling up the barrels. Then disaster as they tried to ram the silk cordite bags in. One was rammed on top of the other, and to our horror the brown macaroni-like sticks of cordite spilled out to begin sizzling on the hot breech. It only needed a slight combustion now and the whole of us would be incinerated to a cinder in seconds, as happened not so long ago on the American battle cruiser's 'A' turret *Missouri* in the Lebanese conflict. There was a blow out and all that was left of the crew was dust, so this might have been the reason. But the TGI's whistle sounded the 'still' as he at the same time quickly drenched the breeches so saving us.

The cast loose drill began from time immemorial with tampions out, bores clear, as to fire with them in would cause a premature explosion in the barrels. These were wooden plugs with a brass ornamental cap. Now it was only done as routine, but nevertheless inspected, as we had canvas hoods on the ends of the muzzles to keep the weather out. Next was to raise both gunloading cages to about 6 feet repeated each time by those concerned. Now they sang out, 'Cannot raise the right gunloading cages with the pedal pressed and the telltale showing not ready,' then the left. Then from the depths of the working chamber came an echoing voice, 'Both gun-loading cages locked,' and again, 'Raise both gun loading cages,' and again, 'Cannot raise both gun loading cages with the pedal pressed and the telltale showing not ready.' Then both breeches were opened, pedals pressed, and both gun loading cages came up fast in a high scream of hydraulics, to a banging stop abreast both breeches. This was done with all the equipment to test it. The voices of Scots, Irish, Welsh, Yorkshire, and West Country people had an almost operatic quality in the different timbres of tone, blended with our youthful ones. We were a truly British guns' crew.

To get to my position as centre sightsetter I went down a small trap door by the gunlayer's position and round a narrow passageway around the barbette, passing the giant-toothed rack that the turret trained round on. My clothing caught up in them once and I escaped only by shedding my oilskin from being mashed up in them. Sometimes I've nightmares over this among the others. Two steps up and I squeezed into my position under the blast bags. At one time they had split and I had staggered out after, high on cordite fumes, rubbing my eyes to find I had no eyebrows. It was a lonely position and I had already accepted the fact that my card would flip up some time, but I hated the thought of being alone when it did, and was resolved to reach Michael in his cabinet.

Then thump and a roar as *Repulse* dug itself down in jerking creaking sounds, thousands of tons over for'd, over aft, with the wretched blast bags leaking drips down on me with that feeling of going down backwards from my position facing aft. I had one of my quiet spews into the bucket at my feet, but we were able to ditch the contents of the latrine bins down the turret's deck hatch, in confidence that it would be instantly swept away.

This was exactly the position of 'A' turret's gun house crew on the battle cruiser *Hood*; my opposite number was probably a boy or ordinary seaman with the same worries, hopes and fears.

Now every now and again a thump ran through the vessel, almost like a stick being drawn across corrugated iron, as the screws raced when they cleared the water. We had reached our top speed of about 25–27 knots, nowhere near her original launch speed of 32 knots, but still fast for this weather and her 32,000 tons deadweight. *Repulse* had been built on the Clyde to stand anything the Atlantic could throw at her.

The 'buzzes' were flying about as usual, and it was amazing how often they came true from things supposed to be top secret, but it was only the Lower Deck's deductive powers. Sometimes however we went adrift, for example when we loaded tropical gear, and found ourselves on 'Winston's Specials', slow and fast convoys from Halifax, Canada, to UK in the winter North Atlantic.

We had heard that the heavy cruisers *Prinz Eugen*, *Gneisenau* and *Scharnhorst* were in Brest but had been damaged by the RAF. Michael and I often looked at the black silhouettes of the German battle fleet posted up in the cabinet and their armaments were explained by Nobby the turret officer, and it looked a formidable opposition, but we kept our apprehension and fear to ourselves. We could well picture the bloody carnage that would be involved when we mixed it with these heavyweights standing toe to toe slogging it out, chucking 1-ton high explosive shells at each other. Bagsy gave us vivid accounts of the battle of Jutland with German units to the south of us.

We were in Arctic weather, the steam heat on after our tiresome mopping down; we were now at our gun positions fairly comfortable in woollen jerseys but still not knowing what we were steaming at such speed to meet.

I observed from my position as centre sightsetter the guns' crew, making up stories about them to keep my mind off seasickness and fear. Bagsy was the No. 2 right gun breech worker, with his heavy pale features and old West Indian straw hat, together with his bandoleer leather belt of percussion cartridges in case of a misfire on the electrical circuits. It was not able to go around his fat waist so was slung under his belly. To me he became a Mexican bandit; as he leaned casually over his breech I detected a tautness about his features: did he know something we did not? No. 3 of the right gun on the rammer, Jan Tucker, with his swarthy good looks and gold earrings, became a pirate. No. 2 of the left gun, Taff Thomas, and Scouse Hogarth were a couple of gangsters. Nobby, the turret officer, was a friendly old bear that occasionally came out of his lair, the cabinet, to amble about in stocking feet and joke with us, but now there was no sign of him, probably dozing in the cabinet. Michael on the phones was not to be seen either, as he usually was in the turret outside the cabinet on an extended lead; we took turns hour about relieving him. So something was definitely up. Smart compared to the rest of us dressed like tramps in beards was the TGI, restlessly padding up and down between the sleeping giants, still giving the appearance of immaculateness in full uniform even though his formerly white shirt was grubby and a smear of oil was on his alert features. He always gave me a smile of assurance now and again in my lonely position. The young midshipman came out and gave me his nod of acknowledgement; in spite of our different status youth called to youth.

There was almost the exact position on 'A' turret of the battle cruiser *Hood* as it was on 'A' turret of the battle cruiser *Repulse*, and fate is what is to be will be.

Beards and old clothes were the fashion, a far cry from our pristine smartness for the Royal Cruise, so I requested to grow a beard as the first early small shoots appeared on my chin and fluff on my upper lip. My name was barked out by the Master at Arms, and I doubled up smartly to the First Lieutenant's request man's table. 'Not granted, shave off, about turn, double march,' barked my friend the Jaunty, hence the expression used as an expletive, 'Well, I'll shave off,' and of course 'seen off,' but used in another context in the RN, where it meant to 'diddle'. From the radio we heard the plummy tones of the BBC announcers, when all in authority talked in this manner. (I notice they all talk like the average man in the street now, the conservative MP Norman Tebbitt sounding almost cockney.) The voice would announce in great pomposity, 'The right honourable gentleman, MP for so and so was "Seen off" at Victoria Station by . . .' It always brought a laugh on the lower deck because we knew it was probably the other way round, MPs being professional 'diddlers'!

You could wear whatever you liked, you could have walked about bollock naked, as long as you had your cap on – very risky in view of Winston Churchill's statement to the House of Commons and the world at large, that we were ruled by 'rum, sodomy and the lash'.

In spite of my severe training I was always in the 'rattle' owing to going about in a dream. I was once accused of drinking Bluebell metal polish, when at that time I hated alcohol. In the tropics on the Freetown run dressed correctly as it was piped 'rig of the day,' negative shirts, I was dressed in shorts and sandals, but of course no hat, as I made my dreamy way languidly across the upper deck, to be suddenly startled out of my wits by a voice that thundered, 'Come here, that Ordinary Seaman!' There was the Master at Arms who had suddenly sprang out from behind a deck ventilator, or so my heightened imagination thought, as he always appeared to wait to pounce on me.

At the First Lieutenant's defaulters table, my name was barked out and I shouted 'Sir!' in reply, doubling up smartly. (I notice they march now.) The Jaunty cried, 'Off caps!' so I seized the brim of my cap with the right hand across the body on the left side, making a pause of two marching paces between each movement, reciting silently to myself, 'Up two three, over two three and bring the cap to the right side on down two three.' The Jaunty now read out the charge as if I'd robbed a bank or worse: 'Was seen on the upper deck, at such and such a time, to the good order of naval discipline, namely out of the rig of the day not wearing a cap.' The Jaunty, my friend, repeating what James had said, barked 'three days' stoppage of pay, on caps, about turn, double march.'

As the centre sightsetter of 'A' Turret, I was the nearest to the bows of the whole of the ship's company, and in reflection of those times as a seventeen-year-old boy, and looking much younger than my years, I felt honoured to think I might be considered the ship's mascot. These daydreams were soon dispelled, however, as *Repulse*, all 32,000 tons of her, took a sickening backwards dive, so to speak, in relation to my position in the centre of the gun house between the guns under the blast bags, my back facing for'd.

Thousands of tons began to bury our bows in a roar and a devilish screech of the wind in triumph. We expected to be buried for ever, as we began to dig our way downwards in short jerky movements. The bedlam of the cacaphonic noises of steel plating under stress of bending movements, and the 'creak, creak, creak' noises were to me most alarming. Then it occurred to me that she had been built on the Clyde, my home port; the steel used was the best, not given to fractures later as those built in Germany and Japan, and the bending stresses had been carefully calculated for each plate to well above anything the North Atlantic storms could dish out. They knew how to build ships on the Clyde when Germany and Japan were building canoes. We ruled the seven seas.

Now there was sudden silence as we reached the extremity of the dive. We had stopped digging down, and the screeching howl of the wind temporarily cut out as we were now in a deep trough, and now rising up, the ears pinging to the difference in pressure. Again came the thunderous roar and scream of the wind as thousands of tons cascaded in white torrents from the bows as now the stern was covered in gallons of water. The bows described sickening circles in wild gyrating swings; into the bucket between my legs I had another of my quiet spews so that no one would know.

In my normal isolated lonely position this would have been possible, but I'd forgotten the Turret Gunnery Instructor, Petty Officer Jan Vanstock, in front of me on the catwalk that separated both guns. His good looks were shielded by the black mirror of his hat's visor, immaculate in full uniform. The comparison between us was startling.

From my position between the huge 15-inch sleeping giants of guns, I looked out to the small catwalk, and could see him turn in his catlike tread as he paced up and down, alert as always, and in my lonely position, always fearful and feeling seasick, he would give me one of his reassuring smiles.

The ship was going flat out and in this weather would normally have been at reduced speed to prevent the risk of damage in these huge mountainous forty-foot waves. The screaming howl of the wind was suddenly cut off as we dived under in a big one. The banging and alarming creak of protesting steel told me something was up as Captain William Tennant was a prudent ship's master and would never have put the 'old girl' through this.

We were not at action stations, but in the first degree of readiness, a relaxed state for those not on duty, such as Michael who was the communication number to the TS. In defence stations and cruising stations, the various stages that led up to action stations, we helped out by doing one hour on the phone and one hour on the bridge wings as lookouts. Even so Michael would have been on an extended lead from his phones in the thick armoured control cabinet to be able to join us in the gun house, now the thick four-inch fireproof steel door was battened shut.

I reflected on that past; why was it always us, the boy seamen and ordinary seamen, who did the dirty work? As seventeen and eighteen-year-olds, about the same age as our paper boys, we thought the war very unfair.

We were in the 'first degree of readiness', that is to say we were in a relaxed state, but ready to go into instant action at the first sign of it. Bagsy, Captain of the right gun, was slumped against his huge breech, but the tense expression on his face denied his position as an old hand who had been a boy seaman at the Battle of Jutland, as the aquatic leviathans had begun chucking tons of high explosives at each other, standing toe to toe, and nowhere to retreat but that wide open space the sea.

Scouse Hogarth was a hard man who 'Tiny' at Portsmouth Detention

Quarters had not been able to break. It was always a mystery how he was ever allowed to come up the gangway of *Repulse*, formerly chosen for the Royal Cruise, but then Captain Tennant was a good judge of men. His lean body of bone and muscle was slumped over his shell ramming levers, likewise Jan Cobley over his ramming levers on the right gun. Accompanying us were the *Prince of Wales* and the battle cruiser *Hood*. We were ordered to find the *Bismarck* and sink her.

After that last silent spew into the bucket at my feet, I felt a lot better but weak from not eating when I should, and I rested my head on my arms on my range and deflection dials. The dim shaded blue turret lights, together with the hypnotic hum of electrical machinery and the stuffy atmosphere, was like a drug on me, relaxing and soothing in this silent void. Suddenly came a sound that seemed to punch itself into your stomach, that instantly catapulted us into a jacknifed motion. It was Michael's 'ALARM!' followed by an ear-splitting crashing bell from the transmitting station and the 15-inch directors.

In a piercing scream of hydraulics, both gun loading cages came up fast from below in the working chamber, to stop with banging loud thumps abreast both gun breeches. Jan and Scouse were already down on their gun loading platforms, even before the cages came to rest. Now they rammed the 1-ton high explosive shells rattling up each gun barrel, making the gun house tremble as the copper driving bands on the shells bit into the rifling that would impart a spin to them, keeping them straight on the target when fired.

The noise was like bedlam, with hydraulic machinery and hoarse shouted orders, the rasping snarl of the huge rammers as they punched the shells, withdrew and in turn punched the bags of high explosive silk cordite bags that contained a substance like brown macaroni sticks. The huge solid drawn brass breeches, almost as big as barn doors, shut with a loud hiss and muffled thumps, with a click as Bagsy and Thomo's intercepters closed the electrical firing circuits to the guns. Then came their long drawn hoarse shouts: 'Right gun ready, left gun ready!' Red lights glowed on top of each breech. *Repulse* was loaded with six tons of H.E. 15-inch projectiles barely a minute from Michael's first shouted alarm.

That cacophony became as silent as the grave. The clicks of my range and deflection pointers on the dials now come from the latest computers in the transmitting station. Here they were magnified out of all proportion, as I followed them with my own pointers: two range dials and two deflection dials; keeping them in line transmitted the range and deflection of the most updated information to both our guns. In the thin pencil light of my gun sights the pointers seemed to scurry about in frantic haste, chattering to me like so many black beetles, first one way then the other, to stop briefly, then dart away again on a life and death mission. These last minute adjustments to the latest range and deflection buffeted me from one side of the right gun to the left gun in short sudden jerks, in an urgent and desperate savagery. Our lives depended on us 'hitting first, hitting hard and to go on hitting' (Admiral Fisher in the 1914–18 war).

In these stops and starts, I shouted out to Smithy in front of me on his centre periscope, where he had control of both guns in laying training and firing if the need arose in the turret's local control, 'Sights moving, sights set.'

(In peace-time *Repulse* won the Home Fleet gunnery competition, splitting the towing target at about thirty miles.)

The stops and starts were caused by the corrections at the last minute from the computer in the TS and were in short abrupt hydraulic hisses, grunts and snorts. Outside on deck the giant gun barrels in the dawn of morning were silhouetted like huge snouts, sniffing the cold Arctic wind for prey. It was now 0300 hrs, the danger time for most attacks, and now soon would be the fatal moment for the battle cruiser HMS *Hood*. At last the gun barrels came to rest after their fidgeting short movements up and down and the turret's short joltings one way then the other, and my final shout 'Sights Set!'

Then at long last drawled the repeated order from time immemorial in the Royal Navy from the TS, 'Broadsides.' The turret guns fired control gongs, two short clangs. I took a deep breath to lessen the effects of the explosion that was about to take place, opened the mouth wide, adjusted my white anti-flash hood to eye level. The guns recoiled, the scream of high pressure air blowing the cordite fumes clear of both gun barrels. The bedlam of hoarse shouting and repeat of orders began all over again; my range and deflection dial pointers went on their mad chattering journeys as before. Then after barely thirty seconds, the drawled, 'Broadsides,' and the noise of the fire control's two short clangs.

Chapter Twelve

FORCE 'Z' SINGAPORE

Admiral Sir Tom Phillips KGB, senior officer of Force 'Z', looked strained and weary as he asked for opinions of his battle plan. The officer Captains from the other ships that were to take part sat quietly round the long mahogany table in the Admiral's great cabin aft, as they had done from time immemorial before a battle, even before Admiral Nelson's time.

Admiral Phillips finally said, 'Gentlemen, we can stay in Singapore, or we can go out and fight. Gentlemen, we sail at 1700 hours.

Captain F.J. Cartwright HMS *Express* from Public Records ADM 199/1149

The Flagship was the latest up to date battleship of the KG5 class and had been recently launched. It took part in the sinking of the *Bismarck* along with battle cruiser *Repulse* and was the battleship HMS *Prince of Wales*. It was hot and humid in the Straits of Singapore and we as ordinary seamen from the crowded wartime complement on the lower decks spent what time we could 'up top', even sleeping and taking our meals there.

Japanese history states that the Japanese Admiral said, 'What is the intention of this British suicidal mission? It is now the 10th of December and America has already declared war on us in Japan after our surprise attack on Pearl Harbour three days ago on the 7th of December. Nevertheless I admire their audacity.'

A Japanese plane spotted Force 'Z' in the Gulf of Saigon and tried to signal to the Japanese Admiral and his Fleet approaching us, but the Japanese Admiral thought it was one of our planes attacking him, and went hard of starboard, right rudder, as we went hard to port left rudder, missing each other by a whisker. What would have been the outcome at night with our radar and speed? The Japanese admit we would have won a night action against their old fashioned Fleet, but their modern aircraft-carriers would have found us in the morning.

In the Admiral's great cabin aft the atmosphere was calm and thoughtful, fatalistic perhaps, to the best of my recollection. I remember Admiral Phillips saying, 'Gentlemen, this is an extremely hazardous expedition, and I would liken it to taking the Home Fleet into the Skagerrak [Germany's front door] without air cover. Nevertheless I feel that we have got to do something.'

There was a long silence after this, and I suspect that others were feeling the same as I. My own thoughts were, yes, indeed you have got to do something, but this is quite against your will and reasoning, and the position you find yourself in must be laid at Winston Churchill's door. I suppose we were all thinking of ourselves and forgetting other priorities: North Atlantic, Mediterranean, Home Defence and so on.

Captain R. Dyer. HMS Tenedos

Midshipman Henry Leach, later Admiral, dined with his father, Captain of the Flagship HMS *Prince of Wales*, who along with Admiral Phillips expressed his fear that the mission would be a disaster, as we on the Lower Deck did at Cape Town in November. Henry dismissed it in his youthful optimism when General Smuts spoke to the ship's company. At 'Clear Lowerdeck!' we had fallen in on the quarterdeck in divisions, but broke ranks on the order to gather round. Captain Tennant was against the formal falling in by divisions as he introduced Field Marshal General Smuts who stood on top of the wooden capstan cover and wasted no time going on in his blunt unemotional Dutch voice which we appreciated. He said that we must resign ourselves to the fact that most of us would not be coming back this way ever again. As youthful ordinary seamen later on the messdecks we dismissed his speech, laughing that the Japs had cardboard planes and anyway suffered poor eyesight and were frightened of the dark; that their aircraft were slow, whereas we were the ship's company of *Repulse*, picked for HM Royal Cruise, and that our ship's motto in Latin inscribed on the crests of our tampions in the muzzles of our guns was 'He who touches shall be broken.' Like some curse this has now passed to us after Japan was broken.

Field Marshal General Smuts sent urgent telegrams, six in number, to Winston Churchill urging and pleading he abort this mission.

As ordinary seamen at that time we did not form any opinion or criticise those above us. We were here to obey orders instilled in us from the age of fifteen at HMS *Ganges*. It is only now that I can see the significance of the events that were to unfold.

Winston Churchill's gamble was to bring America into the war using us as 'live bait'. If it was to win the war and save millions of lives, sadly we can't argue for those of us who were to be sacrificed, but I am now of the opinion of Captain R. Dyer of HMS *Tenedos*, who said, 'I suppose we are all thinking of ourselves, forgetting other priorities, North Atlantic, Mediterranean, Home Defence and so on.' What I don't understand however and surely you must agree, is that the cornerstone of my story is Japanese official history of those events.

The audacity admired by the Japanese Admiral was to cost us two fine battleships and their crews, badly needed to fight the war, and the 'live bait' theory to end the war had now changed to lengthening it and costing more lives. I pointed this out to Lord Trefgaren MOD through my MP Anna McCurley and he refused to comment. I also spoke about HMS *Indomitable*, an aircraft carrier with four squadrons of the modern Hurricane aircraft, an updated version of the famous Spitfire that was to prove itself along with the Spitfire in the 'Battle of Britain'.

If she had been sent through the Panama Canal to reach both ships at Singapore it could have saved the day, including Singapore. I could be wrong but I leave it as a question: Food for thought!

A detailed account of the above is in a later chapter.

Chapter Thirteen

THE PANAMA CANAL

The Panama Canal is a lock type canal across the Isthmus of
Panama, with Cristobal and Colon twin cities at either end of it.
The work began in 1881 by Ferdinand de Lesseps who had built the
Suez Canal, but was abandoned in 1887 owing to the high cost,
corruption, and the death from tropical diseases, and the enormous
size of the task. The representative for the French de Lesseps was the
Hay-Varilla treaty, signed by the United States of America. As another
Hay I myself represent again the Panama Canal, but for very different
reasons.

The Panama Canal is the central point of everything written in the
following chapter. I hope to stress one important point. This canal cost
America 40 million dollars, during the administration of President
Theodore Roosevelt, a very large sum in those days. It allowed their
naval Fleets to sail both in the Atlantic and the Pacific during the
Second World War. What a boon that would have been for Richard
Henry Dana who wrote the American classic *Two Years before the
Mast*. His notes on seamanship in those days of sail, 1836, were
adopted by the Royal Navy in their first seamanship manual. In those
days he had to go the long and dangerous way across the Atlantic, and
by a strange coincidence he wrote of the danger and hardship of seamen
as I do.

HMS *Indomitable*, an aircraft carrier with four squadrons of modern
fast Hurricanes, departed from Key West, Norfolk, Virginia, USA, for
Singapore to back up the Flagship, the battleship HMS *Prince of Wales*,

and the battle cruiser HMS *Repulse*. Churchill did not send her the short way through the Panama Canal, but the long and dangerous way that Dana's seamen had been forced to take in the days of sail. Now for *Indomitable* the waters were far more dangerous with the 'Wolf Packs' of U-Boats having their '*glücklich Zeit*' or lucky time as they played havoc with our convoys. But for our Merchant seamen, however, there would have been no Battle of Britain ceremony today, as our petrol supply would have been cut off.

Churchill had decided, and in the end it was a useless mission like all his other ones that nearly lost the war, that nothing was to prevent the 'live bait' of the two ships at Singapore and the Far East to tempt the Japanese, and so bring America into the conflict as he had done in the 1914 conflict. Japan took the bait to our disaster, attacking Pearl Harbour and sinking both ships with the capture of Singapore and all our Far Eastern possessions.

Indomitable by a miracle made it to South Africa for Singapore but had achieved Churchill's plan. She was too late to help the two ships and Singapore. America was on the point of coming to our aid in any case, and this was a useless sacrifice by a man whose only ambition was not for his country but for political power, and so most of my shipmates, very young men, were needlessly slaughtered.

Now those few who had survived the action by the overwhelming odds of Japanese aircraft sinking both ships stood on the parade ground of the naval base at Singapore at 'Clear lower deck' for the Far Eastern C-in-C Vice Admiral Layton.

He addressed us with, 'Forget you are survivors; you are now Singapore's "Sheet anchor". The native population look to you for leadership and guidance.'

This was what we liked, it was 'fighting talk'; but then he added, 'Keep a stiff upper lip; I am leaving Singapore for Colombo to fetch our Far Eastern Fleet back.' He never came back.

There was a stunned silence from the men, well disciplined in the ways of the RN since they were fifteen years; then they broke into loud angry jeers as the Admiral hurriedly left the scene, to the shouts from the Regulating Police Petty Officers, 'Keep silence', and that silence has been maintained to this day.

Chapter Fourteen

THE NAVAL CONFERENCE 1930

The London Naval Conference put the British Fleet into a strait-jacket, padlocked it and sealed it, not to be unlocked until December 1936. Note *Repulse* was sunk in December 1941. The name of the treaty given by the future Admiral of the Fleet Lord Chatfield was the Washington Naval Treaty of 1922, which was still in force, permitting the modernisation of existing ships within the limits of an extra 3,000 tons displacement.

The technical advances in the design of engines and boilers meant that considerable weight savings were possible through the substitution of up to date machinery. Within these limits, six of the fifteen British battleships and battle cruisers were reconstructed in the period up to 1940. Britain's main requirement was to improve the defence against air attack by thickening the deck armour. If only HMS *Hood*'s deck had been included! The Labour Government concluded, however, that it would be too expensive, and as a consequence a shell from the *Bismarck* went through *Hood*'s upper deck into a magazine.

See the newspaper account in the *Wilhelmshaven Zeitung* by Heinz Gerken 25 May 91 in the next chapter. My comment: it is not clear whether the heavy cruiser *Prinz Eugen*'s shell, or the *Bismarck* sunk HMS *Hood*.

At that moment 1,497 men, 200 boy seamen* and 30 midshipmen under training were incinerated in minutes. Only three men survived.

---

* Most of the 200 boys on *Hood* were from *Ganges* during the time described earlier.

Also then was the augmenting of light and heavy Anti-Aircraft Gunnery. At this period, too, the installation of aircraft was an important development which needed more sophisticated treatment than it had yet received. Many of the large ships in the world's battle fleets already carried aircraft, but except in the latest cruisers these machines, together with their catapult machines, had been added more or less on a makeshift basis.

In the Royal Navy trials had been carried out with alternative arrangements of the catapult either on the quarterdeck (in the beginning on the *Hood*, *Valiant* and *Royal Sovereign* for example), or on the roof of 'X' Turret (as in the *Barham*, *Ramillies* and *Royal Oak*). The trials showed the quarterdeck position to be untenable in bad weather (who on earth would put aircraft on the low quarterdecks in any type of weather?): another insight into the people who are supposed to rule us.

The top of 'X' Turret position was adopted, as the best of the solutions to the problem of carrying aircraft. *Repulse*'s proved the best, having the hangar for two aircraft amidships and above the height of 'X' Turret. This no doubt was planned by a seaman. Although the battleship *Barham* had undergone a major refit during the period 1931-3, the battle cruiser *Repulse* was really the first of the six ships to be reconstructed on the more sophisticated lines now considered necessary. Whereas the *Barham* had her single plane and catapult on 'X' Turret, *Repulse* was to be provided with two hangars in one.

The work on *Repulse* was to be provided at Portsmouth dockyard between April 1933 and the beginning of 1936, at a cost of £1,337,748. This was a large sum in the 1930s. The total cost, including the expenditure on her refit in 1921, reached about £5¼ million.

The first two years of the Second World War were a disaster for our big ships. *Hood*, *Royal Oak*, *Ark Royal*, *Cornwall*, *Barham*, to name but a few, were lost. This was bad enough, but they all carried roughly two hundred boy seamen along with about thirty midshipmen training for officer on each of the ships lost.

As early as 1943 the official records stated that the RN was now manned by sixty per cent Hostilities Only men, those boys described earlier from HMS *Ganges* just before my time and after had been lost, the future corn seed of our Navy. This was of course augmented by *Prince of Wales*'s and *Repulse*'s seamen boys and our midshipmen.

The main features of *Repulse* in 1936 were the large hangar structure, built around the after funnel, and the clear space just aft of the hangars, for a new pattern of fixed crossed-deck catapult. The space abaft of this was where the Royal apartments were later built. She carried four planes, 'More aircraft than any previous British fighting ship', as reported in the *Illustrated London News* of 12 June 1936. The machines were sea planes, two Fairy Swordfish, and two Blackburn Sharks, for torpedo attack, spotter and reconnaissance duties. They could be armed with bombs instead of torpedoes. During *Repulse*'s action in the South China Sea our Petty Officer Pilot went up amongst the Japanese squadrons attacking the *Prince of Wales* and *Repulse*. The fast Japanese planes on what they called their 'go-go' fuel that was the precursor of the jet fuel, disdained to shoot down Petty Officer O'Brian in his slow Fairy Swordfish; later, running out of fuel, he was picked up by our destroyer.

After an early catapult malfunction, the list of volunteers became markedly shorter. Normally one plane was stowed in each hangar of the two, one on the catapult cradle, and a fourth sitting on the catapult rails to be hoisted clear by crane when the machine on the cradle was launched. With this procedure, the first two planes could be in the air very quickly as the catapult could launch to either side.

From 1936 the flying crew of RAF personnel were in the charge of a Flight Sergeant from his Flight Office, a tiny caboose in the port hangar. In 1939 it was Sergeant 'Lofty' Digby who became a friend of Michael and me. As he was the ship's photographer, I have now, thanks to him, the many photographs of *Repulse*, unfortunately only those I'd sent home before the action. Lofty later inherited the family title: Lord Digby. He was only on loan from the Royal Air Force, and not actually in the Fleet Air Arm.

One drawback was that the ship had to be virtually stopped for the recovery of planes, and this could be done only in calm weather. To make room for the catapult, the triple 4-inch mountings in front of the main mast were removed, together with the various deck houses in that area. These alterations left four of the triple 4-inch mountings as a secondary armament. The four single 4-inch AA guns were resited, one each side amidships at hangar level, and one each side amidships at fo'c'sle level. These were the guns my party supplied after the hoists were damaged by enemy action. These were sited outside both recreational doors, port and starboard.

Two twin 4-inch BD mountings were installed as experimental weapons, one on either side of the mainmast. These were the show pieces of the new Anti Aircraft outfit. The matching close-set twin bursts following the drogue targets were far more impressive than the scattered bursts from the single 4-inch guns.

Two eight-barrelled multiple two-pounders, or Pom Poms, called 'Chicago pianos' stood on new platforms abreast the fore funnel. In the action they were devastating, and the Japanese pilots treated them with respect. Practice with these in peacetime was highly exhilarating. From their position above the boiler room vents, the noise thundered and echoed around the boiler room casings, and as there were forty-two boilers in six boiler-rooms, it was always very amusing to see crowds of off-duty engine-room personnel deserting their various hideaways whenever the 'Chicago pianos' opened up. These were our most effective close range guns; of course the 4-inch were our long range ones.

Chapter Fifteen

THE BATTLE OF THE *BISMARCK*

From Heinz Gerken in the *Wilhelmshavener Zeitung*, 25 May 1991

THE FIRST TRIP OF THE *BISMARCK*, A TRIP TO SEAMEN'S DEATH.
After an heroic fight against superior odds, the Battleship sank 50 years ago.

The sinking of the battleship *Bismarck* on 27 May 1941, in three days of heavy fighting against superior hostile sea and air power, about three hundred miles north-westerly of Quessant, ended one of the most tragic sea fights of the Second World War. After scarcely nine days of the *Bismarck*'s first hostile trip, she sank, the Flagship taking with her, after a heroic fight, 1,977 seamen, among them the total Fleet Staff, along with the Fleet Chief Admiral Lütjens, and Chief of Staff Kapitän zur See Netzbandt down to a cool seaman's grave.

Already even at putting to sea out of Gotenhaven on 18 May 1941 for the *Bismarck*'s first eventful trip, its sinking had been programmed by the British, and the British Press were saying that the build up in the Eastern sea would not happen, as the *Scharnhorst* and *Gneisenau* were still damaged and not in a state of action readiness. [But for the fateful oil leak of one of HMS *Prince of Wales*' broadsides, the leak leading the hunting pack to her, and her consequent loss of steering, it might have been a success! Were we the RN ready, or was it to be like their courageous and daring Channel dash, catching us totally unawares?]

At Kiel the *Bismarck* and *Prinz Eugen* started in the direction of the

The German battleship Bismarck.

Kattegat, with destroyers *Friedrich Eckhold* and Z.23, the sky having previously been cleared of enemy British aircraft. That now it only meant keeping a good lookout. Now, under the tactical name *'Rheinübung'* [Rhine exercise] they had long prepared for this outbreak into the Atlantic, and had a few weeks before going up the English Channel in broad daylight under the successful leadership of the Commander, Chief Admiral Lütjens, who would now use this as his model.

The Admiralty under Gross Admiral Raeder, urged a repeat of this success, as he saw a fighting group composed of *Bismarck, Prinz Eugen, Scharnhorst* and *Gneisenau*. However *Scharnhorst* and *Gneisenau* had been damaged by the RAF and were not in action readiness. [Should he have waited till they were ready? Yes, I know it's easy to be wise after the event. However Gross Admiral Raeder leaves this for *Bismarck* and *Prinz Eugen* to decide.]

Gross Admiral Raeder reminded Admiral Lütjens of his previous success, and urged a quick action as he was to be the one to lead it. The fighting group put to sea on 21 May, from the Norwegian Fjord, all British aircraft firmly cleared, and on 22 May left north-westerly from Drontheim, with him in company with the destroyers.

Meanwhile on the English side there was great alarm, and all available fighting forces were mobilised. In March a whole armada was being organised, and now this armada set itself upon the track of the *Bismarck*. Vice Admiral Holland in the battle cruiser *Hood*, along with the *Prince of Wales* and six destroyers, had the first encounter with the German units. Later the Germans sighted the 18th Cruiser Squadron under Rear Admiral Wake-Walker on the *Suffolk*, and that was 23 May about 1920 hours. Fate took its course.

The *Bismarck* fired the first salvo as the heavy cruiser *Norfolk* appeared out of the fog but it was not hit. The feeling on board the German battleship however was that the forward radio measuring apparatus was out. The *Bismarck* and *Prinz Eugen* set off into the fog after this first encounter. On the next morning, 24 May, they came again by Iceland to a heavy fire fight, and both German units

The German heavy cruiser Prinz Eugen.

concentrated upon the British Flagship *Hood*, while the *Hood* took on the *Prinz Eugen*, and the *Prince of Wales* put the *Bismarck* under fire.

After six minutes a salvo from the *Prinz Eugen* hit the *Hood* amidships by the aft magazine and one minute later a broadside from the *Bismarck*, having got the range, blew the *Hood* to oblivion. Only three were saved. Then minutes later the *Prince of Wales* received a heavy attacking fire from *Bismarck* and *Prinz Eugen*. While she came through it unscathed, *Bismarck* received three fateful hits which led to a reduction in her speed and also left an oil track behind her.

The Commander in Chief Admiral Lütjens now questioned himself, broke off the undertaking, and set off for home, in spite of the *Rheinübung* order. The judgement of military historians here is undecided, but the facts of the matter are that Commander Ernest Lindemann of the *Bismarck* entreated his Commander in Chief for a turn round towards Germany for repairs.

In hindsight, one wonders if a turn round would have made any difference to the outcome, the terrible end to the *Bismarck*. Military historians lean towards this concept. They also question whether Admiral Lütjens himself was to blame by being influenced by his predecessors and his own conceit after his success in his daring Channel dash. This is where his downfall lay.

The British heavy cruiser *Norfolk* followed the *Bismarck* track of oil-fuel leak into the Atlantic. On the evening of 24 May Admiral Lütjens dismissed the *Prinz Eugen*, which entered Brest on 1 June. On the night of 25 May *Bismarck* was under heavy attack by torpedo carrying aircraft from the carrier *Victorious*, but repeatedly scored hits and turned the *Victorious* away.

Meanwhile the Gibraltar squadrons of *Rodney*, *Ramilies*, the cruisers *Edinburgh* and *Renown* and the aircraft-carrier *Ark Royal* [later sunk off Gibraltar; few survived] as well as the cruiser *Sheffield*, concluded this Armada. The *Bismarck*, after *Prinz Eugen* had left, was completely alone, and saw a powerful superior force opposite.

Once more the German battleship tried on 25 May to escape in the short time she had left to get to the coast of Brest and safety. However on 26 May in the early morning the first act of the proud *Bismarck* had begun, attacked by torpedo carrying aircraft, and resulted in a fateful hit in her rudder area, which led to her end, and only limited manoeuvring capability possible. She now became the football of the Allied sea and air strike power. After an engagement with the Polish destroyer *Piorum*, it is not clear today why *Bismarck* altered her course from south-east to north-west, so bringing her into the enemy's Armada. About midnight the British 4Z-Flotilla attacked the German battleship. At the same time, Admiral Lütjens announced his position by radio to Brest.

The battleships *Rodney* and *King George V*, the cruisers *Norfolk* and *Dorsetshire*, meant the *Bismarck*'s end.

In the early morning hours of 27 May, in spite of a heavy defence, came the end. At 0853 hours fore main director was hit; 0902 hours, loss of turrets 'A' and 'B'; 0912 hours hits fore director; 0918 hours loss of after director; 0924 hours hit turret 'D'; 0940 again hits and heavy fires amidships (the steel sides showing red hot, steaming); 0950 hit turret 'C', then about 1000 hours the armament was silenced, and *Bismarck* on fire from stem to stern. Some guns kept firing in brave defiance, but *Bismarck* slowly sank as the scuttling valves were opened up, to clouds of steam from the red hot wreck, as the crew abandoned ship.

HMS *Dorsetshire* put in the *coup de grâce*, one torpedo to starboard, two to port. Out of 2,000 men only 118 were rescued, as there was fear that a U-Boat was in the vicinity. The rest died in the icy Atlantic ocean.

Chapter Sixteen

THE BLACK RAIDERS

The Black Raiders were heavily armed and converted merchant ships. Their guns, usually 6-inch, were concealed behind dummy shutters. Our British equivalents were called 'Q' ships on one of which my father served at one time in the 1914–18 war. Of course it was the main task of capital ships like *Repulse* to guard the convoys from these raiders and from heavy German units like the *Prinz Eugen, Bismarck* and *Scharnhorst*.

The destroyer and corvette frigate flotillas were like the old V & W class 1914 destroyers like HMS *Vansittart* which I served on. These vessels were with the convoys, guarding, whereas the big ships were usually out of sight of them. The German MV *Steiermark* was one such vessel, renamed *Kormoran*, when, after an extensive refit and reconstruction, her engines were changed to powerful diesels, six 6-inch guns put in, three each side, together with magazines, four torpedoes on their mountings on deck but covered up, and the means of laying mines on the steel rails aft on the stern, of which she carried 420.

Above decks on the mast, concealed, was the guns' fire control and director, along with a powerful range finder. The crew were not merchantmen, but well disciplined German naval men. The Captain was Kapitän zur See Theodor Detmers, and there were two hundred specially picked men, like our commandos. So in fact the *Steiermark* renamed *Kormoran* was now an auxiliary cruiser.

The *Kormoran* spotted a faint whiff of smoke on the horizon and the sudden crashing bell sounded the alarm as the crew closed up at the double to action stations. At about the same time the Royal Australian Navy cruiser *Sidney* had the *Kormoran* on radar, they to close up to action stations.

The *Sidney* went to investigate and saw what she thought was a normal merchant ship going about her lawful duty on the high seas, but which had no registration or name. *Sidney* therefore asked by international code 'What ship?' On board *Kormoran*, they hoisted a flag that did not belong to any nation, in order to buy more time, or have the *Sidney* move into closer range; this was done by the international code of signals.

Kormoran bought still further time and drew *Sidney* now into her tracking gun director and range finder range by hoisting the Dutch flag. Now to *Sidney*'s expected signal, 'Where bound, where from?', as the German naval battle ensign flew up close up to the yardarm, the shutters dropped, and the first broadside with a roar and flash destroyed the bridge of the *Sidney*. All her bridge personnel, including her Captain, were killed.

The next broadside quickly hit 'A' turret, the next the *Sidney* director, and finally *Kormoran*'s torpedo was destined to finish her off. Instead, though, *Sidney* began to fight back, listing heavily and sinking, but into local control that meant all guns fire independently. The *Sidney*, to the surprise of the *Kormoran*, was now fighting back and scoring hits as a sudden blinding explosion ripped through *Kormoran*. One of *Sidney*'s shells, just before she sank, struck the magazine that carried the 420 mines.

Now, in the bitter irony of war, both crews were helping each other beat off the sharks in the Indian Ocean, and help each other, Germans and Australians, with their wounded. Later they were picked up, the Germans spending the rest of the war as prisoners in Australia.

Translated from the German seamen's news magazine called Blaue Jungs, *Blue Boys, the equivalent to our* Navy News.

Chapter Seventeen

SLOW AND FAST CONVOYS: HALIFAX, NOVA SCOTIA

It is 27 May 1941. Germany's greatest battleship, the most modern and up to date in the world, has been sunk. This had been the pride of Germany, and Hitler would never again risk his Fleet in an engagement with the Royal Navy. The loss of the *Bismarck* did not however deter the U-Boats. This was their 'Happy time', *Glücklich Zeit*, and our convoys were being devastated. Our merchant seamen losses were so great (announced after fifty years) that they exceeded the whole total of the combined three services, the Royal Navy, the Army, and the Royal Air Force by the end of the war.

These seamen signed on again and again, drunk or sober, at the Glasgow, Liverpool or London Dock Street pool, as it was before it was moved from the area of Shark Island to Prescott Street. The U-Boats were now hunting in packs, and getting into and sailing with the convoys, making them difficult to detect. By then we no longer believed we were immortal.

Repulse, running out of fuel after the hunt for the *Bismarck* had ended, was ordered to refuel at Halifax, and that's where we were now. We were no stranger to Halifax, 'New Scotland', as for the last two years without leave we had been on convoy duties and Winston's Specials. *Repulse* had, in the *Bismarck* hunt, been ordered to cut off any retreat to the north if *Bismarck* tried to return to Germany. If this had happened, it would have 'made our day'.

106

Now as we have read in the *Wilhelmshaven Zeitung* of 25 May 1991, we know that the Commander of the *Bismarck* besought Admiral Lütjens to cancel *Rheinübung* and return to Germany for repairs; however fate decided otherwise. What would have been the outcome of a 'Shoot out'? Chucking bricks weighing a tons of HE at each other leaves nothing for the imagination. However if that had taken place *Repulse* could have given good account of herself.

She had won all her 15-inch shoots in competition in peacetime. 'A' turret was on record of having split the towing target in two at twenty miles, and could produce broadside after broadside every minute of six tons of high explosive that would land on the target. Even so, Captain Tennant offered to block the *Bismarck*'s path for its escape home, by being a floating block battery ship. *Repulse* carried the coveted awards of 'Dagger Gunners', and 'Dagger Range Finder Crews', that were left over from being chosen for HM Royal Cruise.

We now gathered round the loudspeaker in the mess that relayed the radio down at meal times from the WT office, this to prevent disturbing watch keepers. It was Lord Haw Haw's half hour, the German propagandist, his heavy sneering nasal accent saying, 'We know where you are, *Repulse*, and will be waiting for you outside.' He had said this every trip we had made, and we had laughed not so much at what he had said, but at the way he had said it. As ordinary seamen the great majority of us knew we were immortal, we were unsinkable, we were the *Repulse*, the pick of the fleet that had once been chosen for HM Royal Cruise, and now Lord Haw Haw only reinforced this. He became as popular as Vera Lynn.

The Battle of the Atlantic was won generally speaking by the Royal and Merchant Navies, without whom the Royal Air Force and, later, the Americans could never have flown. They would have been grounded and we would have lost the war.

Now, back to the Halifax convoys.

On the messdecks we were looking forward eagerly to a run ashore, knowing it would be piped soon, and it was our watch ashore. We had already checked out our shore-going gear as a lap ahead, after two

107

years incarcerated in the steel confines of a war-time battle cruiser. It is easy to explain our eagerness to get ashore. Michael gave me an unintelligible shout above all the excited noise of the others about something of an 'end away'; I shouted back something just as bad as we grabbed towels and soap and joined in the rush for the bathroom.

Now we jogged along the starboard passageway that would soon be fated, ducking through the many watertight doors open in harbour, always ducking as the top clip sometimes slipped down from its clasp and this could give a very serious bang to the head if you were always on the double like Michael and myself. Now the Bos'n's pipe shrilled out on the Tannoy, followed by the Bos'n's mate's call: 'There will be a liberty boat at 1630 for the port watch, Leave to Chief and Petty Officers 0700 in the morning, men under-age 2359 tonight.' A loud cheer followed this announcement.

Michael was to be disappointed, as I wished to go ashore without him. It was with my other mate, Sergeant 'Lofty' Digby RAF, who had a Canadian cousin, and he was taking me to be introduced to her and the family. She seemed by her photograph to about the same age as myself, although that was not important; I did not judge people by their age. I had first seen her picture in Lofty's caboose, where Michael and I were privileged to go in the port hangar. As well as being in charge of our aircraft personnel, he was the ship's photographer, and had utilised the sink for developing films for his own use, as it had hot and cold water. He had also knocked up a bunk, the naval-type fire, which could be stood lying flat, so we had late night fry ups. You could say it was a de luxe caboose. These had always been in the Navy from the days of sail to the present day. Of course they varied; for example gun sweepers, those who kept the gun clean, made their caboose in its support. On *Repulse* these were round with not much room to move around in. Others were the Gunner's store and Bagsy Baker's fo'c'sle locker, which were average; Chief of Stores office and distributing point, which was of the luxury type. It was like being a town councillor: if you had a caboose you went up in the community's esteem; in any case to be in charge of a store you had to be someone of merit. I liked to get away from the hubbub of the mess decks and we found Lofty's caboose a peaceful haven.

Now, as we stepped off the liberty boat, I became transfixed. To Michael's and Lofty's impatient concern, their, 'Oh come on,' made no difference to me as I heard the bird song, and saw the green of the vegetation, and breathed in the peaty smell of the very earth itself. Stepping ashore that moment after the fug on the mess decks, and that stale smell: yes, the sea smells stale out at sea, it's only on the beach you smell the ozone for some reason.

We left Michael, arranging to meet up later, and now I was in Lofty's Canadian relatives' home. I was enthralled; this was my first civilised contact since I'd been on leave at home before joining *Repulse* two years ago. I drank in every moment of the polite comfortable family atmosphere over coffee and biscuits after dinner later. Now it was time to leave. She offered to show me the park and the beach that surrounded it, as I had told them how we had been cooped up on the ship. Lofty, after saying his goodbyes, left us together.

The beach was deserted, I flung my Burberry down on the sand in a sheltered spot away from any prying eyes. In the past my shore leave, up at 2300 as it was now for men under age, made me desperate at the thought of being incarcerated again in the steel confines of a battle cruiser. 'Stowed thick and get lousy,' there were two hundred on our messdeck, but even in prison they are only three to a cell. After two years together we tolerated but hated each other.

One time, it seemed an age away, we had been to Greenock to pick up one of our Winston Special's convoys. Not being able to afford an hotel room, we had made use of a shop doorway, another time a telephone box as it was raining. In peace-time Devonport Park became so popular that a notice on the park gates said, 'Sailors and dogs not allowed.' The next evening the Fleet in port went ashore and tore the park apart. Some people in Devonport accepted this with a shrug: 'Sailors don't care'; this time they did.

Now from my past failures of trying to do it standing in a shop doorway, but failing because of a knee trembler, the more I tried the worse it became, till she left me in disgust. Now as I lay on top of her in this deserted beach supported by my elbows they now began to tremble – I had an elbow trembler! – and my hot passionate breath tickling her ear making her giggle as my elbows finally give way and I fell on top of her. Now there was loud outright laughter, and worse, I'd somehow got sand on it so that it was like doing it with sandpaper. So much for some memories of my youth.

I made my way back to Halifax town square and, meeting Michael and Lofty, went for a drink, only to be refused in the bars as being under age, so we went to the Army club. After three pints I remember very little except trying to eat steak, eggs and chips, our favourite when ashore. We then caught the 2359 liberty bus from Halifax town square to the dock.

It was a good arrangement, it meant shore leave expired on the bus and so avoided people 'being adrift' on leave, especially those under age who were not allowed all-night leave. We arriving at the dockside to board a Canadian fishing boat that had been given to the ship, so as to avoid using our own liberty boats' crews, and was also used for ship to shore duties.

The run ashore had done us all good after being incarcerated in the steel confines of a battle cruiser for almost two years, except for the few times allowed ashore in the barren wastelands of heather and sheep while ammunitioning, fuelling and store ship, by watches, at Scapa Flow.

Suddenly the laughter and singing broke off as we saw with envy Ordinary Seaman McDonald step out from a sports car driven by a girl. She was the daughter of Moir's chocolates, and he was engaged to her; sadly he did not survive. The canteen was kept stocked up with chocolate each time we made our crossing, protecting our valuable convoys not so much from the U-Boats but from the Atlantic raiders *Scharnhorst* and *Prinz Eugen* to mention some that were on the loose. Later the *Bismarck* tried but as we all know failed miserably.

We came alongside *Repulse* with a bang and a crash, the fishing boat's coxswain not used to the small area of our gangway. It could be quite tricky in even our twin screw powerful Thornycraft power boats with the ship at anchor streaming in one direction from her cables, the tide in another direction, the wind in another. Our young midshipman coxswain was waved away by the OOW and ordered to 'Go round again'. Suddenly silence fell to our happy laughter and singing, as far above us on the quarterdeck at the top of the gangway showed the white discs of the faces of the 'Crushers', the regulating Petty Officers, who looked down, barking, 'Keep silence.'

Moir's chocolates were free, except for a small charge that was put in the ship's sports fund for that day if it ever was to come. King Farouk of Egypt donated free cigarettes and the South African government likewise; they were called Cape to Cairo. After that there was a quick run down of the layout below decks, continuing along the starboard passage, leading in an after direction, ducking through the many watertight doors that now in harbour were open, marked 'Y' doors routine. At last we came to a deck hatch that was shut, but on top it had its own little manhole hatch. This we went down to enter the bathroom flat, that comprised the Chief and PO's bathrooms next to and separate from our own; this watertight door had one clip on allowed in harbour.

I watched Blondy languidly soap himself down luxuriously and as we were the only ones in the bathroom, it being late after coming offshore, my eye caught the cold sea water tap and rubber hose. Now he tipped the portable basin over his head, filling up and repeating, then went over to the corner for a cold douche with the sea water one, that was good for the skin, followed by a fresh one. This was our routine, there being no showers. Now I wandered over towards him to do the same.

A very important incident was to follow that was to save my life. Blondy had read my mind and was hosing me down with the cold water hose. Now as we grappled together, I trying to wrest the hose from him, I found it more and more difficult as his slim, slippy, youthful body slipped from my grasp time after time. This is what I remembered just in time when faced by a black belt Japanese Judo

111

expert; as he tried to grasp me I was able to free myself, later told in my story of the Teak House, Johore.

The next morning came the pipe, 'Cable party, muster on the fo'c'sle; special sea dutymen close up; close all "X" "Y" and "C" doors; down "Dead lights".' Now back to our old routine, convoy duty back to UK, as we came belting out of Halifax's long harbour, on all forty-two boilers, leaving in our usual high speed zig-zag.

Chapter Eighteen

THE FACTS SPEAK

'The Navy will lose the war, the Air Force will win it.' Winston Churchill in the House of Commons, 1940.

The Battle of the Atlantic was gradually being won, and at a dreadful cost to our Merchant Navy officers and seamen, from the U-Boat 'Wolf Packs' at La Palance, inland from the Port of La Rochelle in the Bay of Biscay. In later years I served as 1st Mate on *Orion*, an Arctic oil survey ship, after the war. Their 'Killing ground' was outside their front door, the North Atlantic Ocean, but the Battle of the Atlantic was eventually won by our Navy.

Each time we left the long straight harbour of Halifax it gave us time to build up speed on our forty-two boilers, as we would come belting out on a fast zig-zag, too fast for the 'Grey Wolves', too fast for our own destroyers. It was to prove good practice for later in the South China Seas, as Captain William Tennant took avoiding action dodging 19 torpedoes out of 25, zig-zagging at high speed, even after being hit by three torpedoes, like a wounded stag being hunted by overwhelming Japanese air squadrons. He handled *Repulse*'s 32,000 tons like the young destroyer Captain he had once been.

Historians are divided over whether *Repulse* should have left the hapless *Prince of Wales* to her fate, and so saved a valuable ship, a battle cruiser and her equally valuable ship's company, pre-war trained at great expense to the tax-payer. The *Prince of Wales* had dockyard workers on board still working on the damage she suffered from the

Bismarck action. All or nearly all her AA guns had jammed in their training racks, and now the gun's crew, with the courage that was not lacking on the *Prince*, hauled the guns round by tackles, a hopeless situation.

Added to this she had damaged steering and was going round in circles, like the *Bismarck*'s ironic end. We heard the Bos'n's pipe 'Do ye hear,' then Captain Tennant, 'We are now going to stand by the *Prince of Wales*.' From then our fate was sealed.

A ladder led up to 'B' gun deck, the Chief and Petty Officer's smoking area. This space between the turrets is where I was when the vessel lurched savagely to port, clinging to the guardrails on the high side starboard. I lost my footing as I turned at the noise of grinding metal upon metal, as 'A' turret began coming out of its mounting foot by foot. This was a system to prevent the ship's capsizing by allowing the heavy guns to come out and so right herself. Mr Ballard, in his research submarine, found the wreck of the *Bismarck*'s guns miles apart from her.

Now to my horror and that of those watching I was sliding helter skelter down the deck to the low side. Probably it would be the end for me: ironic after all the near misses I'd missed in the action. In those split second desperate moments, I remembered a sunken deck shackle that took the wire for the recovery of our paravanes, and also the block for the ammunition ship. I flung myself sideways, putting myself in line for it, knowing every inch of that deck after the many times holystoneing it the year before war broke out. I grabbed it, stopped the slide and regained my place beside Petty Officer O'Rourke, Michael, Jan Horsford, Blondy, and the rest of 'A' turret's crew.

Chapter Nineteen

BELOW DECKS FOR ACTION STATIONS

This is a brief description of below decks, to help explain the 'Action Stations' in a later chapter.

Down in the sweltering messdecks were two hundred men in these conditions for the last two years without leave. Of course in this sort of crowding we hated each other. Michael and I along with 'Blondy' Garton slept on the deck where at any rate the air was fresher. Later we were forced to move under the mess table to prevent being trodden on by those above us.

Now we stripped and took from our locker doors our towels; it was the only place you could hang them. Now with them around our waists we headed for the bathroom. The fo'c'sle messdeck was on the starboard side of the ship, and the topman's messdeck of also two hundred men was on the port side. Seperating the messdecks was a large, heavy, wide, wooden teak ladderway, wide enough for at least two to pass comfortably up and down. This led up to the next deck above which was called the 'Citadel' a thickly armoured section that protected 'A' and 'B' turrets' magazines and shell rooms.

This deck, apart from the actual 'Citadel', was specially strengthened and ran from the stem to the stern. It may sound confusing, because it was called the upper deck, but it was enclosed. In ship construction terms, both in the RN and the MN ships, it was the strongest deck in the ship, and ran without a break. The deck above this, exposed to the elements, was called because of its position the 'upper deck', but it did not meet the terms of ship construction as it was not a continuous deck ending at the quarterdeck.

The 'Citadel' deck, above our fo'c'sle mess hatch, branched and one passage led up the port side for'd, the other port side aft already described. Another passageway led down the starboard side aft, and passed the Petty Officers' mess and pantry. As we passed we gave a wave to Boy Seaman Sharky Ward, the PO's messman. He gave his very distinctive broad smile. He was just out from HMS *Ganges* and maybe that was why he still smiled.

The Sail maker was an old title; he now did canvas work, like the repair of the 15-inch guns blast bags, the close and long range weapons' gun covers, and the huge quarterdeck awning, and sick bay outside awnings. The other jobs had always been allowed since the days of sail, boot and shoe repairs, suit making, and hair cutting, the book stall, and canteen: we were like a small town.

The Torpedo men, although we had no torpedoes, owing to their qualifications became the electrical branch of the ship.

Next we passed the canteen, with our famous saying, 'Canteen open, canteen shut, mind your fingers,' as we gave a 'Hi' to Canteen assistant sixteen-year-old George Henderson from Kirkcaldy. A bit further on was a watertight hatch that would lead down to the Petty Officers' and separate ships company bathrooms. The passageway continued for a bit and a ladder led up to the recreation space. That also branched to starboard and port, ending in doors each side on to the upper deck. The after end by the ladder just entered was another misnomer, as it was called the fo'c'sle locker, but it was miles from the fo'c'sle, Bagsy's territory.

On the port side of the recreation space, better known as the rec space, was the goffer stall that was run by the NAAFI that sold ice cream in peace time; now there were only soft drinks, called 'goffers'.

The starboard passageway below the rec space led on to another ladder that would take you up to the after end of the rec space and at the top was the starboard rec space door that led out to the upper deck and SI gun. The same on the port side; opposite the goffer stall was the port rec space door that led out to the upper deck and P2 gun.

Back to the starboard passageway after passing by George in his canteen. (By the way the NAAFI never sold socks for some unknown reason, so anybody with no socks was known to wear 'Canteen socks'.) The passageway led on to the boys' messdeck. Across and at the foot of this was the instructors' mess, a canvassed-off part in a corner like the Royal Marine Sergeant's 'Horse Box'. The two Petty Officers, Slater and Jefferies, because PO Slater was the largest were called Mutt and Jeff. They had been our boys' instructors also on the battleship HMS *Revenge*, so they knew Michael, Blondy and myself well, and we could not pull the wool over their eyes, even now we were ODs.

Across from the boys' mess deck, and inboard was the ship's servery. This had several hot cupboards that had the numbers of each mess in the ship stencilled in black on the doors. Outside were the hot boiling water taps for brewing up our tea. The food was sent down from the galley in lifts to these cupboards. At the 'Cooks to the Galley' pipe, Blondy and I went up and drew our mess's trays, about four in number, when it became our turn in the mess. The first was roast potatoes with a joint of roast beef; the second probably cabbage; the third steamed figgy duff with custard; the fourth spare potatoes and cabbage. There was also a mess kettle of soup, so we lived pretty well. We all put on weight after *Ganges*, but this may have been due to no more doubling!

Next to the galley was the ship's bakery, where we baked fresh bread and fresh rolls.

Chapter Twenty

FRIENDLY KIPPERS?

Out at sea, out of sight of the convoy, we were on the lookout for the battleship *Scharnhorst*, the heavy cruiser *Prinz Eugen*, *Gneisenau*, and other 'Black Raiders'. Suddenly the usual signal came over the Tannoy, 'Alarm aircraft, AA and close range weapons' crews close up.' This was relayed all over the ship, so that we in the turrets could also hear what was going on. Now the Air Defence Officer, Lt. Cdr. Jay's voice on the Tannoy came over in his usual contemptuous drawl that always intrigued me in these frightening times: 'Engage.'

He was in the AA director, that square box on top of the fore mast, and now all hell broke loose, as the Chicago pianos joined in. Suddenly his contemptuous drawl, 'Cease firing, Cease firing.' Cease fire bells were rung desperately all over the place, as his voice came again: 'Check Check Check; train fore and aft; friendly aircraft.'

Then a rushing and tearing sound overhead like someone tearing up a giant piece of cardboard, followed by 'Wham, Wham, Wham' as the bombs came down, making us all duck, as they seemed to be right on top of us. A lot of good that would do us, ducking; nevertheless I saw the face of Bagsy Baker, Captain of the right gun, go chalk white.

The bombs came so close as to send up fountains of water and drench the upper deck guns' crews. At breakfast in the wardroom, Lt. Cdr. Jay asked in his usual polite drawl to the steward, 'What's for breakfast?' There came a bitter shout from another officer: 'Friendly Kippers.' After that on the lower deck kippers were always called friendly.

118

Now again up at our old stamping ground Scapa Flow, the Pipe came across, 'The Prime Minister Winston Churchill will be visiting us shortly.' This was greeted by a loud cheer of derision. He had understandably never been liked by officers or men since his outrageous statement in the House of Commons about us.

Chapter Twenty-One

THE CANTEEN MANAGER

The reception party on the quarterdeck comprised the Captain, Commander, Officer of the Day, and our Bos'un Mate's piping party of six. The Boatswain's call had been used as far back as AD 1700 by Admiral of the Fleet John De Vere, Earl of Oxford, it being a badge of high office. It reverted to its original use for passing orders in the days of sail to signal orders in a howling gale.

To use the pipe as a call, the side of the 'Buoy' rests against the palm of the hand, and the fingers close over the 'Gun', 'Buoy', and orifice or hole in such a position as to be able to throttle the exit of air but not impinge on the orifice in the 'Buoy', or all sound would be completely choked.

As the barge arrived alongside we began to pipe on the OOW order, 'Pipe', raising our pipes to our mouths as the Prime Minister Winston Churchill stepped onto the lower platform of the gangway. We began to chorus in a low thrill note, rising to a high note, and coming down the scale to finish timing it as he reached the top of the gangway. He gave a sloppy off-hand salute to the White Ensign flying on our staff aft.

His dress was black and completely featureless: black hat, no badge; jacket with black buttons. In fact it was a copy of our non combatant canteen manager and staff, their bravery sometimes going unnoticed because of this title. Winston Churchill, Prime Minister was known in the Fleet as 'The Canteen Manager'. Our own canteen manager and staff fought alongside us and died in the subsequent action.

Canteen assistant George Henderson, aged sixteen, was in the for'd damage control HQ. We met his party running towards us for advice. *Repulse* was now turning turtle and hearing no 'Abandon ship,' thinking it was our high speed turns, we told them things were OK. They went back to their station and were never seen again; it was a long time before we could rid ourselves of such terrible regret. Captain Tennant had calculated four torpedo hits but instead it was five, one too many.

Churchill's visit had passed, and now we waited to hear at any moment, 'Special sea duty men,' and another convoy duty. One half of the fo'c'sle locker caboose of AB Bagsy Baker had tackles neatly strung up along with full coils from the dockyard of manilla rope, tarred hemp, coil upon coil of heaving lines, buckets one inside the other rising up to the deck head, scrapers, wire scrubbers, and enough stores for a chandler's shop.

At first, as a boy then as OD, I did not get on with Bagsy, as I was either losing gear or forgetting what I'd done with it. Now he had it chalked up on his black board: Hay – boom jockey, one wire scrubber, one deck cloth. 'Boom jockey' meant straddling the lower boom that stretched out from the ship's side, almost as thick as myself. This took the boat ropes from the boats to a long reach up to a bollard on the fo'c'sle and so enabled the boats secured to them to slipstream from them clear of the ship's side.

Now I started from the end with one end tied to my deck cloth dipped it into the sea. I pulled it up and wetted the boom. Then on the other end of the line was my wire scrubber which I used to remove the brown dead wood, to expose the beautiful teak undersides. I repeated this process till I'd reached the end, reporting back to Bagsy, 'Job finished.' I never dared ask questions, as I would only be told his usual, 'ODs should be seen and not heard.' I was disappointed and puzzled, as Bagsy had been an old shipmate of my Uncle Andy, and of course I expected special treatment.

In the corner that was his caboose he slung his hammock, and he bathed regularly by having two buckets of water, one to soap down, with the other to rinse off with, this being not so much different as we did in the bathroom. He only went to the mess for meals, and then he kept us ODs down at the foot of the mess. The young Leading Seaman left the running of the mess to him.

In his caboose along with four of his henchmen of similar vintage, they ran the Tombola, the ship's laundry, the cigarette factory and boot repairs, all this on condition that a small percentage of the profit went into the canteen fund. The cigarette machine took up nearly all the space in his caboose; it operated like an old fashioned sewing machine foot pedal. The tobacco went in one end and came out rolled and filter tipped the other end. We supplied the tobacco in half pound tins called 'Tickler'. In the days of sail the jam was supplied in tins of this size and the manufacturer's name was Tickler.

It cost us a small sum to have this done and also to have them put in packets stamped HMS *Repulse*. In peacetime it was said it was hard to recognise Bagsy in his pin striped suit and bowler hat as the owner of property on Plymouth Hoe. Bagsy ran a taut ship, making sure we washed, and when cook of the mess ditched the gash, etc. Not only were we kept away from the social side by being down at the foot of the mess, it was hard to join in any conversation except among ourselves. We felt very underprivileged not having a slinging billet and having to sleep under the mess table to prevent being trodden on.

Down several decks, in the dog watches in the smoky and tense atmosphere several thousand pounds were being gambled away. The ship's company, having no shore leave except at Scapa, spent their money on crown and anchor, pontoon, roulette, crib and poker. We ODs and boys preferred to spend our money on chocolates from the canteen.

Chapter Twenty-Two

SCAPA FLOW CANTEEN

The 'crazy gang' on board was led by 'Scouse' Hogarth, a large slim hard man, who had done so much time at Portsmouth Detention Naval Quarters and whose record had not been broken by the infamous 'Tiny'. He could have entered the *Guinness Book of Records*. With about a hundred of his followers he would go round the ship, past all the messes, making a terrific din banging on empty mess utensils and chanting like today's Hari Krishna religious group, but quite different as they shouted out obscenities.

At the beginning of these crazy outbursts we had grabbed hold of one little nervous Top man with, 'What's all this in aid of, Jan?'

He replied, 'They say it's an old Chinese custom to frighten the Devil away.'

I looked at Michael and said, 'Are we now all going bonkers?' Just previously another Top man, Leading Seaman Taff Shephard, had started every Sunday to leap up onto our mess stools and address us with a Bible in one hand, his little goatee beard, contrary to regulations that said it must be square, quivering in fervent earnest exortions as his Welsh voice rose. We listened respectfully, as he was so earnest, as he told us to mend our ways or the devil would get us.

We were a good example of a British gun's crew, with Welsh, Scots, Irish, Yorkies, Scouses and West Country Janners, as seamen had been since time immemorial in the RN. We were back again at Scapa Flow, 'The land God forgot to make' as that the Royal Navy had always called it even before we were born, and leave had been granted. With four beer tickets each we headed for Flotta Island naval canteen.

To be British today seems to be out of fashion; nevertheless we now ploughed through the mud after landing like a scene from the Klondike Gold Rush. Gone were our former prestigious smart uniforms for the Royal Cruise; now it was war, and the dress seemed to be anything as long as you wore a cap or hat.

The dress in general was sea boots and oilskins, with duffle coats for those lucky enough to possess them. Our table was now overflowing with beer, and our company included Michael, Jan Tucker and Scouse Hogarth, his size and reputation giving a feeling of security to Blondy and myself. We looked about us at about a thousand men from the ships in at Scapa; *Rodney, Renown, Nelson, Victorious* the aircraft carrier, and various destroyers and frigates.

We looked eagerly towards the stage and, having been so devoid of any social contact or large gathering such as this, we were prepared to laugh at just about anything; and laugh we did, so much that I had stomach pains. On the stage in darkness was a screen illuminated from behind, so that the figures were silhouetted. The first was a Royal Marine who marched in to what was supposed to be a urinal, stamping down in military precision, and doing each movement with a pause of two marching paces between each.

Now the atmosphere was warming up with the cold beer. The next silhouette came in with mincing little steps; next a business man in bowler hat; but last, that was to bring the house down, was a large fat Able Seaman, drunk, cap flat aback, who staggered about doing it all over the place after pulling out what appeared to be fathom after fathom. As I said, we had been so lacking any entertainment over the last two years of dreadful monotony interspersed with dreadful frightening brief moments of excitement, that we now relaxed and had a good laugh, at anything.

Now some fights were breaking out, and glasses were being flung. In the toilets you had to step over bodies seemingly flaked out by the effort of urinating.

In the canteen things were becoming sour with some but the singing of the vast majority was evidence of a happy occasion, until a stoker from the *Rodney* got up on the stage drunk, and began stirring up his pint of beer with his whatnot, shouting, 'This is all it's good for up here in the last two years.'

This made us remember our girl friends, and the others their wives, now the singing had stopped. The mention of the *Rodney* was of the time a leading stoker had been found sleeping with a sheep on Flotta Island by one of the Islanders, which nobody believed of course, but our young stokers on *Repulse* felt very aggrieved and said it was one of our ODs naked in a duffle coat.

Now in the ensuing silence a voice shouted, 'Who shagged the sheep?' and of course the ensuing roar that always followed was '*Rodney*!'

After the duty Royal Marine platoon had sorted it all out the canteen was almost destroyed as *Rodney*'s ship's company bitterly resented this remark on their manhood. We caught our liberty boats back to our ships, paused at the top of the gangway to be frisked for bottles by the Regulating Police, cut one off to the white ensign aft, and fell in on the quarterdeck to be inspected by the Officer of the Watch. As long as you could stand you were all right, the young sub lieutenant going quickly down the ranks of swaying drunk seamen breaking wind and belching.

Now he turned to the Master at Arms, with 'Thank you, Master at Arms, dismiss them!' We turned for'd and dismissed. The Devil and the Crazy Gang had been exorcised, and also Taff Shephard gave up his sermons.

Chapter Twenty-Three

ALARM AIRCRAFT

We were closed up in 'A' turret, when Michael on the phones in the control cabinet, shouted the alarm. As the attack progressed we realised this was no ordinary air attack, and found out, of course, later on, that there were fifty-one torpedo-carrying aircraft, Genzan, Kanoya, Mihoro, and the infamous Bettys and Nells, called by the Americans later, 'one shot lighters,' because of their 'go-go' fuel. There were also thirty-four bomber attack aircraft, making an overwhelming attack on the two ships of eighty-five aircraft involved.

In that first part of the action our casualties were heavy, mostly on the exposed upper deck crews, and down in the magazines, where men were flaking out with the heat. We were told to relieve them, keeping only key men in the turret, like Michael and Bagsy, loading numbers. I joined up with the rest in the queue to go down the for'd 4-inch magazine.

At the head of the queue I could see AB Parkhouse counting them down the hatch, sick bay flat for'd, that would eventually lead down another deck into the boys' locker flat, and my old billet, my hammock slung by S & B port scuttle hole, and then to another hatch down into the 4-inch magazine. As I drew near I was shocked to see Parkhouse's face, almost unrecognisable from the way he used to be in the mess making all the ODs laugh with his son's schoolboy's cap on, reading out aloud 'Desperate Dan' from a comic. Now seeing him in his tin hat and his face as taut and as white as his anti-flash hood, I got my first feeling of apprehension. This was no ordinary attack. Like Bagsy he had been a boy in the Battle of Jutland.

Now it was my turn to go down the hatch. My foot was already on the lip of the hatch coaming, when Parkhouse said, 'Right you are, Ian and the rest of you, join up with the upper deck supply.'

As I went through the huge Citadel watertight door and it closed behind me there was a slight thump, and *Repulse* shuddered.

The torpedo had struck in the vicinity of the 4-inch magazine. As they turned the flooding valves, I thought sadly of those who a few moments ago had been in the queue with me and those others whom I had known. Now with 4-inch projectiles on our shoulders, we entered the Citadel and passed through the barber's flat, then passed the Chief of Stores' office that was now the for'd damage control HQ. We then proceeded along the starboard passageway, leaving the Citadel at the other end and went up a ladderway into the recreation space, the fo'c'sle locker on our left hand. We went along, branching sometimes to the starboard side, sometimes to the port side, depending on which side was under attack, relayed to us by an AB who was stationed at the rec space doors.

These two doors were at the very end of the rec space, and led out to S1 and P2 guns respectively. On the starboard side was the ship's piano in its still heavy wooden protection box, and near it was the ship's diving pump, both secured by wire strops. Separating the two sides from each other, like the Citadel, were 'B' and 'A' turrets' barbettes, making passageways to port and starboard aft and one going for'd, so the rec space had two passageways, port and starboard, so by having the funnel supports doing the same.

The separation in this case was caused by the funnels. However, being signalled by one of the ABs stationed at the starboard rec space door, we went to the port door, took a deep breath and plunged outside as all hell broke loose. The close range having now got the range the 'Chicago pianos' above our heads were blasting away.

Now, this is where we were to make a fatal mistake. At P2 gun, the Captain of the gun, Leading Seaman Jock Devlin, shouted to us above the bedlam, 'Load up S1, we've got enough!' We could now see the ammo piled up on the deck. Now our mistake was that instead of ducking back into the rec space the way we had come, we carried on down the exposed upper deck, crossed over to the other side using the catapult deck and went up the exposed starboard side to S1 gun, where the Captain of the gun was Smithy, another Southern Irish man and a friend of Michael.

Our upper deck supply party of twelve had decreased by about half, through going down the port side of that exposed upper deck instead of turning back and ducking through the port rec space door to safety. This had been our routine in the many ammunition and store ships in the past, never to turn back against the main flow but, having delivered your ammunition box or store, you carried on, so as not to cause a traffic jam.

Ordinary seaman Blondy Garton gave me a look of despair that said we would not make it this time. We had just missed going down the 4-inch magazine, we had just missed it again on the upper deck, and the others had not. Now AB Gibble, our 'A' turret working chamber gun's crew, saw what was happening to us, and must have rushed down the starboard side opposite to us on the port side, and crossed over to our side by the catapult deck to try and head us off.

We saw him at the corner of the catapult deck and port hangar, gesticulating frantically for us to go back to the comparative safety of P2 which, like S1, had a six-foot armoured plated shield round it. The heavy bullets jumped him about as he gave his life to save us. Now we all retreated in desperate haste to P2 where the crew were too busy putting up barrages, as now *Repulse* was fighting for its very life. All around the gun's crews' communication numbers could be heard repeating the order, 'Barrage, Barrage, Barrage.' This meant that each gun fired independently as fast as it could to put up a defensive barrage of exploding shells of steel around the ship. The enemy had broken through; the voices sounded desperate in the situation we were now in.

We lost count of the times we went below for ammunition, also of the number of times *Repulse* shuddered to the thumps of torpedo hits, as we heeled right over in high speed zig-zags dodging them. Now P2 Leading Seaman Jock Devlin was dead and his injured crew were being attended by the first aid parties.

Captain William Tennant stood up in an exposed part at the rear of the bridge, and gave his helm orders, as he watched the bombs and torpedoes fall, timing it so successfully that out of twenty-five torpedoes dropped we dodged nineteen, and numerous bombs of which only one hit.

Now, our dreadful walk along that killer deck over, we concentrated on S1 gun's crew. We arrived to a sudden shout as we all tumbled into the gun well, as the bullets ripped up the boat deck above our heads. As we picked ourselves up we heard Bob Hewlet shouting in anger and pain with a bullet-shattered arm, 'Don't just stand there, load the f– practice and starshell.' We did this now in fevered haste from the ready-use lockers around the gun. It was essential we gave the appearance that our sector was still open, otherwise they would all soon descend on us like a horde of hornets. The enemy had twigged that by coming in just above the sea level we could not get sufficient depression to hit them.

We loading numbers were in the rear of the gun's breech waiting to load, cradling 4-inch projectiles in our arms that were similar to the miniature .303 bullet. Now came the communication numbers' report: 'Commence, commence, commence.' We loaded in the fuse setting machine to the sound of the fuse setters' handles cranking double crunch. As the fall of shot gave its double hoot, we loaded the end of the brass cartridge case rim, and tripped the catches retaining breech block open. Under the powerful springs the breech shut, to the distinctive sound like a cup and saucer being brought together, 'Clup, clup', and the click of the electric circuit's interceptor being closed by the Captain of the gun.

Then came the sudden explosion and the blast of flame and thick brown cordite smoke from the breech as the steel deck gun bounded from under the feet. The empty brass cartridge case was ejected, hitting the rope matting of the gun deck with a thud, to be kicked away as it went merrily tinkling and clinking into the scuppers, as the loading was quickly repeated.

As a young junior seaman on the training ship HMS *Cornwall* I had found this all very alarming, and put my fingers in my ears when I heard that double hoot signifying the gun firing. I would begin to shuffle back, fingers in the ears, only to stop suddenly when came a roar above all other sounds: the gunnery instructor's shout: 'Stand still, boy Hay!' and a stinging cut with his whistle chain across the seat of my tight canvas duck trousers would halt me.

Now on *Repulse* in that critical moment, when Bob Hewlet shouted angrily, 'Don't just stand there!' we positively revelled in the sound of our gun firing; it meant we were at least keeping them from attacking us. Although firing only practice smoke shells, our fire sector was open once more, as our ammunition was replenished.

Bob Hewlet was later given first aid and survived to sail again with me when I was a POGI on HMS *Daring*.

Now as we made our way below for the umpteenth time we passed AB Brown, a torpedo man from St Andrews, Fife, the first aid party by his side, so badly injured we could see he was dying. As he recognised Blondy he whispered for his gas mask; inside the face mask was a photograph of his newly married wife. Brown had before risked his life going into flooded compartments to jamb the breakers down so that we had lighting below decks.

Now there was a sudden frightening lurch. We thought at first it was the ship heeling over in our zig-zags. This was when we stopped the rush of young stewards and others in the damage control party, headed by sixteen-year-old George Henderson, canteen assistant, with worried looks on their faces. We told them that things were OK as no 'abandon ship' had been given, and it was only the ship slewing on a turn. They returned to their damage control station and were never seen again.

Captain Tennant's Damage Control had told him there had been four torpedo hits; this was the limit calculated in the ship's stability sheets that the ship could heel to before reaching the angle of point of no return, therefore it was not necessary to give 'Abandon ship'; but it was in fact five, and this was one too many. We began to turn turtle. When he did finally announce, 'Everybody on the upper deck' it was too late. Even so, no abandon ship would ever have had the time to be given as we went so quickly. The old girl did try to save us; as she reached the point of no return in her list to the gunwales she seemed to be balanced there, so giving hundreds like myself those bare moments to leave her.

Or was it, as Leading Seaman George Lawford, the man on the wheel, had said, that Captain Tennant's last order to him was to lash the wheel to starboard, so that with our engines still turning over at a speed of about, they said, 8 knots we were gradually slewing to starboard, keeping us up, but at the same time slewing the dreadful propellors away from us going over the high side to starboard. The Engine Room were trapped below but he said the repeat revolution counter showed they were still working.

As we passed saw the Chief of Stores sitting in his office swivel chair, his feet up on his large desk against the list. He had a jar of neat rum in its wicker basket cover, and was drinking back in huge gulps, as this was the way he wanted to go, he had told his young friend Blondy. Now, as Blondy knocked the rum jar away, I could see it was too late, as Blondy and I desperately tried to drag the heavy Chief from his chair. That, being a swivelled one, just twisted about, and I now had to drag Blondy, almost hysterical, away. I realised his past 'Hi Chief!' whenever he passed was not flannel.

Now we scrambled and crawled along the starboard passageway, and then up the ladder that led into the rec space, as another savage lurch shook down from above the peacetime awning stanchions made of heavy cast iron from their racks above. The only warning was the sound of a rasp as they slid out, coming down on us like bolts from the blue.

On our trips through the rec space before, we had seen Leading Seaman Powell sitting on his haunches, his back to the side party's locker, his head heavily bandaged, and obviously sedated, as when we shouted to him each time we passed, 'All right, Sandy?' there had been no response from him. Now in the distance we could see him in the same position as before. Further on we could see our aim: the starboard rec space door to the upper deck.

Now, we scrambled desperately in a fever bordering on panic, but remembering from the past that this was when we were at our best. All systems were 'at go' as we were now on our hands and knees at a deck angle of about 50 to 60 degrees. Blondy shouted as the heavy diving pump broke its lashings in the next savage lurch, and just missed us, passing by like an express train to hit the bulkhead with a tremendous thump. Then to our horror, after just shouting to Sandy to see if we could at last get a response, the ship's piano broke free from its lashings and pinned poor Sandy to the bulkhead. We slid down to him but it was impossible to move the heavy piano from him against the list also. The piano was always kept in its heavy wooden case, only allowed out to be played; this added to its weight.

Getting outside, we shouted to our Royal Marines above us on 'B' gun deck for help to shift the piano, but they were too busy trying to free the huge Carley float, using foul language as was usual with them about whoever had secured it with sizing wire. Now it was apparent with the list, as we stood with our feet in the scuppers holding on to the guard rails, that to rescue Sandy was impossible.

The sizing wire had been put on by myself, as the cod lashings had soon become frayed 'Dutch penants' and I had been highly complimented by PO Brown, captain of the fo'c'sle, for my bright idea. However, I was glad to see the Marines eventually freed their float.

It was remarkable how these little incidents always remained with you at a time like this. 'Dutch penants' should be furthest from my mind; and the time I'd lit up a cigarette amongst the smoke, fire, death and destruction, only to be put in the OOW report for smoking during action stations by Acting Leading Seaman Billington, with whom I'd been in the same class for Leading Seamen. Now I worried briefly about that report: would it stop me trying again for Leading Seaman? He later was quickly to become advanced to Petty Officer and Admiral Spooner's Coxswain at Singapore.

As we stood together in the scuppers, now joined by Leading Seaman Jan Horsford, the list increasing, another dreadful thing happened of the many that were taking place just after Captain Tennant had shouted down to us from the bridge wings, 'God bless, thanks for fighting the ship!' We heard sickening thuds like, as one described it, bags of wet cement falling from a height. It was the tragic mistake of our twelve boy Anti-Aircraft lookouts high up in the foremast on that square box structure. From their position it looked as if you only had to jump and you would clear the ship's side easily; we knew, as we'd been up there painting in the past.

This was an illusion as it was about a 50-foot wide jump. If only they had jumped the port side that was leaning over towards the sea owing to the list they would have been saved. Now we stood there, our faces as white as our white anti-flash hoods, under our tin hats. Nothing was said from us, this was a situation beyond words. As we side-stepped our way along for'd we could now see Petty Officer O'Rourke standing at the guard rails in full uniform, so that he would be recognised, directing men away from the deadly unseen torpedo holes as men going overboard had been sucked into them never to reappear.

Now as I approached Petty Officer O'Rourke who was standing opposite the space between 'A' and 'B' barbettes, I could hear the sound of metal grinding on metal, and I half turned to look. To my horror it was 'A' turret slowly coming up and out of its barbette, in a system for righting the ship: as she turned turtle the guns were supposed to fall out. Suddenly I lost my footing and went helter skelter down the wide expanse of deck with nothing to grab. I knew it was the end if I reached the low port side, but in those micro-seconds remembered a sunken deck shackle that took the block for the wire in our ammunition derrick and PV wires. I knew every inch of this deck, having spent a great deal of my time down on my knees cleaning it.

Slewing myself towards it in my death slide, I grabbed the shackle, stopped my fall, and regained my position beside Petty Officer O'Rourke, to everybody's relief, and my joy of meeting Michael, Bagsy and the rest of the gun house crew.

Now Jan Horsford and Blondy Garton decided to go for'd, and down the paravane chains on the bow. PO O'Rourke was against it so as he was my old seamanship instructor I obeyed his order without question. How ironic could it have been for Blondy and Jan; they had gone for'd with the express desire to avoid the torpedo holes and were never seen again. The Japanese survey later showed a torpedo hole by the paravane chains on the bow with two skeletons inside.

Now standing beside PO O'Rourke and as the youngster I felt loath to leave him, as amongst all this turmoil he represented order and discipline. To his, 'Come on, Ian, over the side you go,' I replied 'Sir!' as I could not forget my boy's training under him. 'Sir, what about the sharks?' This, we found out later, was the birthplace of the Great White Shark, so what we had seen was a few of them; the explosions had only attracted them.

Petty Officer O'Rourke's voice rose up to a high octave with, 'Ian, get over the f— side!' I went, knowing this would be the last time I'd ever see him. Petty Officer O'Rourke stayed at his post directing men away from the submerged torpedo holes, and did not survive.

As I climbed over the guard rail to go overboard, the Petty Officer's last words to me were, 'Remember, Ian, don't jump and go deep.' I now hit the ledge, sliding down, such was the list now; this ledge was the top of the armoured belt that went round the ship. I took off my gas mask and tin hat, leaving them on the ledge for some unknown reason, and now, only a few feet up from the sea, I took off. Such was my fear and with PO O'Rourke's warning I was already swimming in the air before hitting the water, and hardly went to any depth. The warm China Sea and the knowledge that the nightmare was at last ended put me in a happy relaxed frame of mind.

That was until I heard the 'Thump, Thump, Thump,' of the huge propellers coming nearer and nearer. My nightmare returned, of being chopped up in a mincing machine, as some had been from the quarterdeck. In desperation I struck out wildly, and to my immense relief I could hear them gradually getting fainter as *Repulse* slewed away from me to starboard. Captain Tennant's last order, 'Wheel to

134

starboard.' I struck out for the three destroyers in the distance; they seemed about a football pitch away but they were slowly moving from the possible threat of a Japanese submarine. Now the thick oil came out in a black cloud, as the cry went up, 'She's going.' Half turning I saw her bows rise up steeply, showing the still recently red-leaded bottom put on in Rosyth dockyard. That had been when we went in for repairs to the bow.

Now *Repulse* seemed to slide down backwards and pause as she hit the bottom with her stern. She had sunk in only a hundred feet of water, the same depth our submariners practised free ascent in the deep tank at HMS *Dolphin*. Many of our ship's company were trapped in watertight compartments, and the tragedy is that some reported hearing the clanging of spanners as people in the engine room were trying to escape. Some probably got out but the sharks would have finished them off in the night.

They had all the gear at Singapore Sultan Naval Base for 'Sub smash,' and the salvage tugs, but no order was given to use them. Ironic the time before the war when HMS *Thetis* sank in Liverpool Bay doing trials. She was renamed *Thunderer* but was sunk in the Med. I did not dare to tread water as the rest were doing, watching *Repulse* sink. Sub Lt. J.O.C. Hayes, later Admiral, saluted the Flag as she went down. As for myself, I struck out, believing that he who lives fights another day, and I had no great love for *Repulse* after two years without leave in the close confinement.

The first destroyer went slowly past, I'd missed her, and the second the same. Various people swam past me, shouting, 'All right, Ian?' How they recognised me in my black oil-covered anti-flash hood I don't know. Petty Officer Lofty Rodger was one of them, and he is still in communication with me today. I was a self-taught swimmer; from the 'dog paddle' the Navy considered I could swim, but I made slow progress.

Now I was getting groggy with the oil fuel fumes. I could see in the distance the last and final destroyer coming up and I knew this was my last chance, but I was slowly dropping off. The thing that saved me and brought me round was my mouth getting numb, and with a start, remembered the terrible time I'd had once as a boy at the dentist, I began to strike out with fresh vigour. I could now see a figure on the destroyer's fo'c'sle, I paddled in my dog paddle with my right hand and held up my left arm. The heaving line must have gone the full length as the end knot, a monkey's fist, fell over my left shoulder. All I had now to do was to twist my arm round it in a jamming half hitch. Just in time, as I was all in.

The figure on the fo'c'sle had now moved down from there to the waist which meant it was not so high for me to climb. As he pulled me into the jumping nets, like a hooked fish, all I could do was hold on as the destroyer was still under way and the under tow was dragging me down. Others who had no heaving line support were dragged under and down for good.

After the others had clambered over me by stepping on my head, using it as a step up, my friend above on the heaving line pulled and I climbed up and over the guard rails; my stomach bounced me on deck. At last I was safe on board the destroyer *Electra*. *Electra* in Greek mythology incited her brother Orestes to murder their mother, who had already murdered their father.

The shout went out again, 'She's going!' but this time for the *Prince of Wales*. Now there was silence except for the sound of people blowing up their rubber life belts, and one youngster wailing, 'Oh no, not again!' Above me was the *Electra*'s flag deck, and we could hear the PO Yeomen of Signals singing out to the bridge, word for word from the International Signals code book, 'Stop firing, pick up survivors,' so saving our lives as he took his squadrons off. This has been contested, but from an old International Code Book of Signals, we find for example, in all the countries' languages: B10 = Pick up, C2 = Survivors, S10 = stop firing. That's not exact but it will do to illustrate.

The oil fuel burning our eyes we showered. The *Electra*'s crew turned their lockers out to give us clothing, and now after a tot of neat rum, we were spewing up the rum but ridding ourselves of the poisonous oil we had inadvertently swallowed. Going for'd to the messes I passed Bagsy and his henchmen, unconcerned about the past incident, drying their pound notes off on the galley range. In the mess decks acting as a first aid place, our 'Sticks', the Royal Marine boy bugler, was almost in hysterics, with the body of a Chief lying on the mess table. Sticks had put his finger in the Chief's mouth to prevent him swallowing his tongue but the Chief had died and his mouth had shut, trapping his finger.

Now we were tired and happy to have survived that dreadful nightmare and to be on our way back to Singapore. The *Electra* was so crowded with survivors that at one time the Pipe was, 'Move over to starboard,' as we were in danger of capsizing. I saw a quiet place on the fo'c'sle of six forms stretched out and as it was cool on the foredeck they had blankets covering them. If I'd not been so tired, and with the effects of the rum, I might have thought differently, but I said something like, 'Move over, Jan, for a small one.' On the crowded mess decks of *Repulse* it had been commonplace for us to sleep together on the deck, so now I crawled under the blanket and snuggled up to the one beside me and in no time was fast asleep.

It was dark when I was awakened by a voice that shouted, 'Stop, this one's alive!' I have often visualised the bitter irony of that scene: after having miraculously escaped death now to become shark meat, and I could hear the splash and the flurry of white phosphorescence as they fought over me. They had told me you couldn't feel the shark's bites as he has in his teeth the same nerve-numbing substance as the dentist's cocaine, but I did not think that was any consolation.

I wandered down to the mess decks to the sound of voices, warmth and companionship and met Michael, whom I'd thought lost. I flung myself into his arms.

Chapter Twenty-Four

HMS *REPULSE*:
SOME OF HER SHIP'S COMPANY

Top left, Leading Seaman Sandy Powell, fore anti Aircraft Director's crew; below him my mate from *Ganges*, Michael O'Hern, Southern Irish, 'A' turret's gun house crew along with myself as centre sightsetter to both guns before the attack by Japanese aircraft; below him, Leading Seaman Jan Horsford – all West country men were called 'Jan' – 'A' turret's range finder for local control. Next to Sandy at the top right, 'Slinger' Woods, gun crew of the 'Chicago Piano' ('They tried to fly straight down our gun barrels'); and between him and Michael, 'Scouse' Bob Hewlett, Starboard S1 4-inch gun's crew, his cap flat aback against regulations with a fag in his mouth. Below him and next to Jan is Ordinary Seaman Billington, later Leading-Seaman and later still, after the fall of Singapore, Admiral Spooner's Coxswain as a Petty Officer. Next to him on his left Petty Officer O'Rourke, Boys Int. and above him Junior Seaman 'Sharky' Ward the only one with his hat on square. He had a perpetual grin having just joined from the training ship HMS *Ganges*; maybe that was why he's happy. Next to him on his left is Leading Seaman Smithy, captain of S1 gun, another Southern Irish man, and below him an ordinary seaman whose name I can't recall.

HMS *Royal Oak* is in the background, later sank in mistake for *Repulse*. On deck by the bollards is our mine degausing gear before it was installed below.

HMS Repulse: some of her Ship's Company.

Myself.

Sergeant Digby.

The photo of myself was taken by Sergeant 'Lofty' Digby, in charge of aircraft maintenance, the RAF forming our first Fleet Air Arm. Most of the photos which I sent home were taken by him. (He later inherited the family title.)

Chapter Twenty-Five

TORPEDOMAN WALTER FARQUHAR, HMS *REPULSE*

It is 1937–8 in Glasgow. The steelworks and shipyards are going flat out. Every so often a roar rings out and the sky at night is lit up with a red glow in the vicinity of Beardmore's Parkhead forge. The smog from this gives out a sour stale smell, and day sometimes turns into night; the street lighting remains on all day and night. Coming home from school with eyes rimmed in black soot, our white shirts, clean in the morning, are grubby.

Walter Farquhar lived near me but we were unknown to each other till we joined *Repulse*. Like many, we were glad to leave Glasgow and its rain, bitter climate and gang fights, for the Royal Navy. Sunny, warm and clean with happy holiday makers, Plymouth was a marvellous change. After getting over our homesickness at fifteen years old, well warranted having never left home before, in this now strict discipline but fair regime, we gradually drifted from our families; unbelievable a few short years before. Now we always looked forward to going back south when our leave was up.

When we arrived at Newton Abbott station, Devon, the porter with a strong west country burr would shout out the name and we, about a dozen of us northerners, would mimic him, ending in rhyme with, 'You can have it,' but our happy laughter belied this. The Royal Navy had become a part of us, or was it we had become a part of it?

Walter was older than us having been at *Ganges* before Michael and me, but naturally we three became close friends. After qualifying

Walter Farquhar.

Seaman Torpedoman, and there being no torpedoes on Capital ships, they took the place of electrical staff because of their knowledge of electrics. We saw Walter only occasionally now as he moved aft to messes next to the 'horse boxes': the Royal Marines' messes.

The first time the ship arrived at Singapore, Walter and another young torpedoman were sent ashore on temporary loan to HMS *Sultan*, the naval base. The contrast between the two was remarkable. Walter was thick-set and even as a boy shaved; the other was slim, nervous and quiet, but we noticed the two were inseparable. I was happy for them both as a friendship like that is a precious thing, even more so in danger and death in war.

The next two occasions we were to meet, I was to remember, now as vividly as then. I stumbled down HMS *Electra*'s gangway at midnight at the naval base dock, and at the foot of the gangway with stunned looks on their faces were Walter and his mate David. I was given a tot of neat rum at the base, which I did not spew up like the one on *Electra*. This one had immediate effect, and I remember faintly them both putting me under a shower to try and rid me of the oil fuel, and then to bed under a mosquito net. I had arrived at the naval base HMS *Sultan*, Singapore.

The base closed and we were evacuated. We were now at the RAF Seeleter air base camp, going into Singapore docks to load up a small coaster with drums of aviation spirit which the aircraft had no further use for. They were lying in wooden crates all over the dock side, as they were in the country lanes around Seeleter air field. That was the air cover we were supposed to have had. We gathered at the bottom of the hold, and as the drums came down we swung them in a stevedore manner to the after end, shouting 'Lower!'

Now suddenly the air raid began. The first sign was the small local Singapore defence 4-inch anti-aircraft guns going off; the sirens had long ago packed in. We rushed to the ladder but when we reached the top of the hold we were only to be met by the immaculate Petty Officer Pascal in smart pressed green denim, his service revolver strapped to his slim waist. With his usual dry caustic voice he said, 'Where do you think you lot are going to? Get down that hold and carry on loading!'

He then shouted after us that there was no place to run for, the dock had piles of drums of aircraft gasoline, and it was safer not to draw attention by running about the dock. We saw the logic of this but still felt very uneasy.

Now came the second occasion we were to meet Walter and Dave. They had been searching the dock for us even during the air raid, as it was important to tell us that they were on their way home, being specialist ratings. They told us with undisguised joy that they were on their way out of all this, which we understood, and they promised to see my mother and give her my message.

Here was the terrible irony. After missing the action on *Repulse* where few of the torpedo staff survived, being caught below decks as most of our ship company were, their convoy was shelled just outside Singapore by the waiting Japanese Navy and sunk with no survivors. Those that escaped, the sharks finished off. I've often thought of what those terrible last moments were like for them but comforted in the knowledge that whatever happened they would have stayed together till the end. Sadly and ironically, I was the one who saw their mothers in the end.

Back in Seeleter air base camp, Petty Officers Pascal, ex HMS *Prince of Wales*, and 'Ginger' Wilkinson, ex *Repulse* approached us saying that they required volunteers for two Royal Navy Dutch former motor gun boats. Michael looked at me and we silently agreed: anything was better than loading aviation spirit during an air raid. There were about two hundred naval ratings in the camp, and when they heard of us crewing two motor gun boats for a 'hairy' job up in North Johore, the usual Navy micky-taking took place by the usual few, of 'Any one want to swap drafts?'!

This was the second bitter irony as they all left and their convoy, like that of Walter and Dave, was shelled and sunk with the few survivors leading a dreadful life as prisoners of war. We, who were destined not to stand a chance, survived *Repulse*, and escaped from Singapore to live and fight another day.

145

Chapter Twenty-Six

HMS *SULTAN*, NAVAL BASE SINGAPORE

We docked at the Base around midnight. It was situated at the other end of the island, close to the Johore causeway linking it to mainland Malaya. The following day, dressed with towels around our waists, waiting to be kitted up, we lay on the grass of the beautiful landscaped gardens, the perspiration already beginning to bead on our faces, with a small film of oil fuel that no amount of showerings for weeks thence seemed to remove; by drawing your fingernail across the skin you could still see it.

The kaleidoscope of colours, the vivid startling beautiful flowers, and the tropical plants with their very deep tropical green only seen in these climes, formed a glorious backdrop to the bright reds, blues, and yellows, dazzling more brightly than any we had seen in our lives. The many species of tropical birds with their strange and beautiful cries, the musical pleasant bedlam of the insects together with the strong scents of the flowers, and undergrowth all tended to be erotic and dull the senses to pleasant relaxation, like a powerful drug. It was the drug of life, of very life itself, after the living ghastly nightmare we had recently experienced. The small cheeky green parrots with their heads cocked seemed to look down on us in friendly curiosity and wonder. As I hugged the earth, burying my head in its dry earthy smell, as I breathed it in, a single blade magnified out of all proportion in all its splendour, I formulated a silent prayer of gratitude, vowing never to be dissatisfied with life, come what may in the future.

At particular times when the humidity was low Singapore could be a paradise, and now we fully appreciated this beautiful planet of ours. Lying naked devoid of all worldly possessions, it was sufficient just to enjoy every vital moment to its full; the message, 'Give up all your worldly possessions and follow me,' was in its true perspective.

Suddenly we were startled out of this pleasant reverie by the shouts and barks of broken voiced NCOs. To our complete and utter amazement our Royal Marines, 'The Plymouth Argyles', were being fell in, already with new uniforms, boots shining, webbing blancoed sparkling white, rifles at the slope, fixed bayonets glittering evilly in the sunshine. As the hoarse gravelled voice of the sergeant marched them off in close column, we could almost hear their hardbitten caustic remarks when things went a bit awry on board ship, 'That's fuck all on a big ship, Jack.' We stood up and cheered wildly and loudly our beloved 'Bootnecks'; as seventeen- and eighteen-year-olds they were our natural heroes. They were to fight their way down Malaya along with the Argyle and Sutherland Highlanders in the best traditions of our Highland Regiments with bayonets.

The second battalion of the Argyle and Sutherland Highlanders were later to be commanded by 'Mad Mitch' – Colonel Colin Campbell Mitchell – with whom I am proud to claim kinship. The Plymouth Argyles Royal Marines of *Repulse*, on being picked up by *Electra* covered in oil fuel and exhausted like us, all immediately relieved the exhausted ship's gunners and continued the fight against the swarming Japanese attacking the *Prince of Wales*. They had to fight back down to Singapore through no air cover with bayonets and few survived.

The revelation that material possessions are of little value compared to life itself was soured by our bitterness about the deaths of our comrades and we suffered an angry vindictiveness against the enemy as well as everybody and everything. We were now misfits of the very worst kind, intent on destruction for destruction's sake against the Japanese, and anybody else that got in our way. That included our own people. We felt utterly ruthless and vicious. The butchery of the past having wetted our appetites, as if hooked on some horror film we

147

looked forward to more and that was soon to come. We now had a gangster's mentality.

Sadly we were again to witness time and time again the results of the lack of air cover, as when the crack Indian AA gun battery at the foot of the naval base that protected the dockyard, brand new and with stores to equip a fleet together with the newest largest floating dock in the world, were all later given to the Japanese without a thought of demolition. This Indian regiment we watched in our spare time, admiring their snug dugouts, sandbagged, as opposed to our own on *Repulse* completely open and little protected, and their own small sandbagged range finder, which was to prove so accurate in making the 27-wave formations waver coming over from Johore to bomb Singapore, something we had not been able to do on *Repulse*. We were also intrigued at their drill as on completion they stood back stamping their feet in military precision to attention. All this was done while we were waiting for repatriation, as Captain Bell of the famous HMS *Exeter* River Plate battle against the *Scharnhorst* had picked us out as being too young for active service. Next day we found this fine Indian gun battery dead, stood to attention by bomb blast, testifying again to our lack of air support and to the Japanese precise bombing.

Now we were employed on sentry duty at Admiral Spooner's residence, and during an air raid took cover, only to have Lady Spooner, armed only with a Chinese parasol against the shrapnel, say, 'Come out of there, you rabbits, what will the natives think?' We did not care what the natives thought as they were quicker at taking cover than we were, but we admired her courage, took stock that we were bolting at the slightest sign of danger and rectified this. Our story resembled that of the rabbits of *Watership Down*; six of us, fleeing an equally terrible tyrant, were to escape, and I identified myself with Fiver, the smallest and most nervous, later when I read this charming, classic story.

Later in Australia, over a schooner of beer, I was to hear from Petty Officer Billington, the Admiral's coxswain from *Repulse*.

They had left in a fast motor launch although a signal had been sent saying no one was to leave Singapore and although he had told us we were the sheet anchor of Singapore and it would not fall, could not fall. The Japanese Navy were waiting outside sinking all that left including the last of the Royal Naval draft, whom we had heard taunting us: 'Anyone want to swap drafts?' as we had volunteered for a motor gun boat's crew and had to remain behind to pick up a government agent. Unknowingly, this was to lead to our safety. Billington returning with some head hunters from Borneo found Admiral Spooner dead from dehydration.

We had been picked for the motor gun boats by Petty Officers Wilkinson and Pascal of *Repulse* and *Prince of Wales*, two Petty Officers of the old school, although firm disciplinarians. They were friendly and tactful and we owed our survival to these two very fine NCOs. The Service way of volunteering was, 'You, you and you.'

With the Royal Naval Base closed and empty, we were billeted in the Union Jack Club, Singapore, and travelled down to the boat moored at Princess Pier each day. This was before things started to hot up. We called at the dockyard stores at HMS *Laburnum* at Keppel Harbour, where the official required us to have a requisition form in triplicate, until a smartly dressed PO Pascal with his revolver holstered in its green webbing, his usual quiet sardonic smile and those unblinking, unsettling, staring eyes, changed the man's mind as we loaded up with camouflage nets and stores. Unknown we also loaded up with white tropical shorts, shirts, stockings and shoes in our own sizes, about a hundred for each of us, so that later we were the best dressed seamen ever seen, much to the amazement of our NCOs who had called us scruffy. When one set of gear became slightly soiled, after a shower we changed into a complete new rig. The old Sikh watchman, our friend at the UJC, did a roaring trade in cast-offs.

The dockside was now filling up with cars abandoned by their owners leaving, most with their keys in the ignition, so that we indulged to the full our youthful vandalism. After driving them around, every make under the sun, we pushed them over the dock. Never having driven a lorry, we set off for our posh hotel and, forgetting the

149

sides of the lorry sticking out, brought all the ornate pillars and canopy down on top of us. We left in a hurry. Most of these types of hotels were for officers only, but we were tolerated as we were smartly dressed and quiet, content to sit and soak in the genteel civilised atmosphere, with the quiet murmurings and clink of glasses. There was one exception as the famous snooty Raffles Hotel was definitely out of bounds. One of our members however put the rickshaw boy inside and, taking up the shafts, drove into the hotel, just as the 'pukka wallahs' were having their first drink, the sun 'being over the yardarm'. It was said two retired Service Officers almost had a heart attack, as well as the rickshaw boy. We enjoyed the sods opera, and the rambustious service clubs UJC, New World, etc. where you crunched up to the bar on broken glass and had to step over drunken forms flaked out in the toilets, but we liked a change. At this point, changing our car which we used for transport from the UJC to Princess Pier where the boats were moored, to an old fashioned MG which took my fancy, we put on the windscreen 'requisitioned for naval services'; now in spotless whites we looked the part and very official, and we were left alone by the Red Caps (army police) who had been known to shoot looters dead. In the past we had been on a hair-raising chase by them, burning rubber and two wheels, only narrowly to miss being killed.

This I repeat was in the beginning before things got out of hand. Stalling at the traffic lights opposite Raffles Hotel, a smartly dressed Eurasian gentleman in spotless whites and tropical topee pointed out in faultless English that we had spelt requisitioned wrong and furthermore it was his car. This was to set the scene later for some horrific happenings. He was a member of the Sultan's exclusive company. The Sultan was to be later taken out and shot as a traitor. At the time we did not know what a dangerous acquaintance we had made. This was Mr Rangi whom we were to meet often later, and from whom we were barely able to escape with our lives. HMS *Sultan*, nearby his country house the Teak House, was renamed HMS *Terror*, a fitting title for what was to happen in the Teak House.

Arriving at the boat we would proudly hoist our small white ensign at the yard, and in our spotless whites created quite an impression on the public who leaned down from the pier with such comments as, 'It's good to see the Navy here.' Little did they know we were all that was left of it. The many leafy lanes around Seleeter air base were crowded with exhausted troops who had fought their way down Malaya without air cover only to find they were sheltering from the sun against the many oblong crates of aircraft that were never used and which could have prevented this sad spectacle. Again, in complete contradiction to the book *Battleship*, aircraft was for the asking. It stated that Admiral Sir Tom Phillips, that stubborn old sea dog, did not ask for air cover as there was none to ask for so the battle was lost together with Singapore and all our Far Eastern possessions.

We always had a rousing cheer from the Army, and they appeared to think we would get them out in a Dunkirk operation. We were told very little as the less we knew the better and we shuddered at the horrible pictures of torture. We knew we would never stand it so it was just as well we knew nothing, but we cherished the hope that the Army might be right. It was good to see they were in good shape and held grimly on to their rifles.

The whole jetty was like a bomb; we returned and carried on loading the high-explosive fuel. From Lady Spooner's rabbits we had swung the other way; we now believed we were immortal after the horror of *Repulse*, and we were subsequently picked for Pascal's crew as much for this as for the fact we were all ex boy seamen from HMS *Ganges* and after that training it was hard to resist saluting and turning somersaults to railway porters when on leave.

Our next operation was sabotage over in occupied Johore with PO Wilkinson so now we became a natural choice of both POs, but to our dismay at the time missed being repatriated home with the other younger ratings. However, it was to save our lives as the last draft all perished, though that seemed such a long time ago.

We were now living on the boat as the UJC was closed up, and dressed not in our whites but in khaki so as not to draw attention to ourselves. We dressed in coloured sarongs, sandals, straw hats and sunglasses ashore for the same reasons. We flip-flopped through the teeming masses of so many mixed races of Singapore with the best of them, the cacophony of sounds and the erotic spicy smells of so many different national foods stimulating us; we enjoyed this unusual unfamiliar garb and anonymous appearance.

We were now acting as a ferry boat taking the last of the base officers wives who had previously refused to leave out to the last ship to go. I was suddenly startled to hear a voice say, 'I say, you there, yes, you boy.' It was a very formidable lady, standing opposite the smoking ruins of what once had been the Bank of Singapore, with a huge pile of luggage. Doubling up smartly with a respectful, 'Yes, Mam!' she ordered me to take this mountain of luggage down to our small craft. Her parting remark was, 'Don't forget the tennis rackets,' as I sweated with the heavy cases, handing them down to Michael. It was like a scene from Laurel and Hardy as in my best Hardy voice I said, 'The lady said don't forget the tennis rackets,' to Michael's stammering rage as he went from one side of the boat to the other, dropping the luggage overboard. The harbour was now littered with floating luggage of every description. He remarked 'She will be lucky to get out herself,' but in fact, like Lady Spooner's spirited remark, 'What will the natives think,' I suspect this was said in the same context. We admired both ladies for their stiff upper lip of the British Showing the Flag in very trying circumstances. Later in Australia I was to recall this incident so solving a puzzle of banknotes.

Shortly later we were under air attack again but the expression, 'No bloody air cover,' was worn out long ago, as we closed up at the rush on our for'd Oerliken machine gun, Michael manning the gun, I acting as lookout and helper.

Our first indication was from the gallant volunteer Singapore defence gun battery with its sporadic firing, as the sirens had packed up long ago. They were the other side of the pier from us where we lay in deep shadows. He came in low and unsuspecting and we could not miss; another 'one shot lighter' went away in a blaze of glory, but our position was given away. Thumping hard on his shoulder, pointing this one out diving straight for us, Michael sweated and cursed with a jammed gun, clearing it too late as we fell into each other's arms behind the gunshield. The 'ice candles' searching us out in screaming ricochet against the pier behind us, cut the water and deck up like a giant lawn mower, 'The lips smile but the eyes are saying farewell,' once again. Suddenly the howling scream stopped and I was savagely pushed aside, as he swung the gun up and got him in the underbelly.

After that it was imperative we change billets as now our position was known. We moved to Keppel harbour where we tied up near the old wooden hulk HMS *Laburnum*, now long deserted, where we had got our kit, it seemed so long ago. Now, to our ever-increasing desperate position and our natural enquiries, 'When are we getting out?' we were simply told this was a mission to pick up someone.

Before the shift from Princess Pier to Keppel harbour, we had been regular visitors to Mr Rangi, a member of Raffles Hotel, the gentleman whose MG we had borrowed, at his Singapore air-conditioned flat near by the pier. The main attraction was Lani, his beautiful housekeeper or mistress, we could never decide which. He showed little interest in her and was more interested in myself for some reason, probably my experience on *Repulse* of which I eagerly told. I tagged along to be with Michael and more for the air conditioning than anything else, as when the sun shone it was pleasant. Singapore became almost a paradise with its vivid and startling tropical scenery, but strangely, when there was no sun and it was overcast with low cloud, the adiabatic lapse rate went crazy, reaching such a saturation point that it was like someone throwing a bucket of water over you, drenching shirts and shorts. You could almost hear the perspiration squirt out, followed by my agonising prickly heat, so I was more than content to sit hugging my drink of iced crème de menthe and listen to the sparkling conversation, with the wonderful Oriental dishes cooked up by Lani.

It took a while at first to convince Michael that it was not 'Red Biddy', a favourite tipple in some parts of Glasgow of methylated spirits, boot polish and cheap wine.

153

We were both very much attracted to Lani who was Eurasian, the most beautiful girls in the world, said many, and spoke all the languages that made up her many nationalities, Dutch, Chinese, Malay and Javanese with ease, and who had a sparklingly brilliant personality. No wonder we were in love with her, but her eyes were only for Michael and I had long ago given up trying to chat her up as she pointedly ignored me to such an extent that I felt like shouting, 'Listen, I'm speaking to you!' To make matters worse she had confided to Michael that I looked cute. With a bitter smile, I thought, so does Mr Rangi. I had accepted the fact that I was not one to set the party on fire, with my quiet reserve and nervous selfconscious manner, together with the unconscious habit of screwing my face up in anxiety in repose till they would ask if I was suffering toothache. I always seized eagerly on the excuse and said yes, but they cured me of this. Rangi and Lani had now moved from Singapore owing to the air attacks and futile opposition against them, and above all the lack of air cover. It obvious to all now that Singapore was doomed, in spite of the banner head lines, 'Singapore will not fall, cannot fall,' and 'the Far Eastern fleet is on its way.'

They had moved out to his country house by the Johore causeway that linked Singapore with the mainland and was coincidentally near HMS *Sultan*, renamed 'Terror' as the Sultan was later shot as a traitor. The house was called the Teak House, but after the events to follow could have also been renamed Terror.

After passing the deserted HMS *Sultan* a country lane branched left, and after passing through several small native villages arrived at the impressive decorated wrought iron gates. On the mantles either side were two oriental lamps. The gravelled driveway curved gracefully round giving you glimpses of the sea separating Singapore from the mainland, sparkling through the tall graceful palm trees and thick dark green foliage like glittering diamonds. It was a large wooden structure built of teak, about fifteen feet from the ground on stilts on the native style, but it was no native hut. A wide veranda encircled the house with huge green venetian blinds that could be raised or lowered to suit the occasion. Being off the ground it was cool and pleasant: I was surprised at first that there was no air conditioning but realised it was not needed because of this.

Inside the house, leaving our sandals at the door, we were met by a wide expanse of polished teak floor enhanced by the absence of carpets and chairs. We sat on high cushions in our sarongs with our iced drinks under the gaze of an almost life sized Buddha, the burning joss sticks giving off a pleasant scent to his wise all knowing smile. With a cool sea breeze rustling the palms it was very pleasant after the sweltering heat of the town, and I was not troubled by my prickly heat. Adjoining this, departing from the traditional oriental style, was an up-to-date kitchen in modern western mode and showers and bathrooms as in his Singapore flat. After our service way of life and uniforms we revelled in sarongs and these surroundings.

This was of course in the past, now, and we had not paid a visit for some time, being ordered not to stray too far from the boat where we now lay at Keppel harbour docks near the old *Laburnum*.

Chapter Twenty-Seven

THE TEAK HOUSE

There was plenty of activity in the fore cabin. When I had the excuse to poke my head in on some pretence of a routine enquiry, the scene told its own story. The overflowing ashtrays, the half empty bottle of whisky; Boy Signals Andrews with his head-set on busily sending and receiving signals from our powerful radio set; the lieutenant, our CO, decoding them. As a former Singapore Johore yacht club member, his prime function was to navigate as he knew all the islands and country from Singapore to Java and to decode signals which were now coming from as far afield as Colombo and Batavia where the last of our naval resistance was.

The running of the boat and a great many of the important decisions were left to Pascal, so we naturally looked to him, not having too much faith in a lieutenant RNVR, but this quiet officer and his polite concern for our welfare and his knowledge of small boats eventually won us over and we were later to owe our lives to his quiet leadership. We had two former Dutch naval fast motor gun boats P10 and P12, each with twin Thornycroft powerful engines, one lieutenant and three hands to each boat. Boy Andrews, Michael and I made up for our youthful inexperience by our eagerness and very vigorous training from an early age of joining the Royal Navy, and now *Repulse* which had hardened us as veterans.

I immediately spread the 'buzz' that our important passenger was expected and we all breathed a sigh of relief: soon we would be getting out of this 'rat trap'.

It was at this point that Michael on the spur of the moment decided to bring Lani back to the boat. I was against it, but could not convince him of the danger not only to the mission but to all of us. With my face screwed up in its customary toothache expression of anxiety as I fretted and worried after he had gone, I was indeed Fiver, the smallest nervous rabbit from *Watership Down*. Reporting this to Pascal I was prepared for his customary words on occasions like this as he exploded in rage with a, 'What! That's all I need to bloody well know now!' and with his hard, uncompromising, unblinking, disturbing stare and his cruel sardonic expression, he said, 'That's too bad; if he is not back in time we go, all right,' and, stabbing a forefinger at me, he added, 'And you're staying put, all right.'

I turned and left, my mind made up to go after Michael. Quickly I stripped from my uniform of shorts and shirt on the upper deck, as it was too stuffy below which would bring on my prickly heat, and donned my longhi, sandals, straw hat and sunglasses. Pascal had no objection to this rig ashore, the Japanese tortured and killed you no matter what rig you were in. I placed my uniform cap neatly on top, wryly thinking that in spite of being not in uniform, without your cap on the upper deck you were improperly dressed. The lieutenant insisted that the small white ensign be hoisted right on eight o'clock in the morning and taken down at sunset, and kept us busy from morning to night in all kinds of activity: down on rope gun mat stripping the guns and cleaning them; putting them together again blindfolded with nothing left over as he timed it with a stop watch; this along with wood scraping, polishing brass etc. and stopping us taking our stand-easy cups of tea when we felt like it. Now we had something to look forward to, and bring order into our lives in the chaotic and tense conditions of ashore. We welcomed it all to have someone to tell us what to do. He was against favouritism, bullying and sarcasm, as I was to find out when driving him to one of his many foragings for the boat, food and equipment, in his acquired powerful old Bentley. I said, trying to make friends with him, 'Thanks, Pascal,' over something or another, and he nearly took off in his anger. In the deserted naval stores of *Laburnum*,

157

our eyes lit up like jackdaws in this Aladdin's cave of everything from a small pin to cries of 'Just look at this!' His terse comment was, 'Concentrate on the Chief Engineer's list and our own. We haven't the room or the time for anything else and keep your eyes off those uniform shorts. The boat already looks like an old clothes shop.' We also loaded up with cases and cases of tinned food of every description, picking out what we fancied ourselves – tinned tongue and ham, chocolate biscuits, also biscuits for bread etc. As we only had a small fridge, all the food was necessarily tinned. Those of us smitten with 'this may come in handy' Pascal shot down.

Now, having changed dress for this very comfortable attire to go after Michael, I heard him call softly, 'Ian,' but remained stubbornly with my back towards him, pretending to fiddle with my sarong, feeling intense disloyalty as up to now I had obeyed him without question. But then, he had always impressed on us that if we thought something was wrong to obey our judgement and always question it. Gripping my shoulders and turning me round gently to face him I was surprised to see for the first time the hard uncompromising stare and faint sardonic twist to the lips had disappeared as he said, 'Look, I don't want to lose either of you. I need you for the Oerlikon gun forward, all right, but after considering the news that they will not in all probability attack till late tonight or early morning, it's a risk but I have decided to let you go. If anyone can do it, it will be you, all right, and the round journey to the Teak House should take just over an hour, all right?' I had often mused in the past on what would have happened if you had replied, 'All wrong,' to his habitual idiom, but I was not careful to reply as formally as I could, 'Thanks, Petty Officer Pascal.' He might call me Ian, but I knew it was fatal to reply in any other way. Now he gave one of his rare smiles as he said, 'You would have gone anyway.'

'Take one of the Lewis machine guns and spare ammunition magazine clips; use the Bentley,' as we all had our own acquired cars. His was the fastest. Getting quickly into the car I started to do my checks on the gun, unaware he was standing beside the car watching me, as I pushed down with my thumb on the cartridges to see they went up and down under the pressure of the magazine springs. I knew all the stoppages by heart but a jammed gun could waste precious seconds. Recocking and releasing back easy the firing pin I banged the magazine on to its satisfactory click, recocked and placed it on the passenger's seat beside me. A harsh grating voice almost in my right ear made me jump: 'Safety catch.' I stammered, 'Sorry,' pushing the safety catch to the on position; I had forgotten the most important function, that might have had the result of shooting my foot off or someone else's. Starting up, I turned to see he had resumed his old hard unblinking stare and faint sardonic expression as I speedily left to his parting shout, 'Keep it to the front of your mind at all times: if you're not back we leave, all right!'

Clearing Kepple docks, I made practised sweeps with my left free hand from the wheel to the sub machine gun on the passenger's seat without looking so that I could find it in a hurry. Entering the main stream of traffic I had to slow down exasperatingly for the teeming multitudes of the various nationalities that made up Singapore, the babble of many tongues, their smiles of flashing white teeth, the slow moving bullock carts, the old buses with the occupants on the roof as well as clinging to the sides, all in happy disorder in their oriental outlook on life. The critical situation seemed to make no difference, life going on just as it had always done in the past.

As I sped on to the sounds of Chinese music the echo suddenly seemed to cut out to be replaced by Indian, then Javanese, then Malay, each one shouting out as I sped past, each with its distinct aromatic smell of the different national dishes. There were the raucous cries of the bean soup and rice pedlars, pedalling their wares to the all night sittings of the Mah-Jong players who banged their chips down with a clatter, along with the cacophony of tooting and blaring horns, everyone seeming to blow whether it was needed or not. All coming over the still tropical cool night air, as was usually the case when the day had been hot and oppressive, the sounds were very distinct and clear, all blended together in a cacophonous sound pleasant to the ear, which was Singapore, a very fascinating place to be in. All lived cheek by jowl in perfect harmony, an example to the world.

Clearing the native quarter, I was at last able to speed up, and crossed the iron bridge into a more select and quieter quarter of green swathes of lawns and statues, with the famous Raffles Hotel with its invisible sign: 'East is East and West is West, but never the twain shall meet.' The place was deserted and gone were the long queues of rickshaws and taxis waiting for the gentlemen in bow ties and cummerbunds, the ladies in evening frocks. It was only a few weeks ago that they were socialising as if nothing had happened. I was glad someone had believed the headlines: 'Singapore will not fall, cannot fall,' because we had not. As was my custom on passing, I gave Churchill's famous salute to them.

Now as the countryside opened up I switched on the headlights, not to see as the moon was so bright you could read a book by it, but for the natives to see me coming, as they had a habit of wandering happily down the middle of the road without a care in the world, and for the old water buffalo who for some strange reason was always waiting for you round a corner.

I pushed the safety catch to the rear and off in spite of the almost normal goings on of the native population in their oriental outlook on life. The situation was critical and I was not lured into thinking otherwise. I went into my old routine, what of this, that and the other, the flexible alternatives and finally the alternative last resorts. It was not needless worry as it had always helped in the past, enabling me to act without thinking when in some unexpected, frightening position. It was not the fleeting shadows caused by the moon across the road up ahead or the appearance of the palm trees on either side of the road like monsters sweeping out to grab me, but suppose we were not in time and the boats left without us or Michael missed me, coming back by a different route! My foot pressed down unconsciously.

The old, but still powerful convertible gently responded immediately and wonderfully as it pressed me back hard in the cushions. The comfortable monotonous tyre hum suddenly became a howl, the moon shadows were contorting everything and up ahead I was just in time to see a sharp bend which I cursed obscenely for daring to come up to me so fast. Taking a pause of two marching paces between each movement, up two three, over two three, down, I changed down, braked smoothly, stamped on the gas, and was round to only a slight slither and smell of burning rubber. Changing up, I shouted in the sheer elation of being alive, the wind in my hair, breathing deeply the scented tropical night air, and feeling as on that day when the small green parrots looked down in wonder and curiosity at me. I shouted out as the Company Commander on Naval Battalion manoeuvres did: 'That last movement was very well carried out, with the exception . . .' The proviso always amused me, but here I merely said, '. . . of a slight slither, and burning rubber,' and, shrugging, gave myself top marks.

Like our Marines we were trained to fight on land and sea. That, few people realised. The sudden thought: what if some natives had been there, as they were wont to do, right in the middle of the road, or that poor old water buffalo? I eased back on the gas, lit a cigarette from the portable cigarette lighter from the dashboard which I was surprised to see on this old Bentley, but they had had them as far back as the thirties. From its glow, I glanced at the time. With the speed on that last stretch I must be no more than five minutes behind Michael; the road was clear and straight again, the tyre hum changed to a howl.

Slowing down as I sped past HMS *Sultan* and HM dockyard which were completely deserted, to be given to the Japs intact, I was now approaching my destination. I branched left onto a country road that led me past a small village to see in the distance the ornamented finished electrical lamps and elaborately wrought iron gates of Dr Ranji's residence, the Teak House. I drove quietly and stopped outside the gates as I had no wish to go crunching up that graceful gravelled driveway, I parked the car on the grass under some palms out of sight. Slipping the ignition key into the pocket fold at the top of my longhi, I remembered Lani's coloured silk scarf in the glove compartment and bound it round my face. Now, with my straw hat pulled down, the only places to reflect the moon beams and give me away were my legs and ankles but these were covered up by the longhi and were anyway sufficiently sunburned. I caught a whiff of Lani's perfume from the scarf spurring me on and Petty Officer Pascal's parting remark with his cold unblinking, unsettling stare, with its cruel sardonic smile. Punching the air with his fore-finger he had said, 'If you're not back we go, all right.' I was quite well aware he would sacrifice us all for the mission to succeed, including himself.

I stood stock still and listened to the noises of that paper scratching rustle of the palm fronds in the soft tropical night air, together with the sing song of the crickets and the croaking bullfrogs and the deep rumble and sighing sound of the surf in the small cove behind the house, thundering in from the South China Sea. Not far away, the waters rolled over *Repulse* and our dead shipmates, the tumbling drifting tumbleweed sweeping and weeping past them.

Timing my movements to coincide with the fleeting moon shadows, and moving only when the palms rustled, I stole like one of them at the same speed, flitting from cover to cover, stopping again as my heart started to beat faster. There was something wrong; in the past at this point the dogs with their 'Who goes there' barking had given away my presence till they had later recognised my scent. Even then they had sent one of their members out to check, they remaining hidden in the shadows, as he came out in a belly-scraping and furiously wagging tail of friendly obedience. Now there was no sign of him and the servants' quarters were dark and empty. I pushed the safety catch off, skirting the servants' quarters, seeing them deserted, their belongings gone with the dogs also. I came across Michael's car, cursing as I covered his gun with the old car rug, but with a slight rise in my hopes as if there was trouble he would have taken the gun with him. Maybe however the trouble started later and he did not have time. I fretted as I glided like one of the moving shadows up the inside of the steps to avoid creaks up to the veranda, still moving smoothly, relaxed but alert, the sub machine gun balanced easily in my right hand. Now I turned the handle carefully and, slowly unlatching the door but not opening it, I heard someone moaning and sobbing softly. My blood boiled over in terrible raging madness – someone was being slowly tortured.

I went in fast, low down on my haunches, kicking the door savagely as it exploded inwards, in a fast low bouncing leap-frogging zig-zagging hop, the gun at the ready. Clint Eastwood would no doubt have made it in a more dignified fashion. I rose to my feet with a gasp of horror at the scene that met my eyes.

Michael related to me later that when he had arrived he had found that Lani had left for Seleeter village to stay with friends where she would be safer from the expected Japanese invasion. Now he realised that if he left immediately he would probably miss me in the many winding roads connecting the various villages surrounding the house, so he sat down to wait, discussing over a drink with Ranji the critical situation, urging him to leave with him when I arrived and pick up Lani at Seleeter village. His quiet reply to all this did not sink in at first: that the Japs would not touch his house and it was safe to remain. At first he concluded it was because of Ranji's important job in the Sultan's Cabinet and that the Japs would require him to run things later. This seemed reasonable to him at the time, but events later were to prove quite different and almost fatal. He fretted and worried over what had been said, the phrase to 'run things' or something more sinister.

He began to fret now and worry as other discrepancies came back to him; one was Ranji's enormous interest in what our mission was about. We could not tell him anything even if we had wanted as we just did not know, and again we shuddered at the pictures of torture we had seen, realising how hopeless it would be in our case.

The next thing was to ask Ranji a question about his relationship with Lani. He had always wanted to ask this, but had declined out of politeness, as he appeared little interested in her. Michael was amazed that anyone could show such lack of interest in such a charming, sparkling, beautiful girl, and at the mention of her name was surprised for the first time to note in the inscrutable oriental impassive face a look of tenderness, but was now too preoccupied with the immediate situation to draw much attention to it. The word 'safe' here rang the alarm bells and his stomach went into its old routine as he sidetracked his question with amusing incidents of Lani in the past which he'd heard at least half a dozen times before. He now stood up and put more ice in his drink, to try and think out the growing implications.

Stepping out on to the wide balcony, the huge green venetian blinds raised to let the cool tropical tangy night earthy smell of the undergrowth air come through, he saw the young Chinese boy called Vange. Vange had been on good terms with us in the past; I used to chase him as he gleefully ran off shouting, 'Ian, you all same monkey,' as he tried to pluck the fine fuzz that stood for hairs on my legs. Hair on the body to Chinese was a novelty as they had so little themselves. As he gabbled excitedly to Ranji in some strange tongue of half Chinese and half something else that was Singapore, he naturally turned and repeated it in English. He noted again in concern, as Ranji tried to suppress it, that the boy with all the emotion and distress in his face which dispelled the myth that the Chinese were impassive and inscrutable, said how a Japanese patrol had been seen coming out of the huge water pipes that supplied Singapore from mainland Johore nearby and not across the causeway as expected.

This stunned Michael momentarily as he realised the vital importance of informing our authorities, but how could he do this? He was not going to leave me to walk right into it. He looked desperately at his watch: I should be arriving soon. The cool and scented air wafting to him collected his thoughts together. Lani had been the bait all the time and, whether Ranji was a fifth columnist or not, he would be held to suppress this vital information, at least for safe passage from the Japs for Ranji himself. As he turned he was aware of the small pathetic figure of Vange staring up at him waiting anxiously, and he vowed that, in spite of naval regulations and Petty Officer Pascal, he would take him along with Lani to the boats.

Out of earshot of Ranji, he whispered quickly and desperately, 'Get your bike, using the Bunkta road, go to Seleeter village and wait for

Lani for us, but keep an eye for us on our way there in case you do not make it in time,' and also to stop me and tell me what had happened.

Vange knew the old Bentley and this he would recognise. Michael's first duty should have been to leave and report this immediately but he could not forsake me, leaving me to walk right into it by taking the chance of meeting me on the way. There were so many village cart tracks like a maze connecting the various villages by the Teak House. Listening now, all his senses alert and acutely aware, he heard the music of the beautiful tropical crickets with their high and low wavering music, the small bullfrogs seeming to intervene in perfect harmony with their own musical croaks. Suddenly the small conductor of this orchestra seemed to have swept his tiny baton down in a dramatic flourish for silence, as they seemed to listen also with bated breaths to the cold wind of change blowing through the palm trees. His iced crème de menthe turned more icy in his hands as the full implications dawned on him.

Placing it on the sill of the veranda he strode into the up-to-date kitchen and put some of Ranji's excellent fresh ground coffee on. Remembering, coffee boiled, coffee spoiled, he put it on a low flat oil burner tray of oriental style on the table, in spite of his preoccupation, to simmer. He pondered with the almost futile hope that he could be wrong and there might be a perfect explanation to it all. After all, he remembered with a twinge of heart, Lani seemed attached to Ranji. If only it could be so then he would take him along with Lani and the boy Vange. But what would Petty Officer Pascal think, knowing too well his strict outlook on service matters. After all, to be fair, we were not on a mercy mission but one apparently of desperate urgency to pick someone up. That's all we could gather. The Chinese boy Vange could, he knew, be signed up as a naval mess boy, as was the custom on some ships on the Far Eastern station, more in pity for these beguiling boys who dogged your footsteps everywhere in their eagerness to be with you, offering to work for nothing. Our hearts warmed to them in their obvious happiness and how quickly they adapted to our way of life albeit in a crowded naval messdeck, the first real home and kindness they had ever known.

But Ranji was another matter, and Michael smiled to himself in spite of the new critical situation he was in. We could put him in the rope store! The warmth of the kitchen made him take off his long-sleeved tee shirt, which he wore for protection from flies as there were few mosquitoes about, owing to the continual treatment you could see being done during the day by natives with tanks on their backs spraying the ditches. Singapore was enjoying health since Raffles came for the first time. Now Michael stood naked but for his sarong, having no wish for a return of the prickly heat, and turned to confront Ranji with his suspicions, hoping he was wrong. But he started in sudden fear as Ranji was no more than a few feet from him, having stolen bare-footed up behind him unawares. There was no need for confirmation as his intentions were unmistakenly clear. Now the piled up cushions where he had sat were at some distance from him, and his aggressive half crouch, the arms hanging loose, of a black belt expert told him everything he needed to know now about Mr Ranji. Ranji, making a grab, seized him and made a Judo chop at him. He missed thanks to Michael's naked shoulders, and Michael stepped back, releasing his sarong, and slipped out of it, standing naked and in terrible defenceless chilling fear before his adversary.

With a small sob beginning, which forebode ill for an adversary, something stirred in him, a very savage primitive sensation, and as Ranji grappled with him again he was able to repeat the action. His body was slippy with sweat and fear, enabling him to do this again and again, but having each time to retreat till suddenly his bare buttocks touched the kitchen table, tipping him unbalanced backwards on to it in a half spreadeagled position on his left side, his left arm trapped under him by his own weight and that of his adversary, his right free arm held upwards and bent backwards.

With no movement to the front, blows and obscenities raining down on him and with his mind reeling, in desperation he began to sob in a growing terrible anger at this impossible position he was in. As in the past the anger seemed to send his brain raging but at the same time he was icy cool as he thought, trying to remember the thing that nagged his mind. Suddenly he remembered the coffee and stretching his arm backwards slowly so as not to give his intention away, he searched with his hand to where in his mind's eye where the coffee pot lay. Feeling the heat on the back of his hand he slipped his hand in backwards round the handle, the only possible way because of the position of his arm. Now in this cack-handed way he lifted the boiling coffee pot. Bending his wrist and crooking his arm with the little movement allowed, he poured the boiling coffee over his opponent's head and in this awkward manner took the first rush of the boiling coffee on his own hand and arm. The coffee struck his opponent on the back of the head and neck, vital nerve centres. In a high agonising animal scream, he flung himself back as if electrocuted, rooted to the spot screaming, as without waiting a second Michael smashed the empty coffee pot into this screaming face. He repeated this in a frenzied sobbing savage howl until the pot broke and splintered. He still continued with his right fist, not daring to waste a second, unaware of the first degree burn of his hand in taking that first impact of the coffee. He continued smashing his fist into the new screaming mushed up face as his own knuckles popped through the skin like soft tomatoes. He became aware that the screaming had stopped, replaced by a pitiful moaning as Ranji stood there shaking like a huge jelly. Michael realised he required urgent medical treatment for a serious burn and, looking feverishly and frantically in the kitchen cupboards and drawers did not find that small butcher's cleaver but a thin wire with two handles.

Slipping it over his opponent's head in a cross loop he pulled steadily with his knee in the small of the back, his opponent straining and stretching the opposite way to counteract. Now he savagely and viciously hacked and sliced with the blade of his bare hand at the toppling mushed up head with one hand still retained. Pulling steadily, he said in a gasping, sobbing, chuckle, 'Now, nod your head.' The head fell off.

In a high howling scream he tried to kick it, but slipped in the gore and blood. Picking himself up covered in the dreadful sticky mess, still screaming he kicked it again with the bare instep of the sole of his foot where it skidded away obscenely, bouncing off a wall to land right side up staring up at the Buddha. The mashed up face was like a porcupine with the bits of coffee pot sticking out of it like a grotesque scene from John the Baptist, the eyes with an expression of amazement to the Buddha's all knowing smile: I told you so.

Now Michael's own burn was taking effect. His arm and hand were enveloped in a balloon of thin skin. From this as well as from the nightmare experience, he sat and broke down sobbing but remembered to be prepared for burn shock reaction as he knew that being prepared lessened the shock. As he clenched his teeth for it to happen, that cold sick shaking began.

Now I had arrived outside the door and, turning the handle carefully and slowly releasing the catch but not opening it, squatting down low on my haunches, I kicked the door savagely open, going in fast in a low bouncing leap-frogging zigzagging hop, the gun at the ready. I rose to my feet with a gasp of horror at this scene and with ghastly, tasteless, grotesque humour thought, this is taking football too far.

As I softly called his name, the sound of my voice brought on those deep gasping terrible sobs in between repeating in choking gasps in a high wavering childlike pitiful voice, 'I'm not, I'm not,' over and over again, 'I'm not a psycho.' My compassion overcoming my horror I took him in my arms shouting hoarsely and desperately, 'Let's get out of here.' I pushed him under the shower and, finding his sarong untouched, he was dressed as we hurriedly left, his youthful grace striding before me. It was hard to imagine he was responsible for such savage carnage and butchery till I noticed he had found what he had been looking for before. Swinging by a leather thong from his wrist and glinting evilly was the small butcher's cleaver.

Michael picked up his sub machine gun and ammunition from his car, as we were to use mine down at the gate, flitting like fleeting silent shadows back the same way I had come up before. I set off at breakneck speed, only to hear him from behind whispering excitedly from high up in his chest, excited as if hooked on something, and I shuddered as I knew what it was. He told me to slow down to a normal speed; that would at least give us the element of surprise as the patrol seen was probably an observe and report only, but it was imperative that one of us should reach our people and report that the Japs were coming through the huge waterpipes from Johore to Singapore and not over the causeway as thought. It was, sadly, not to make much difference anyway which way they came as only a third of the causeway had been blown, for another of those unexplained unaccountable reasons.

Now we trundled along at this exasperating speed, but realised its importance. It was soon to pay off, as up ahead we saw the same confusing moon's fleeting moving shadows I had seen on the way up, the clouds passing across the moon like evil thoughts and I shuddered again at them. We both saw at the same time one of these shadows sweep across the road and we instantly recognised it as a group crossing an exposed place the best way undetected, smoothly and in line abreast way up ahead. But I heard the barking ear-ringing bursts from the sub machine gun resting on the sill of the rear inside passenger's door opening up just behind me. Instantly, without a word between us, as in the past in these situations, Michael and I worked on some kind of telepathy. He was hosing this section like a gardener up and down. Hearing the bang clip of a fresh magazine go in, I was already changing down, easing the clutch as I kicked the gas. The old Bentley leaped forward to a scream of spinning wheels spewing gravel and burning tyres.

Now passing the patrol, the gun still firing, I was able to see the familiar sight of *Repulse* of the broken, ragged dolls suspended like puppets on a string, momentarily kept up by the heavy bullets, but we did not weep as we had on *Repulse* when the young men were strewn over gun barrels, barely alive, calling for their mothers. Pulling up, I sweated trying to find the reverse gear to Michael's obscenities and curses from behind. When I did find it we shot back fast in a high whinnying howl of protest. Now in silent sickening horror I listened to the hacking, chopping thump clump like the sound on a butcher's block, to the screams and pitiful pleas in Japanese for mercy, then blessedly all was silent again and the tropical insects and bullfrogs resumed their beautiful music as if nothing had happened. One NCO would have on his clip board, 'Nothing to report,' as it was essential he did not. The main body of the Japanese would probably not move until they had some sort of confirmation, they being, no matter what we thought of them, first class soldiers, the finest in their fighting abilities. This might however give us valuable breathing space to reach the boats and Lani; knowing your enemy was paying off.

We had still two clips, one each, left for future engagements, as we sped towards Seleeter village for Lani and Vange. Speaking of the devil, we saw him ahead, peddling furiously with his small legs on his bike, his most treasured and only possession that we had brought out to him months before to his unbounded joy. We pulled up a few yards ahead of him. Getting out, I met him running and he sprang into my arms, his small arms clinging tightly round my neck, his small cheek with its salty tears pressed against my own as he cried, 'Ian, don't leave me.' Disentangling him, I gently placed him in the car beside Michael, noting he never gave a backward glance to his bicycle. I know how he felt as on that day of the small green parrots who looked down in wonder at us, I had understood what are possessions compared to life itself.

Now we sped off towards Seleeter village for Lani to Vange's excited chatter as he knew exactly where she was staying. In the distance we could see the billowing flames and thick black smoke of the oil installations enveloping Singapore as they committed their scorched earth policy which did not include the dockyard or naval base or many other important sites, like only one third of the causeway blown for again some unaccountable reason. More important for us at the time was the deadly silence. The guns had stopped firing in Singapore and the problem that had beset us all along was why had we not seen any of our troops to pass on our vital information. If we had, dressed in coloured shirts, sarongs and straw hats with two sub machine guns and no ID, how would the police interpret it, possibly shooting us dead as army deserters. Rumour had it that they had shot a whole platoon who could not explain their absence from their unit, leaving them as an example to others. We had witnessed ourselves in Singapore town them shooting two army looters dead without the slightest compassion. We decided it was too much of a chance to take and if told to stop we would drive on in any case. If they did eventually believe us after a long interrogation we would jeopardise the mission and other lives and end up in the bag as prisoners of war.

The notion that a stand could be made against the Japanese now, without air cover or the Far Eastern Fleet that had never arrived as promised, we could see was ludicrous. We did not have to be Admirals or Generals to see that. In any case, we thought bitterly, they had all got out long ago. Thanks to the few good officers who from Nelson's time to Lord Louis had stepped in and filled the breach, we remained supreme on the high seas. Distinction must be made in the chain of command for discipline purposes but now it was grossly overdone and was leading to bitterness and consequently was far short of the efficient service we could have been. Sorry if I have upset anyone by this but at the time we were very bitter about the needless *Repulse* deaths, for the bluff of Churchill that did not come off which we were later to be blamed for. Now there was this rat trap of Singapore where the signal sent and also delivered verbally by Admiral Spooner meant no-one would leave, 'Dead men tell no tales' and the ridiculous conditions. At Raffles Hotel they were still ginning up and stuffing themselves right up till the end – a prime example of what I have said. The naval base and dockyard, all brand new at huge cost to the British taxpayer, were given to the Japs intact, together with much else.

Now our problem was about to resolve itself. Michael placed Vange on the floor, as up ahead we saw an army Red Cap sergeant wave and flag us down to the side of the road where other drivers were being interrogated, a tall man looking very important. In our coloured shirts, sarongs and straw hats pulled well down we looked no different from the natives. As before, no word passed between us as I changed down, the first burst blasting and slicing him in half, in a jack-knifed fast articulated fold up, punching him off his feet backwards as if under some invisible force. The sweeping vicious arc continued and caught the others, about six, totally unprepared. Accelerating at speed we crashed the flimsy barrier, my ears ringing from the savage blasting bursts from the rear seat. I breathed the smell and tasted on the lips the acrid cordite fumes in appreciation like an experienced connoisseur. Vange had risen from the floor, not being able to resist a peep, and in a childish wail said they were our soldiers, but we pointed out that they were Japs. Did he not see the rising sun on their caps? He seemed satisfied, and curling up to Michael went back to sleep, the incident instantly forgotten as only an interruption to his very necessary precious and valuable sleep. We now had the vicious outlook and gangsters' mentality not of our own making, from two happy teenagers to now two very dangerous psychopaths on the rampage, good against a ruthless enemy but not for peacetime.

The foot went down and the old Bentley again responded as it set us back in the seats, and to its comforting tyre howl, now with Vange safe and on our way to pick up Lani, the flames of Singapore beckoned us to the boats and safety. I reflected on what had happened so far. I would never know whether Ranji was a fifth columnist or whether he was just trying to protect his own safety in trying to hand me over the Japs, and I shuddered as to what that would have meant. At the thought of all that had taken place I found myself racked by those body-wrenching sobs but silently within and, feeling Michael's consoling arm, felt a weight fall from me as also a weight glinting by its leather thong attached to my wrist fell: you see, it was not Michael in the Teak House. A wind seemed to be blowing down my soul through the countless ages of time to centuries ago to a thing that had lain dormant and evoked and was not extinguished. This dreadful reverie was cast aside suddenly, as it was replaced by the thought: would the boats still be there? The thought of them leaving without us after all we had been through was too much to contemplate, and I took the corners in a wide slewing slide to screaming tyres and the smell of burning rubber, stamping clutch, brake, stamping the gas, the gears going up and down in regularity and precision; fighting the wheel out of the corners was as terrifying to me as it was to my passengers.

Soon we pulled up at Seleeter village, parking the car under the palms on the grass in the shadow. Michael and Vange hurried off to find Lani. I sat in the car, slouched down in my seat almost from view, the safety catch off. Making a rapid check using a tall palm as a reference at twelve o'clock, I checked off the various features in a clockwise direction, noting the shadows, and had a quick look over the village. The few villagers I could see were sitting crossed legged on their framed roped beds in sarongs with their oriental calm and indifference. Was it because they thought they would be no worse off under Japanese rule than under the British? I observed their tin shanties and open sewerage gutters and dreadful poverty in the light and smell of their kerosene lamps and scented wood fires. Everything seemed normal enough but something was wrong as my mind nagged at something I had forgotten. Now as I saw a dog trot out to me I remembered there had been no barking, as in the past they had done when we approached these villages from as far as half a mile on foot. They set up a tremendous din until passing through it reached bedlam as if to say, don't you come into our village. I noticed none were ever seen and I concluded dogs were all cowards at heart but realised now it was because of Lani and Vange; they knew them and in their wonderful dog sense treated us as friends. Now a dog trotted over in his stiff legged gait and I recognised the expression, 'Advance and be recognised, friend or foe?' As he sniffed satisfied, he seemed to say, 'Pass friend,' as he cocked his leg over the front wheel, baptising and blessing us all at the same time. Now he trotted back to the others to make his report. I could make out faintly in the shadows, the light catching their eyes red, about six of them sitting quietly on their haunches looking in my direction with friendly wonder and curiosity. It was a relief to know now that we had an early warning system of anything for at least half a mile and with a smile said, 'Dogs, stand at ease, that last movement was very well carried out, keep it up.'

Raising myself to a sitting position and pushing the safety catch on,

I lit a cigarette to the pervading smell of burnt rubber and hot oil, and fidgeted and fretted, cursing, as my face assumed its toothache expression. Now I tried to relax, my watch seeming to have stopped at two minutes past. Then I heard Vange's boyish chatter as he appeared to be consoling Michael about something, and before starting up waited that brief second. At the footsteps my heart sunk: there were only two sets. I started the Bentley with its powerful guttural growl, opening the rear door for them so that it would be ready, in gear. My hand on the brake was ready as they bundled in and we shot off, resuming our mad dash. Vange, not giving Michael a chance, chattered excitedly that Lani had left for Singapore and the boats. This cheered us immediately as she would probably be already there and waiting for us. Sadly, what we did not know at the time was that she had gone to Princes Pier, the last place she had known us to have been at, not knowing we had had to move to Keppel docks after the air attack. We had had no contact with her since then and owing to the recent horrendous events which had taken place we had forgotten.

Now another fateful twist was taking place as I branched off to the right, by-passing Singapore and going right across country, avoiding the main road to the coast road and further patrols to reach the main Keppel harbour road which would take us quicker to the boats. If we had only continued on our present course we would have undoubtedly passed Princes Pier and seen Lani, now probably looking for us in desperate puzzlement and sadness, and with a feeling of deep betrayal that we had gone without her. Now, to sliding lurches and screaming tyres, I felt I was hurting our old faithful friend and I patted the wheel consolingly, saying, 'It won't be long now.'

Then to our great relief the boats showed up in the distance with Andrews commencing to single up on the mooring ropes. He shouted happily to the others, and Pascal hurried out to us, while my eyes were searching desperately for Lani. Pascal said, 'Where is the girl?' and continued with a quick, 'What's all this, Ian?' which included everything. As he glanced at Vange I tensed, but all he said, to my surprise, was, 'You makee tea then chop chop, all right.' Vange, as he had seen done in his many foragings in the Naval Base said, 'Yes, Sir!' and sprang to attention, saluting smartly, and scampered on board as we did also, Pascal dismissing me with one of his hard smiles. My heart warmed to him as we were well over our time but he had refused to go without us. No doubt the long rebuke of how I'd jeopardised the mission and other people's lives would come later.

My mind was in a turmoil as we slipped and moved well out in Kepple harbour, tying up to one of the many empty junks there, spreading our camouflage nets over the boat which made it indistinguishable from the other junks. With slip ropes rove and one engine ticking over we remained below out of sight waiting for night to fall for our escape. My mind was in a sort of dazed numbness of despair as I wondered what had happened to Lani.

We now had our agent on board. Petty Officer Wilkinson, ex *Repulse*, was on his boat with his three hands and the CO, a young Lieutenant RNVR, on one boat, and on the other Andrews, Michael, myself, Pascal and our CO and his father who was a rubber plantation owner, the CO being a former member of the Johore Singapore Yacht Club who knew every island and tide and current from here to Java, so he was to be of immense value later. Also at the time we had another very useful volunteer, a young Chief Engine Room Artificer who acted for both boats. They are the highest paid men in the Navy as with their skills they could have built us an engine from scratch.

Now we remained below, the perspiration drenching us in the close confinement, playing the old gramophone with our own record, 'Drifting along under the tumbling tumble weed,' it having a morbid fascination for us. We played it over and over again as it reminded us once again how privileged we were to be alive. If the worst came to the worst we had had a good run, more so than those of our comrades on *Repulse*. As we waited tensely for nightfall playing 'uckers', a two dice game, it appeared the government agent had been escorted to the boats by a British Army Officer who advised us to surrender by the Geneva Convention as we would stand little chance outside. Unknown to him was our powerful radio with which were in constant contact with our authorities and an escape route had already been laid on. Now, as I reflected on *Repulse* and all the other hairy moments, I thought of the time hugged in Michael's arms behind the gunshield after clearing a jammed gun too late and it struck me with a start that we had forgotten to tell Lani of our move, and to my anguish pictured her on Princes Pier in her desperate misery. We had betrayed her and she had loved and trusted us; we had left her to the mercies of the rampaging soldiers now in Singapore. We occasionally heard the sound of broken glass and shouts and screams denoting this, but how could I ever explain this to her about the Teak House if ever that was possible. You see she was not Ranji's mistress or housekeeper as we had thought, but Mr Ranji's daughter.

Night fell quickly in the tropics as if the curtain rings screeched as the curtains swept closed on the final act and now concealed the dreadful things being enacted in Singapore. We quickly slipped our moorings and almost silently on one engine each boat stole out of Kepple harbour, gliding like two black shadows. Standing on the stern I looked back at Singapore lit up by the billowing black smoke and flames of the oil installations flickering past. The Cathay Buildings like a huge buddha oversaw the gigantic grotesque sacrificial rite that was HMS *Repulse* and *Prince of Wales*.

The powerful twin Thornycroft engines' gutteral throbbing hum went up an octave as the stern went down in a flurry of white foam. The bow went up as the speed gradually increased to the flickering flames astern of Singapore. I looked at my watch. It was five to the hour. I went for'd to relieve Michael on the Oerlikon gun.

Diana stirred in my arms, her naked flesh against my own like adhesive, her long slim legs and arms entwined about me with a possessive gesture. Now with a seemingly protective embrace she murmured, 'Please go on Ian, what happens next?'

In an emotionally exhausted mumble I replied, 'Later, darling, later.'

Chapter Twenty-Eight

SARAWAK TO AUSTRALIA

The sound of our Dutch installed Thornycroft engines went up another octave as we began to leave the islands outside Singapore. The adiabatic lapse rate as usual had reached its saturation point; the sweat simply as usual spurted out from us. Sometimes the climate could be paradise, other times it was like this, and the darkness was like breathing through cotton wool.

As I had relieved Michael before on the for'd Oerliken type Dutch naval gun, he came for'd and relieved me at five to the hour; Pascal was a stickler for punctuality. Now, as I passed the fore cabin, I could hear below the sound of a morse key's staccato rhythm, belching away as Telegraphist Andrews, ex *Prince of Wales* boy and ex *Ganges*, sent and received vital messages in code from our HQ now in Colombo, that had been transferred from Singapore long before it had fallen.

The tropical dawn broke in a savage outburst, and as suddenly as it had fallen in darkness, the harsh sounds of bird and insect life coming to life seemed appropriate, giving signs of a new beginning, a new hope of life, another fresh start to our sometimes abject life of danger, death and destruction. The cool morning sea breeze after the heat of the night seemed to say so.

We took turns lying back in the deck chair, searching the sky for aircraft. As some were spotted droning away in the distance and we instantly recognised the sound as Japanese, we sheared close in to one of the many little beautiful tropical islands that were sprinkled about, too small even to be on a chart. Dropping our kedge anchors both boats came to rest in clear sandy water that you could have read a newspaper under.

Spreading our camouflage nets over both boats, leaving some on board to watch, we dived overboard. Sharks – well, the great whites did not like me before, so why should I worry now? On the silver grained beach, sand trickling between our toes, we settled down to wait for nightfall.

The Filipino great white shark hunters had reported that after the sinking of *Prince of Wales* and *Repulse*, there were no great whites seen for twenty-four hours, so the reports from those on board at the time that they had seen them, and my cry going over the side, 'Sir, what about the sharks?' may have been correct.

We swam, sunbathed, and relieved those on board. On board, I began to scrub out our mess. Before that I had a good look at everything, and, lifting the side floor deck boards, found a hoard of tinned food that I added to our store of tinned bacon, tinned cheese and cartons of Jacob biscuits. It was of course Dutch food, and some of the tins were very tasty, with what appeared to be savoury rice balls, but there were also some large brownish earthenware flagon type jars, with a label that said in bold black letters, 'Bols'.

I thought it must be some kind of disinfectant, so I poured a liberal amount into my scrubbing out water, just as Michael arrived. 'Bejesus, Ian, stop, that's gin,' he exclaimed, pouring out half a glass for me to taste. It looked clear like water, so I drank the lot down in one go before he could stop me. Now dressed in sarong and sandals with a tray of biscuits and cheese, I arrived in the fore cabin. Staggering about, I said to the sub lieutenant and the other officers, with an elaborate bow, 'Dinner is served,' to their laughter as they knew my intoxication was accidental.

Night fell suddenly like a black curtain, with the sing song sine wave of the chirping crickets. The smell of the vegetation changed to a deeper scent. Our former route to go to Batavia had been changed as it was now in Japanese hands. The decoded signal said for us to head for Kuching in Sarawak, where there were head hunting tribes, but who were on our side.

We got under way, following P12, their tiny pencil of a stern light, and the turbulence of the white water at their stern. The town had a small Dutch oil refinery and, unknown to us at the time, Admiral Spooner and the Air Commodore in a fast motor launch had also been here when Singapore fell. Coxswain Petty Officer Billington later told me in the naval base HMS *Flinders*, Australia, that after leaving Kuching they had run aground and, after swimming ashore, came back to find Admiral Spooner dead from dehydration and the Air Commodore very ill.

We arrived in Kuching in the early morning, refuelled and stored ship, with extra barrels secured on the stern. Now we nearly suffered the same fate as coxswain Billington. We were aground also; the stern was free but the boat touching for'd. This was the highest tide in the world, rising and falling twenty to thirty feet. We should have been prepared, as this had nearly happened at Princes Pier, Singapore, that time when we were secured alongside it, the boat in that case almost suspended by its bow lines.

This time we were lucky as the water at the jetty shelved away from being shallow no doubt by the amount of debris collected through time. With one keeping guard with a rifle for the crocodiles we went overboard, pushing the stern, and as others pushed on deck with long poles, we came free. Now the signal ordered us to proceed to the entrance of the river Jambi in the Island of Sumatra, about a day's travel south and west of us.

The plan slowly emerged that we would go three hundred miles up the Jambi river, where fresh orders would await us, and proceed overland from east to west to the town of Pelembang, from where a ship would take us to freedom to Colombo. It was not going to be as simple as that. Night fell and we shoved off, thanking them and again telling them to get out themselves; however they seemed happy to remain, as they believed the Japanese, when they got round to take this small unimportant refinery, would need them to run it.

Dawn broke as we entered the mouth of the river Jambi, passing the little straw-hutted villages of Sembang and then Tangoung. On either side of the river were the brilliant coloured deep tropical greens and reds of the rhododendrons, blended with the muddy coloured river.

It was now the agent's turn to lie back in the deck chair, scanning the air for aircraft. The binoculars around his neck were on the strap that in the Navy was always insisted upon. A knock can give them double vision, then you do get a headache. Later as a Navigating Officer in the Merchant Navy I found this impractical as some companies insisted that you took fixes of the ship's position every fifteen minutes, and what with going out to the wings of the bridge to the gyro bearings mounting, then poking your head down in the radar screen, then taking Decca fixes in the chart room and laying them off, to have the binoculars all the time dangling around your neck was not practicable.

This was one difference between the two Navies. Now I watched the agent with interest as he did his sweep coming down in stages to finish with a quick up and down above and below his horizon, a trick that we had learned on Arctic patrol, sometimes disclosing things you had not picked up before. There was more to this fellow than met the eye.

I recalled the time after we had moved from Princes Pier in the heart of Singapore, after we shot up a Jap plane, to Keppel harbour. I had seen a slim athletic figure in what had once been spotless whites, but who was now hatless, dishevelled and smudged with dirt, as he sprang down easily into the boat, his jacket opening showing a heavy type service revolver, clutching a service type canvas holdall that was weighted with holes in it.

On the jetty was the senior Army officer, who had requested our sub lieutenant to obey the Geneva Convention and we would be given fair treatment. It was 14 February, Singapore was to fall on the 15th, but we were already in contact with HQ Colombo. Like so many the Army officer genuinely believed fair treatment by the Geneva Convention would be carried out.

Now we were in a dilemma, as we had a signal to turn back to Tanjoung, the village we had passed on the river about forty miles downstream. This called for volunteers as we might walk straight into a Jap reconnaissance party. A naval nursing sister had somehow contacted HQ Colombo; as a young seaman that's all I knew. However Michael, boy telegraphist Andrews and I all volunteered to go back down in P12 boat with PO Wilkinson.

Andrews was required because of his knowledge of communications, Michael and I for the gun for'd. It was another trying time but it passed without incident, and we rejoined the other boat in about five hours. Proceeding once more we arrived at our destination, the town of Jambi. Here we were ordered to turn the boats over to the Dutch resistance army by HQ Colombo. Night fell quickly and we were put up in the local Dutch hotel, and now we watched the headman of the native village kill an old tapir, a distant cousin to the horse.

The resultant meal we recognised as the seaman's 'scouse' or 'pot mess', a kind of Irish stew. After so long on tins of bacon, cheese and other tinned food, we could feel the strength flowing through us. Michael and I went for a swim, only to jump out fast as the young Malay Sumatran children shouted, 'Crocodile,' and ran off. A baby chimp startled me as he crawled into my arms, gently putting his little arms round my neck. The boy returned, greatly concerned that I would keep his pet, so to make up for the crocodile scare I pretended to keep him.

In the morning there was an old Ford with a soft top for the officers and passengers, and an old lorry for us, into which we loaded up our boxes of ammunition and Lewis machine guns. We wore over our heads cotton bandoleers of 0.303, every other one a tracer, and of course rifles. It was a poor swap for two valuable boats plus their equipment and heavy machine guns, but the Dutch resistance would put them to good use.

The lorry led our party, PO Ginger Wilkinson and a native driver in the front seat, and the old Ford followed with the nursing sister, sub lieutenant, the agent, the old rubber plantation owner, and PO Pascal.

181

They gave three on the horn as farewell, that set off the orangutans trying to keep up with us in the trees, their 'Woopwooping' seemingly wishing us luck. We were going to need it more than in the past.

We crossed several rivers by native raft ferries, then steadily climbed the mountains that separate east and west Sumatra, the temperature dropping to a pleasant cool with magnificent scenery of what I remember most, the giant ferns as thick and as big as trees. The constant worrying thought, what if these old transports break down, was offset to a degree as we knew that most of the mountain jungle was unexplored, and we knew there was an abundance of fruit and game. Years after the war some Japanese troops still survived here and were surprised that the war was over.

Descending from the mountains, we arrived at Bukiftaggi. We left our Ford car and lorry, thanking our native driver for showing us the way, and caught a train for the coast town of Pelembang. Boarding the train, there seemed to be more people on the platform than on the train, with their babble of voices and the easy Far East way of, 'Go day, come day, God send pay day.' Even the imminent Jap invasion could not change their way of life, or I should say their approach to it.

There was the hoarse cry of the hawker with his cart selling hot tea, a gooey sweet mess I'd noticed before in Singapore; they mixed the lot together, tea, sugar, and milk. Pascal and Wilkinson served us out for a change from tinned Edam cheese and Jacob's cream crackers with sardines. The seats in the train were bare wood, and I think in this heat cushions would have been unbearable. The last signal had told us Pelembang was in Japanese hands, but although the train was routed for Pelembang we were getting off at Padang. It was going to be close, as all our experiences had been, as Padang was only two hundred miles from the Japs' occupation.

Leaving the train we formed up single file each side of the road leading into the town with our rifles and Lewis machine guns at the ready. This little town was predominantly white and of course Dutch. They put us up in the school gym, and for tea we had the Dutch version of Irish stew, or seamans 'scouse'; it was delicious. Now came the tension as we waited the return of the sub lieutenant from signalling in code our arrival. We slept in the gym, rifles at our sides, sentries posted.

In the morning HMS *Daney* arrived. She did not even tie up, but passed a heaving line down from the fo'c'sle with the spring hawser on its end, which we passed over a bollard. *Daney*, going dead slow ahead on the spring, brought the ship alongside, and we all quickly climbed on board. Then she went slow, then half speed astern and was soon clear, the whole operation taking no more than minutes. Michael and I spurned the stuffy messdecks because everyone wanted to know how we had got out. We were heading in a north-westerly direction with the sun on the port bow, that was the direction of Colombo.

Suddenly she was altering course, turning 180 degrees from her original course. The sun was now on the starboard quarter. We thought that she was returning to Padang to pick up more people, but a few hours later were to hear the pipe, 'Special sea duty men to your stations, cable party muster on the fo'c'sle,' as was usual for entering harbour, but it was not Padang but Cilape in Java, and there we were disembarked.

We were dumb with despair and speechless. The question dominating everything was, 'Why, after all we had been through, why?' The *Daney* proceeded on her original course to Colombo and safety, with the agent and the naval nursing sister. Lord Trefgarne, through my MP Anna McCurly, refuses to believe an RN Captain would do such a thing. Did someone in our party know too much? This was a sentence of death on us or terribly much worse.

After trying several merchant ships at anchor in the harbour, the Chief Engine Room Artificer writing them off, we found down at the docks a Dutch sea-going tug called the *Khoen Hoea*. The native crew having deserted her, the Captain was only too willing to take us. We shoved off immediately. Now the plan was for us to run down well clear of the coast and Japanese shipping, past that beautiful necklace of tropical islands that had begun with Sumatra, then Java, Lombok, Flores, Sumba and Timor, stretching all the way to Darwin, Australia.

The stoke-hold was manned by us and we shovelled the coal from the bunkers. By having a rope attached round our waists, the other end attached to a stanchion, this enabled us to swing with our shovel of coal from the bunker to the furnaces. After our stint we washed down with salt water, and were allowed a very small quantity of fresh to rinse off with, otherwise the salt water became sticky and could cause skin complaints.

On the low rations the work was hard on us, but we were spurred on now that we could see for the first time light at the end of the tunnel, and could hardly wait to tell of the dreadful genocide; did we know too much? Michael and I loathed being below decks so we slept and spent our spare time under the lifeboat, and at night crawled under a spare lifeboat cover, as like a clock it would downpour a tropical cloudburst at about four in the morning.

Admiring the beautiful evening cloud formation and evening sunset, we thought we were seeing the usual tropical lightning as it gave its zig-zag flickerings across the horizon. Above on the bridge wings PO Pascal was timing the flickers, and now shouted down to us, 'Get everybody up!' Those flickers turned out to be gun fire, and later we found it had been the Coral Sea action.

Our course due south from Cilicape had now led us well clear of the islands that were strung out in a beautiful tropical necklace, in a shimmering green sea with hardly a breath of wind. All very well: it looked very nice, but ashore would be that sweltering humid heat, the flies and stink of rotting vegetation giving you a sick feeling of lassitude. Their names: Bali, Sumba Flores and Timor at the tail end, where we altered course for Australia, conjure up romantic versions of Hollywood, but they were anything but.

The famous Coral Sea action took place over to our port side. Six of our destroyers, including HMS *Electra* who had rescued us from the thick suffocating black oil, were under attack by the Japanese Fleet who had been waiting outside Sourabay for them. I can imagine Captain 'D' saying, like Admiral Phillips on board his Flagship to his other Captains, 'Gentlemen, we can stay, or we can go out and fight; gentlemen, we sail at 1700 from Singapore.' Now it was Sourabay and destroyers. They came out in a belting fast zigzag, guns firing, putting up a thick smoke screen; only as fate would have it, as they came out of their own smoke screen, one by one they were sunk.

Now that in a short while we would be safe off the coast of Australia, we put the last of our tinned boiled bacon into the huge native aluminium pot that you could have taken a bath in. The top portion that contained the rice was perforated, the bottom half had water for steam. This, with the last of our green cooking bananas that were now ripe and Jacob's cracker biscuits made our meal. To follow was a native Javanese cigarette in its triangular thick rice paper; one drag almost blew your head off.

We had scrubbed clean shorts and shirt with saltwater soap, and they had quickly dried on the after hatch, so that we were presentable entering Fremantle harbour, what a fateful name. Now, as we trouped down the gangway, we could hardly believe what we saw and heard. On the jetty was a lorry with a steel cage, and the spectators shouted, 'Pommie bastards, deserters from Singapore.' Then they fell silent, as one remarked, 'They're a bunch of kids.' To make up for this reception, and instead of taking us direct to Port Lewen naval barracks at Fremantle, they put us up in a hotel, where, not being used to food and drink after so long, we flaked out on the thick lounge carpet, and slept the sleep of the gods.

Kitted out in new uniforms, hearing the pipe, 'Hands to dinner,' my mind fleetingly recalled all the 'other hands to dinner', beginning with HMS *Ganges* as we were fell in outside our messes waiting to be marched in. Now the boys' piping party came down the long covered way, their high pitched voices after the trill of Bo'sun pipes shouting, 'Hands to dinner, rig of the day sports rig' and my thoughts went over all that had happened in the subsequent traumatic events, only to be interrupted by the many questions from the Australian seamen clustered around.

I toyed abstractly with an untouched piece of steak, and chased it round my plate, a disappointment to those watching for the huge meal they had prepared for us. I glanced towards Michael, remembering again how this story began with us as fifteen-year-olds in the RN as we stood at our clean scrubbed wooden mess tables obediently awaiting the instructor's order, 'Say Grace,' looking down at our battered tin plates that were always to smell of metal polish. I met Michael's steady gaze, as he silently mouthed the words we had said at each meal, and I knew exactly what he meant as we both said together to ourselves: *'Thank God for what we are about to receive.'*

Diana stirred in my arms again, her corned coloured hair and blue eyes blending with my brown hair and hazel eyes as it flopped over on my chest. Now the former protective hold of legs and arms wrapped around me were tightening. My story had done something to both of us and I knew we were in for one of our all-night sessions.

Chapter Twenty-Nine

HMS *VANSITTART* 1943

We were the B7 support escort group, with Commander Peter Gretton and comprised HMS *Duncan, Vidette, Vansittart, Tay, Alisma, Loosestrife, Pink, Snowflake* and *Sunflower*.

It was not so happy a time for the U-Boats; their *Glücklich Zeit* was finished. We sailed from Londonderry to Nova Scotia in Canada with both fast and slow convoys. This had been our old stamping ground on *Repulse*, but then we had been out of sight of the convoy, guarding it from the heavy units like the *Scharnhorst*, and other heavy cruisers like the *Prinz Eugen* and the *Tirpitz*, sister ship to the *Bismarck*. Thankfully the RAF had put them out of action later on. Now we, as the escort group, escorted the convoys and guarded them against the 'Wolf packs'.

I recalled the time in heavy weather when I was closed up as Captain of 'B' guns, twin 4-inch, on 'B' gun deck below the bridge in a surface action, after being stood down to defence station, observing *Vidette*. We must have sunk into one of those white-topped foam-covered huge troughs at the same time *Vidette* did, so that she appeared to have disappeared. My heart seemed to stop. Was she ever going to reappear? Last trip two American 4-stackers, lease–lend 1914–18 destroyers for the use of Bermuda, had just disappeared in a flurry of white foam.

Then suddenly she reappeared, white seas cascading in torrents from her upper works, and like an old sea dog, she seemed to give an angry shake ready for the next one. I thought of AB Albert Tonner, her Asdic operator. He had been seasick on *Repulse*, and you could put the

Alan, Olive and myself.

Vidette on her FX. On *Repulse*, in the over-crowded war-time complement, it was only the senior ABs that had swinging billets for their hammocks, so we ODs had slept on the mess tables stools or where we could. Albert and I had chosen under the mess table to stop ourselves from being trodden on. Now I wondered how he was faring on a V & W. The *Vidette*'s crew had told me how Albert would be actually green with seasickness, his bucket jammed between his feet, refusing to be relieved doing his Asdic search sweep. His determination paid off as he got three U-Boats.

At Smiths Docks, Middlesbrough, I was joining my first destroyer after completing seven days' survivors' leave from the battle cruiser HMS *Repulse*. As I stepped aboard, cutting off a smart salute to our White Ensign aft, to my delight and surprise she moved under my feet very slightly, rolled and gently pitched. I was so captivated that I missed the significance that she was alongside the wall. She appeared to welcome me with open arms, and now, feeling the throb of her engines, she had become alive. This was after the vast cathedral-like messes on the capital ships I'd served on after leaving HMS *Ganges* as a junior seaman: the battleship *Revenge*, a Cornwall County Class cruiser, and the battle cruiser *Repulse*, so maybe you can excuse my endearing remarks about this little destroyer.

Before entering the fo'c'sle mess deck at the break of the fo'c'sle, where the fo'c'sle deck drops down, called the shoulders, and on each of the shoulders were two watertight doors so that one was opposite to the weather one. However, nothing on *Vansittart* was watertight. By both doors were long head-high steel hawsers that were set up tight with 'bottle screws' that led to the depth charges aft. Hanging down from them were safety hand pennants which you could grab in the middle of the night in a howling gale trying to sweep you overboard. You were glad of them as they were free to run aft with you to man the depth charges.

Entering the FX, the deck-head seemed so low you thought you might have to duck, but this only added to the friendly informal

HMS Vansittart.

outlook. Looking the full length, you could see it gradually narrowing to the bows like a sailing ship, and now, looking at it, you could see how graceful she really was, the perpendicular frames that took the ship's side placed like the ribs of a sailing ship curving in gracefully towards the bows. No. 1 mess was right up in the bows and on top of our kit lockers on each ship's side were thick red cushions with the mess table between. We were the driest mess in the ship, I was told, and to give us even greater seclusion was the FX capstan engine which smelt of old grease. I was simply ecstatic and again missed the significance of being up in the bows of a V & W class destroyer.

Coming through the ship's public address system Tannoy as an early warning was the harsh clashing cymbal-like sound of the asdic's electronic pulse going out in its search for a target. If it struck anything the echo returned in a sharp 'Ping' but if not it returned in a sighing sound. How did we put up with it night and day? and how did Albert put up with it going through his head-set for four hours? The result was he became what we called being 'ping' happy.

My acquaintance was renewed with Albert when I was the ship's postman for *Vansittart*, now dressed in a borrowed jumper that was too small, wearing shoes instead of boots with green gunnery gaiters. The gunnery school at Whale Island would have had a fit if they had seen me. My hair was so long that my cap perched on top looked ridiculous.

I passed the Shore Patrol of the infamous or famous (depending on whose side you were on) Provost Marshal Diablow. I with youthful rebellion was enjoying myself as I slouched past them, my ship's post bag over my shoulder. I had a smug look as I knew Captain 'D' had given orders that we were not to be bothered with as we spent so little time in port and our clothes were soon ruined by salt water. We saved up our dirty washing 'dhobying' each trip and bathed at the public baths. Water was for the boilers. We all smelt the same so we did not notice it.

On the dock side at Londonderry were sheds that were used to train myself and other newcomers loading the heavy depth charges which were about the size of a large dustbin. In fact, that was their nickname by some. They were too heavy to lift manually, and were hoisted up by a small tackle, no mean feat in bad weather as they swung about trying to knock you overboard. They were put into what appeared to be an old muzzle-loading gun angled at about 60 degrees but which was in reality a giant howitzer with a tube at the side in to which a powerful cartridge was loaded. On exploding it pushed the depth charge into a graceful curve well clear of the ship still attached to its piston that went down the barrel of the thrower. The practice ones were quite startling even after the *Repulse* action in that they exploded in a huge flame and cloud of thick brown cordite smoke. The very filling of the depth charge could be dangerous. We got rid of our left-overs by exploding them on the old wreck outside Derry, and the hundreds of huge stunned cod we sent up to the hospital. That night fresh cod was delicious.

Old depth charges could become dangerous. On one ship an eager young sub lieutenant told a young OD to scrape off the salt crystals and paint the depth charges; it blew the stern off. Now I was passing the training sheds, where there was also a section for the asdic operators to practise plotting targets. Now a loud commotion was taking place, and I observed a small tubby AB being struck on the head by the hat of a Chief Petty Officer Asdic Instructor who was shouting at him, 'Repeat after me, "I'm a fool!" ' It was Albert and he'd made a mistake. His instructor was however a good one as Albert was later the best asdic operator in the group.

I did not sling my 'mick' for some time but slept on the mess side cushions till I'd got over my seasickness. The old 3-badge ABs took me under their wing as this was not only my first 'boat' but my first as a leading seaman. Thanks to them I survived those beginning days. I would jam my left leg and foot into the boot racks at the side of the cushions to try and sleep – correction, lie in a dull stupor – my bucket handy. It took only one to start making those dreadful wretching noises to start me off. As that bitter bile came up in my mouth I'd fight it, but at last I'd give in and join the club. It was a consolation that I was not the only one. The fo'c'sle capstan that had blocked us off from the other messes, giving us privacy and seclusion, now was giving off its old greasy smells and did not help either. That saying 'Give me the boats and a bucket' had its down side.

Now in my dull stupor, lying with my leg jammed in the boot racks against the heavy roll and slamming bang and thump as the bows went under, the steady hypnotic harsh cymbal clash and its returning sighing sound of the asdics, I heard a subtle change in tone. We were running as it began to quicken, splashing through the evil smelling floating gash in the lower messes, banging the clips of the lee watertight door with our bare hands even before the alarm bells had gone down. We grabbed our safety pennants that hung down from the lifeline that ran aft to the depth charges. The ship's speed accelerated together with the force of the waves coming inboard to sweep us off our feet. We had to maintain 14 knots otherwise we could blow our stern off with the depth charges. Now, aft, it was just as bad trying to hoist the heavy depth charges in the black of night in this as the waves came in at waist high and the charges swung about on the small derrick.

The settings were deep, medium and shallow; we couldn't remember the exact sequence but we were not allowed lights so we put them on by the sound of the clicks on the gauge on the depth charge. The officer in charge had a torch with a pin hole of a light. Right aft were two sets of racks filled with depth charges that could be rolled off; on both sides were two throwers. Now came the order 'Fire 1' and one rolled off aft from the racks, 'Fire 2' and one fired from the port thrower and in a belch of flame and thick brown cordite smoke went up in a graceful curve clear of the ship. At the same time No. 2 starboard went up, then No. 4 port, then No. 4 starboard, then No. 1 aft, so forming a diamond of pressure. Anything caught in this was crushed like an empty can.

The U-Boat aces had earlier waited with great courage till we were almost on top of them, and then went deep hard a-starboard or port, then stop, and crawl away, stop, and crawl away till they were clear. Now we had the hedgehog gun for'd where a gun had once stood. It was an apparatus composed of, I think, twelve spindles that could be angled to about 60 degrees. On these spindles the bombs were placed. They were filled with fulminate of mercury, and were so sensitive you could blow on them and they would explode. Sadly, this is what happened to the Leading Seaman I'd replaced, because the last time they'd fired, the gun's crew were never seen again. Now they were fired by remote control from the bridge. This apparatus prevented the U-Boats trying to dodge us for'd as it only took one bomb to hit and it set the others off. They rose in a graceful arc to fall well ahead of the bows.

Sadly, on one occasion we picked up the human remains floating in the sea, sadly because they were seamen also, to be put in a bucket for proof of the kill back in port, I don't know if it is true that the bucket was kept outside the galley, but it put us off our meal.

Now it was 'tot time' and a gill of neat 'Pusser's' rum in those days was a life saver. We were now in a steady easy North Atlantic swell and pitching and rolling easily, and we could see our fat AB 'rum bo'sun', Ginger, coming the length of the fo'c'sle towards us. He seemed to be waltzing gracefully to the ship's movement with practised ease, when someone shouted, 'Stand By!' which meant we were in for one of those sea milestones hitting us, as they did from time to time unexpectedly. We started to go up and up to a big one, the ears pinging to the change in pressure, and now descending quickly leaving our stomachs behind; now she hit the bottom of the trough of the wave with a bone-jarring bang. Our problem mess table, which was always jumping out of steel shoes on the deck, so that we had rigged up securing rope and small handy bill tackles to prevent this, was once again collapsed in spite of this, lying flat on the deck in a tangle of rope lashings. Earlier, the experts, with their seamanship manuals out, said this could not possibly happen. Worse was Ginger, lying under the mess shelf covered in flour, tea and sugar (we were canteen messing) and broken cups and plates, but unbelievably still holding the rum fanny horizontally, not a drop of the precious liquid spilt.

At both ends of our escorted convoys, Derry and Nova Scotia, Canada, *Vidette* and *Vansittart* crews would celebrate ashore a successful convoy, and Albert, going up for a round of drinks, spewed over the barmen. We compensated the barmen generously for this and excused Albert as being 'ping happy'. Another time he returned on board in a hurry with no trousers on.

Now once again we were back in Smiths Dock, Middlesbrough for stiffening plates to our bows and also to reinforce plates that were beginning to 'pant' after the poundings we had taken. The girl welders came on board aged about nineteen or twenty, and as they came up the gangway we suddenly remembered to our embarrassment that the condoms we had put on the end of the Oerlikon barrels to keep the weather out had been left on.

When they had finished we told them about our problem mess table, and asked if they could weld the steel legs to the steel shoes that they fitted into. It was tot time or, as some called it, 'gibbering-time' and neat pusser's rum when it went down. To me, not a heavy drinker, it so altered my speech no one could understand what I was saying. Now we gave these young girls 'sippers' all round. 'Sippers' meant, for an example on someone's birthday, each man gave him a sip of his tot and if there were eight in the mess as we had it was quite a considerable amount. The girls went down the gangway singing and they held a party for us that night in the Station Inn, Middlesbrough.

We now returned to Londonderry to resume our convoy work. The mess wooden table, supported by its legs with steel welded to the deck was our pride and joy; now we could sit at it without fear of everything landing on the deck. Then one of those extra big ones hit us. Our pride and joy gave a terrible loud crack and split right down the middle, to land in its usual place on the deck. The legs remained upright with a 'told you so' look. We were showered with broken plates and cups, tea, and flour. We numbered eight in the mess and there were only four plates left, so four meals were put, one in each corner of the mess tray, and we used empty milk tins as cups.

Now we sat huddled together in our duffle coats and sea boots. It was no use undressing; there was never time, so we stayed in our clothes from one trip to the next, cold, hungry and miserably listening subconsciously to the hypnotic monotonous harsh clash and the sigh of the Asdics coming through the Tannoy as an early warning. When it began to change tune and quicken, we were already running for the lee door, splashing through the water and gash of the lower messes, to bang the clips off for the depth charges aft.

On my certificate it reads, 'Paid £5 7s 4d, Naval Prize Remittance in respect of assistance rendered to SS *Tahihee* by HMS *Vansittart*, 22-25 August 1943.' The SS *Tahihee* was stopped and helpless, and for days we trudged round the decks with towing wires, not daring to make a sound. It was a worrying time as we were both sitting ducks for the 'wolf packs'.

Each time we left port, the speed gradually increasing, black smoke belching and streaming aft, the funnels encrusted with white sulphur with too much steaming time, the ship's sides coated in red rust, we loudly played our leaving port record on the ship's Tannoy on the upper deck: the Andrews sisters singing 'The Bugle Boy of Company B'. If the Capital ships could have their Royal Marine bands playing 'Rule Britannia' leaving port, so could we!

Chapter Thirty

THUNDER SHOAL SINGAPORE

I returned to Singapore after the ward as Navigating Officer of the 18,000 tons bulk carrier MV *Rossetti* of Bolton Brothers, head of the British shipping at that time. We departed USA for Singapore through the Panama Canal like HMS *Indomitable* that fateful time, with a huge oil rig accommodation lashed and welded down with steel hawsers to bottle screw slips to the fo'c'sle. This impaired the vision from the bridge for'd. That twisting narrow channel of the Straits of Singapore with sandbanks on either side made it almost as frightening as when I escaped when it fell to the Japanese, and for that reason the other time was far from my mind, as I dived from the bridge wings taking gyro bearings, then Radar and Decca fixes to put on the chart every fifteen minutes, and double checking each movement: no sooner altered than I was on the next alteration.

The 'old man' sat in his bridge chair silent as usual. That I was always grateful for, having served with others who had been master nit pickers. He gave me confidence because he had confidence in me, leaving me to it. The man who should have been on the wheel was on deck, topping derricks with the mate to back up crew and as I preferred to do my own alterations on the automatic gyro repeater compass. On it was a small hand wheel that could be turned by your index finger to alter course, the 18,000 tons of ship pivoting almost instantly to the alteration, and I never did get over this novelty as once I had been an Ordinary Seaman helmsman. Then the huge wheel had been almost as big as yourself, and the old routine of

Qualifying gunnery instructor.

orders time consuming as the pilot shouted from the bridge wings, 'Port twenty,' and you repeated 'Port twenty,' and when on, 'Port twenty of wheel on, sir,' then 'Amidships,' and 'Steady' which you repeated as the gyro repeater headings flashed across the screen and you put on opposite wheel, steadying and slowing its mad rush to 'How's your head?' You sang out the heading that momentarily flashed past, '240, sir.' The Pilot, 'Steer 240,' you repeated again, 'Steer 240, sir.'

So now all I had to do was to turn the small wheel with my finger 20 degrees and the vessel span around on a pivot to hard a-port to cheat the advance or skidding motion outwards just before the desired alteration.

The ship's speed of about 15 knots gave very little of the Admiralty advance turning circle outwards to the dangerous shoals or sandbanks on each side of us, which were never reliable as they constantly shifted. That was why the vessel was brought round so quickly and just before the alteration of change of course. The gyro repeater compass made alarming frantic clacking noises as the vessel swung in its turn, gradually gaining speed, as the flashing lights of buoys and shore lights flashed dizzily past. Now as the vessel came up to her new compass course, I gave a few turns of my finger on the small gyro repeater's handwheel of opposite wheel to counteract its mad rush. It slowed from the mad clacking noises to intermittent sounds of gentle clacks, and I was round on to the new compass heading. No sooner round, and I was on to the next.

This to my intense relief even though I'd been doing it for years in the past on super-tankers of Court Line. I have described the process to show the difference to the old way of helm orders. On one of these frantic dashes, I had to take visual bearings from the gyro on the wings of the bridge, into the Radar plot, then Decca plots, laying them off on the chart, done every fifteen minutes, and with double checking, I always not being afraid of being chicken, each movement. It gave little time before I was on the next alteration on the winding channel to the approaches of Singapore's Keppel harbour, so I depended on our seventeen-year-old Apprentice Officer stationed at the depth recorder to sing out the depths as we went.

As I shouted for him to call the depths out, I saw for a heart-stopping moment the depth recorder graph plunging. The vessel was beginning to shallow depths, but only momentarily, to both our relief, as she steadied up again. I quickly shouted time and position to him and he scribbled it onto the depth recorder paper.

On our escaping from Singapore when it fell to the Japanese, I was not much older than our Bridge Apprentice when we crept out of Keppel harbour in one of those black cotton-wool nights, the sweat spurting from us like an orange being squeezed, or was it fear as we held our slippy sub machine guns. From dead slow ahead on engine, the speed was gradually increased as we cleared the port, till at last in these same winding straits our bows came up and the stern went down in an angry white froth of foam, as our motor gunboat's twin Thornycroft powerful engines burst into a THUNDEROUS ROAR and we were free. As I had looked astern I had seen the Cathay buildings, 'The old man of Singapore', shrouded in billowing flames and the black smoke from the oil tanks we had set alight before we left. He looked like a gigantic Buddha residing over the sacrifice that had once been my shipmates on the battle cruiser HMS *Repulse* and the battleship HMS *Prince of Wales*.

Now once again I returned to Singapore, and on deck, unloading our cargo with a dreadful hangover from a session in the saloon bar the night before as, free from the bridge duties, I was able to recall those terrible times I'd kept repressed for so long. When I had a moment I looked for the Cathay buildings, and, if I'd not known where to look, would never have found this famous landmark dwarfed as it was by the tall glass shiny fronted skyscrapers. Singapore was bursting at the seams with prosperity, we were glad to see. Months later 'The Admiralty Notices to Mariners' stated, reported by 2nd Officer I. Hay, MV *Rossetti* 'Thunder Shoal Singapore'.

Chapter Thirty-One

SUMMARY

Midshipman Leach, now Sir Henry Leach GCB, Admiral of the Fleet, made the disclosure when dining with his father on the last night before sailing on his last fatal voyage, on a TV interview about Fortress Falklands and the *Belgrano* in the South Atlantic Seas. The comparison with Fortress Singapore and *Repulse* in the South China Seas was significant.

We had been closed up at action stations night and day since leaving the Naval Base at Singapore; now two-thirds of the ship's company had been stood down, Admiral Phillips satisfied that no landings or Japanese activities had taken place.

Many were catching up on sleep or showering, the heat very oppressive and the temperature in the boiler rooms into the hundreds. Some were at breakfast even though the time was 11.00 a.m. There was a general air of relief after the tension of the past days as the ships turned south for Singapore and safety. No one liked the idea of facing the might of the Japanese Fleet and aircraft with our pitifully small number. Unknown to us, the day before, towards nightfall, in heavy mist, the Japanese force was steaming towards us. We were as little as five miles apart when a Japanese plane spotted us and dropped a flare, reporting it to Admiral Kondos. The immediate concern was thinking the plane had mistaken him for us; now he was sending hurried signals, 'Don't attack, it's we who are below,' and Admiral Phillips, seeing the flare, went hard aport, so we missed each other by a whisker. The outcome would have been devastating for Admiral Kondo, Japanese

200

official history admitted; with his old fashioned fleet, *Repulse* and *Prince of Wales* outgunning them and with their speeds of 30 knots and radar, a night action would have seen a glorious victory that would go down in the history books, but the result sadly would have been the same when the aircraft found them in the morning.

Japanese official history. What was the objective of the northward moves of the British ships? Was it to hinder our landing in the Kota Bharu area? Or was it a manifestation of the British Navy's principles of war to manoeuvre the enemy cleverly into an unfavourable position? Did they know or not that we had torpedo aircraft and a number of large cruisers and destroyers?

The movement of the British ships might have been reckless but its audacity was to be admired. The Japanese force was: Vice Admiral Dono: 2 battleships and destroyer escorts; Vice Admiral Ozawa: 4 heavy cruisers, 1 destroyer flotilla, 1 light cruiser, 4 destroyer flotillas, 4 squadrons of aircraft.

Repulse included in its complement 200 boys between the ages of sixteen and seventeen; officially it should have been about 120 for each capital ship. This was got round by rating up the 17½-year-olds to ordinary seamen. In 1 hour and 27 minutes most would be dead, a great number trapped in watertight compartments in the sunken ship in only 108 feet of water. No attempt was made to rescue them, although at the brand new naval base and dockyard recently opened at a cost of £60 million they had the gear and the experience of HMS *Thetis*, a submarine sunk in Liverpool Bay just before the outbreak of war. All this was given to the Japs without thought of demolition to be used against us and taking more lives.

The attacking four squadrons were of Mitsubishi heavy industry's type 96 G3 M2 'Nells and Betties,' fast for that time, 300 miles per hour. The special fuel they carried they called 'go-go' and was very volatile; later the American Navy called them 'one shot lighters'. Incredibly they dived through our constant barrages, virtually a wall of steel, without wavering. Their courage will never be forgotten, nor will the memory of standing in the shoulders of the deck of the destroyer *Electra* below the flag deck when we heard the Yeoman of Signals sing out as he decoded from the International Code of Signals, 'Stop firing, Pick up survivors.'

It is apparent that Admiral Phillips took the blame for the Labour and Conservative parties who were concerned and responsible, a political embarrassment even after forty-four years, which I can show by documentary proof, a series of catastrophic blunders. There is no hope of ever getting them to admit them, but hope that when the evidence is presented to them, they will in natural justice vindicate him and give those men their proper bravery awards. As you will see, some got a mention in dispatches but all deserved far greater; this then is the object of my writing.

Repulse was at sea three months before the outbreak of war, serving on Northern Patrol and Iceland, based at Scapa Flow. She guarded against German naval units trying to get out into the Atlantic, a successful blockade, Hitler refusing to risk his Fleet against our Navy. She also sailed on WS Convoys, Winston's Specials, and took part in the hunting down of that pride of the German Navy, the *Bismarck*. Short of fuel, *Repulse* put into Newfoundland, and missed finishing her off, to avenge HMS *Hood*. *Repulse* had two extensive refits costing over £2 million, the last just before the projected Royal Cruise in 1939. She was as up-to-date as any in the Fleet, but for her old outdated hand-operated Anti-Aircraft armament which was in the process of being replaced. This was made up for by her pre-war Royal Navy complement. Their drill, not laid down in any field manual, gave them a loading cycle of 22 rounds per gun per minute. In comparison, the fully automatic and latest design at Fortress Falklands in the South Atlantic was only 18 rounds per gun. Her main armament consisted of six 15-inch guns in two turrets for'd and one aft; 8 barrelled multiple 2 lb machine guns; Oerlikon guns; one Swordfish aircraft with its hangar; twenty single 4-inch AA guns. Displacement deadweight was 36,800 tons and to push this colossal weight were 24 boiler rooms each with its own lifts. She had a speed of 32 knots, 29 during the action. With her graceful lines, the most pleasing in the Fleet, the largest flared bow in the Navy (devil to paint) and slim yacht-like beam, this fast battle cruiser was the fastest in the Fleet, a match for any German equivalent. Special accommodation had been fitted called the Royal Apartments to take King George VI and Queen Elizabeth on the 1939 Royal visit to Canada. The last minute order not to proceed with it disappointed us as we had just joined her as Seamen Boys 1st Class, but not as disappointed as Captain Spooner, later Admiral of the Naval Base Singapore; he had bought six new uniforms.

DIARY OF EVENTS

The Public Records Office show quite clearly that Churchill, well backed up by the Foreign Office and Antony Eden, had insisted on sending *Prince of Wales*, *Repulse* and *Indomitable* to Singapore in the hope this would persuade the Japanese against any move in South-East Asia. The Admiralty, Admiral Phillips with Field Marshall Smuts' advice, had opposed it repeatedly but they were over-ruled by the Foreign Office, when they had found out that *Indomitable* had run aground and the Far Eastern Fleet was not available.

3 November
HMS *Indomitable* carrying four squadrons of modern aircraft on board, is on passage to join HM ships *Prince of Wales* and *Repulse*, three destroyers, *Electra*, *Express* and *Vampire*, *Tenedos* later dismissed. *Indom* runs aground on a sandbank entering Kingston harbour, Jamaica. With a few plates sprung, is sent to Key West, United States, for a fast refit; in about a week's time she arrives, to be away again in twelve days again to proceed to join *Prince of Wales* and *Repulse*. It was about this date and time, that the War Cabinet and Foreign Office made their decision to stick to the plan to send the ships alone with no support, that General Smuts sent his telegram to Churchill urging him to change it, and his speech to us on our quarterdeck, warning of the consequences.

1 December
HMS *Indomitable* could have finally reached *Repulse* and *Prince of Wales* at Singapore, but is diverted to the Sudan to pick up more

aircraft. Public Records do not explain this; however the two ships never saw her again. (Diverted halfway round the world! away from us.)

7 December
Pearl Harbour, war declared on Japan, so much for the Foreign Office persuasion.

8 December
The ships sail to Gulf of Siam without the air cover that could so easily have been had with *Indomitable*.

10 December
Both ships sunk with great loss of valuable professional seamen, badly needed to pursue the war with the Hostilities Only men.

11 December
Indomitable returns too late to help Force 'Z'.

HMS *Indomitable* again diverted away, and not retained for the defence of Singapore Fortress Island, now not only deprived of naval units but of air cover as well.

[By now the reader must be aware that something is seriously amiss with the Foreign Office, not just mistakes but any form of Public Records of explanation are silent.]

19 December
Nine days later after the sinkings a secret debate is held in the House of Commons. There are many rumblings at the way both ships have been handled. Churchill is away at the time in the States, and it is left to Mr A.V. Alexander, the first Lord (Labour), to answer criticisms. He gives a reasoned statement, adding that because of the stubbornness of an old sea dog, in never an appeal for aircraft, the battle was lost. Never once does he mention the crucial part HMS *Indomitable* could have played or ever mention her name to the secret debate in the House

of Commons. There is complete vindication of Admiral Phillips without anything else in this damning statement by the First Lord.

20 December

At Singapore, Naval Base Admiral G. Layton, Commander-in-Chief Far Eastern Fleet, at 'Clear lower deck' says that we had to stiffen up our backbones etc.; this is war and we have to forget we are survivors. From one who has up till then spent it in the Raffles Hotel, it is a bit strong; however we respect him for his fighting talk. We do not however a few days later at the next 'Clear lower deck' when, saying 'Keep your heads high, stiff upper lips,' he adds that he is leaving Singapore, going to Colombo to fetch the Eastern Fleet back. It is an unfortunate phrase after his previous one. There was a stunned silence, then all hell breaks loose as the very strong disciplined pre-war active service men nearly break ranks in derisive jeers and laughter, the rest of his speech being drowned out by barking regulating Naval Police shouting, 'Keep silence.' Admiral Layton, Commander-in-Chief, leaves the next day along with Air Chief Marshall Brooke-Popham. It is said they had to obey orders like anyone else. We wonder what the punishment would have been if they had disobeyed orders by refusing to desert their men in the face of the enemy even before the battle had begun.

25 December

Admiral Spooner 'Clears lower deck' and tells us we are the sheet anchor of Singapore. Singapore will not fall, cannot fall, the native population look to us for guidance and leadership. Again we respect our old Captain of *Repulse* for his fighting talk but we are now beginning to wonder where that leadership was coming from as he leaves in a fast ML. Petty Officer Billington, a former shipmate, his coxswain, related this to me in Australia. The only leadership we find is while doing sentry duty at Admiralty House, taking cover during an air raid, to be challenged by a fearful apparition standing outside with the shrapnel pinging all around, holding a Chinese paper parasol aloft

206

for protection like an old fashioned Naval cutlass. About to board us with grappling irons is Lady Spooner who shouts down to us, 'Come out of there, you rabbits, what will the natives think!' So we do so at the double. If we had had more of these stalwart ladies, Singapore would not have fallen, but this was the only leadership we had then. Fortress Singapore was packed with troops, out-numbering the Japs 4–1 with a huge arsenal of weapons and ammunition, but absolutely leaderless. What can the troops do when the generals flee the battle field before it's begun?

15 February
Singapore falls without a shot, metaphorically as the remnants of the Battalion of the Argyle and Southern Highlanders, along with the remnants of the Royal Marines from both ships, fight on side by side in desperate bloody hand to hand encounter with fixed bayonets. Now this has passed into the proud annals of their history.

Our party of twelve, some former boys from both ships, under the hardbitten leadership of Petty Officer Wilkinson of *Repulse*, refuse to surrender, leading us to freedom, fighting our way out through the jungles of Sumatra and Java and reaching Australia to be told we had not reached the calling up age, and to be sent back to UK. To return and recapture Singapore and free our former shipmates and now prisoners of war.

SUMMARY OF THE FACTS PRESENTED

3 November

The sending of two of our finest battleships, one the most up-to-date in the world, and the most modern aircraft carrier with support from the Far Eastern Fleet that outnumbered the Japs – details can be had on the original plan agreed by Admiral Phillips – could have succeeded. When *Indomitable* went aground, and it was discovered that the promised Far Eastern Fleet was not ready and the plan still to continue, sending two ships without support and air cover was protested vigorously by Admiral Phillips and Field Marshall General Smuts whose advice to Churchill was sought. The two ships alone might even then have succeeded as a deterrent, stopping the Japs entering the war, but the war had already broken out when they sailed so the deterrent was lost. In spite of this the Foreign Office and the War Cabinet sent them unbelievingly on what was really a reconnaissance, that could have been done with two old destroyers. This was the gist of Admiral Phillips' and General Smuts' protest. This then was the beginning of a catalogue of catastrophic tragedies and blunders – or were they?

1 December

The repeated attempt of *Indomitable* to reach the ships was foiled, at one time sent halfway round the world to the Sudan. The last time, failing again, was not retained to defend Singapore, now completely defenceless. *Indomitable* was again diverted. Public Records are silent on this as to why.

19 December
The secret debate in the House of Commons, and the First Lord's outrageous statement that Admiral Phillips was to blame in not asking for aircraft. This was ludicrous in the face of the evidence otherwise presented, which above all completely vindicated Phillips. Furthermore, in the House of Commons' secret debate there was not even a mention of HMS *Indomitable*'s name or the part she could have played.

20 December
The withdrawing of all senior Naval staff and military and Air Force Officers, was construed by many as desertion in the face of the enemy. Much worse, they deserted the men they were supposed to lead and at an early part in the campaign ordered by the War Cabinet and Foreign Office again.

15 February
The outrageous scandal of it all, the debacle culminating in the surrender of Singapore without a fight, although the forces there were prepared to fight. The Battalion, or what was left of them, of the Argyle and Sutherland Highlanders, together with what was left also of our Royal Marines, fought on desperately side by side with fixed bayonets, proving this. For the rest they were left utterly leaderless by the Foreign Office and War Cabinet in withdrawing from Singapore all leadership on 19 December. The compass can be boxed round on all points on this but the point remains that Admiral Phillips was not to blame and the reader must now be aware that something was seriously wrong.

CITATIONS FOR MENTIONS IN DISPATCHES IN HMS *PRINCE OF WALES* AND HMS *REPULSE*, 10 DECEMBER 1941*

Sick Berth Attendant H. Bridgewater HMS *Prince of Wales*
For remaining down below in the fore medical station for several minutes after the order 'everyone on deck' in order to help a wounded man on deck. Although he failed in this he only abandoned this attempt when the ship had a very heavy list and was about to sink.

Midshipman A.C.R. Bros, RN HMS *Repulse* (Posthumous)
For showing great calmness and leadership in causing the 15-inch TS to be evacuated in an orderly manner when the order 'everyone on deck' was given. It is considered that Midshipman Bros thereby saved many lives.

Lieutenant-Commander K.R. Buckley, NN HMS *Repulse*
For outstanding calmness in action under trying circumstances.

Chief Stoker Cameron HMS *Repulse* (Posthumous)
Was outstanding in maintaining the efficiency of the damage control throughout the action. He is not a survivor.

Corporal W.R. Chambers RM HMS *Prince of Wales* (Posthumous)
The successful supply of ammunition to the 2-pounder guns was

---

*Based on Public Record Office A D M 1/12315.

largely due to the efforts of this NOC and his ability, coolness and example were outstanding. When conditions between decks became very difficult he continued to carry on, closing down magazines and shell rooms in the final effort to keep the ship afloat. His work in assisting to limit the spread of water when S3 and 4 magazines were flooded were most useful. He was lost with the ship.

Chief Petty Officer F.T. Crittenden HMS *Repulse*
Was outstanding in maintaining supply of HA ammunition under difficult circumstances owing to bomb damage.

Midshipman R.I. Davies, RAN HMS *Repulse* (Posthumous)
This very gallant young officer was last seen firing an Oerlikon gun at enemy aircraft when he and the gun mounting were slowly submerging.

Commander R.J.R. Dendy, RN HMS *Repulse*
For outstanding calmness in action under trying circumstances.

Writer J.I. Griffiths HMS *Repulse* (Posthumous)
When the ship was listing heavily and about to sink, showed great calmness in continuing steadily to wind the winch to raise the armoured hatch over Y Space leading to the after medical station. Water was pouring down the hatch; his coolness under trying conditions enabled eleven men to escape of whom nine are survivors.

Lieutenant-Commander H.B.C. Gill RN HMS *Repulse*
For outstanding calmness in action under trying circumstances.

Surgeon Lieutenant S.G. Hamilton, RNVR HMS *Repulse*
For outstanding devotion to duty on board when in action in tending the wounded and in continuing to do so for some nine hours in the destroyer *Electra* after he had been picked up.

Chief Petty Officer W.E. Houston HMS *Prince of Wales*
This Chief Petty Officer showed fine qualities of leadership in charge of an electrical repair party. He carried on his work to the end under conditions of extreme difficulty, setting a fine example to those under him. He was wounded in the last bombing attack, but is a survivor.

Lieutenant Commander (E) R.O. Lockley HMS *Prince of Wales*
This officer displayed great initiative and coolness under action conditions and it was due to him that many essential services were maintained. He showed great powers of leadership and example under arduous conditions. Although wounded, he was of great assistance in helping survivors and maintaining the high standard of morale after the ships had sunk.

Chief Mechanician Lugger HMS *Repulse* (Posthumous)
Was outstanding in maintaining the efficiency of the Damage Control throughout the action. He is not a survivor.

Commissioned Electrician E.H. Marchant HMS *Prince of Wales* (Posthumous)
This officer displayed great devotion to duty in conditions of extreme difficulty. He showed fine qualities of leadership and continued his electrical repair work to the end. He was last seen in an exhausted condition between decks.

Boy W.T. O'Brien HMS *Prince of Wales*
The ability, courage and coolness of this boy during the action was outstanding and his work in assisting to get up ammunition when conditions below deck were both serious and difficult, was an example to senior ratings. He remained to assist in closing down the magazines under most trying circumstances, finally taking charge of ladders and controlling the traffic leading to the upper deck. He survived and is believed to have reached Australia.

212

Gunner J.B. Page, RN HMS *Repulse* (Posthumous)
As the ship was about to sink, Mr Page found Ordinary Seaman J. MacDonald on the upper deck and without life-saving belt. Mr Page took off his own belt and put it on MacDonald. Mr Page was not picked up.

Writer W. Rees HMS *Repulse*
When the ship was listing heavily and about to sink showed great calmness in continuing steadily to wind the winch over Y Space leading to the after medical station. Water was pouring down the hatch, his coolness under trying conditions enabled eleven men to escape of whom nine are survivors.

Chief Stoker S.J. Ridgeway HMS *Prince of Wales* (Posthumous)
Always a man of untiring energy and devotion to duty, this Chief Petty Officer showed great qualities of leadership during the action. He was invaluable in taking charge of pumping operations and in the supply of good fuel to boilers in spite of damaged tanks and trying conditions. He continued his efforts to the end and went down with the ship.

Chief Stoker A. Russell HMS *Repulse* (Posthumous)
Volunteered to enter D Boiler Room and fan flat to shut off steam in a steam filled compartment. He is not a survivor.

Petty Officer J.S. Spencer HMS *Prince of Wales* (Posthumous)
This Petty Officer was in charge of lookouts and remained at his post to the end, going down with the ship. By his example and leadership he was instrumental in maintaining the high standard of concentration displayed by the air lookouts under trying conditions.

Shipwright 1st Class A.B. Squance HMS *Prince of Wales*
This shipwright was sent to the scene of the greatest damage from his station forward. He displayed great resourcefulness and skill in stopping leaks and in organising repair parties. By his inspiring energy,

example and initiative, he proved himself a fearless leader. After the action, although wounded, he continued to further morale by his cheerfulness and morale.

Lieutenant (E) L.F. Wood, RN HMS *Repulse* (Posthumous)
Was outstanding in maintaining the efficiency of the damage control throughout the action. Not a survivor.

Chief Shipwright L.J. Woolons HMS *Prince of Wales* (Posthumous)
This Chief Petty Officer was in charge of No. 3 Shipwright Repair Party and displayed great initiative and skill in the ordering and carrying out of the shoring of hatches and the stopping of leaks. He set a fine example of leadership, and carried on to the last moment despite of his exhaustion. He was not saved.

Winston Churchill decreed that as there were so many outstanding acts of bravery, a mention in despatches would be awarded to the HM Ships *Prince of Wales* and *Repulse*. This is the first and lowest bravery award that is given. The cynical suggested otherwise, that in his gigantic blunder, he was trying to make it look as if the two ships had acted against his wishes and proceeded on this foolhardy mission, which General Smuts warned against and about which the C-in-C, Admiral Phillips, stated, calmly and thoughtfully as the officers sat around his long mahogany table in the Admiral's dining cabin on board HMS *Prince of Wales* when Captain Tennant of *Repulse* was there: 'Gentlemen, this is an extremely hazardous expedition and I would liken it to taking the Home Fleet into the Skagerrak without air cover.'

'Without air cover' let the cat out of the bag, as the first thing Churchill accused us of was not asking for air cover, when there was no air cover to even ask for, now borne out by Admiral Phillips' statement in front of reliable witnesses. It was a monumental blunder costing thousands of lives and death in the Japanese war camps. This has never before been published, my request in my time in and out of the RN having been refused.

LIST OF OFFICERS WHO ARE MEMBERS OF HMS *PRINCE OF WALES* AND HMS *REPULSE* SURVIVORS ASSOCIATION

Commander G.A.G. Brooke — *Prince of Wales*
Lt. Commander OMB de Las Casas, LVO OBE RN — *Repulse*
Commodore Sir John Clerk, Bt CBE — *Repulse*
Commander I. Forbes, DSC — *Prince of Wales*
Vice Admiral Sir John Hayes, KCB OBE RN — *Repulse* (President)
Sir Geoffrey Hulton, Bt — *Repulse*
Surgeon Lt Commander S. Hamilton — *Repulse*
Sub Lt. G.L. Kipling — *Prince of Wales*
Commander J. Longworthy — *Repulse*
Lt. Commander E.R. Monaghan — *Repulse*
Commander R.A.W. Poole, RN DSC — *Repulse*
Captain D.G. Roome, RN — *Prince of Wales*
Lt. N. Twigge, RN — *Repulse*
Lt. Commander R.V. Ward — *Prince of Wales*

LIST OF MEMBERS OF
HMS *PRINCE OF WALES* AND
HMS *REPULSE* SURVIVORS
ASSOCIATION

Aish, Ivor	*Prince of Wales*
Allen, J.	*Repulse*
Ash, Alf	*Prince of Wales*
Avery, George	*Repulse*
Barron, J.	*Repulse*
Barton, Ron	*Prince of Wales*
Bell, W.	*Repulse*
Blackburn, J.C.	*Prince of Wales*
Blackmore, Roy C.	*Prince of Wales*
Blundell, C.	*Prince of Wales*
Broad, G.W.J.	*Prince of Wales*
Chivers, Fred H.	*Prince of Wales*
Clarke, D.J.	*Prince of Wales*
Clarke, F.	Not known
Claxton, F.A.	*Repulse*
Close, H.A.	*Prince of Wales*
Coaker, R.S.F.	*Prince of Wales*
Coulson, Jack J.	*Repulse*
Court, H.L.	*Prince of Wales*
Crozer, W.T.J.	*Repulse*
Crumlin, J.	*Repulse*
Cutler, A.G.	Not known

Dawber, Mrs. E. (Wife)	(Husband on *Prince of Wales*)
Dodgson, Arthur	*Repulse*
Doidge, Bill	*Prince of Wales*
Donoghue, Steve	*Prince of Wales*
Dykes, J.	Not known
Edwards, N.J.	*Repulse*
Edwards, W.A.	*Repulse*
Everson, J.	*Prince of Wales*
Fitzsimmons, H.T.	Not known
Frost, J.H.	*Prince of Wales*
Galbraith, Frank	*Prince of Wales*
Garner, John	*Repulse*
Gartside, Ron	*Repulse*
Gomerey, C.J.	Not known
Gordon, Jim	*Prince of Wales*
Mrs. L. Goudy (Assoc. Member)	
Wife of Eng Commander	*Prince of Wales*
Goulding, T.	Not known
Green, Edward	*Prince of Wales*
Green, T.F.	*Prince of Wales*
Grindley, E.	*Prince of Wales*
Hadfield, H.	*Prince of Wales*
Hardy, F.M.	*Prince of Wales*
Harrison, R.	*Prince of Wales*
Hatherall, I.J.	*Repulse* (Royal Marine)
Hay, Ian	*Repulse*
Heath, David	*Prince of Wales*
Howell, J.	Not known
Howes, F. (Father)	*Prince of Wales*
Hughes, Mrs. Barbara (Assoc. Member)	*Prince of Wales*
Ingham, Eric	*Repulse*
James, J.N.	*Repulse*
James, Raymond	*Prince of Wales*

Jenkins, Tom	*Prince of Wales*
Johns, W.R.	*Prince of Wales*
Johnson, C.	*Repulse*
Jones, E.D.	*Repulse*
Lawrence, Wilf	*Prince of Wales*
Livall, H.W.	*Prince of Wales*
MacDonald, Rob	*Prince of Wales*
Macmillan, John	*Prince of Wales*
Malkin, W.	*Prince of Wales*
Marshall, G.	*Prince of Wales*
McCall, Jim	*Prince of Wales*
McCoy, T.	Not known
McGrath, H. (Bert)	*Prince of Wales*
McIvor, Alan R.	*Prince of Wales*
McLellan, K.	*Repulse*
Mercer, Fred	*Prince of Wales*
Millard, B.N.	*Prince of Wales*
Miller, H.B.	*Repulse*
Mills, G.H.	*Repulse*
Moss, W.E.	*Prince of Wales*
Nelson, R.D.	Not known
Newton, A.J.G.	
(Father was Peter Newton)	*Repulse*
Newton, Miss Patricia	
(Assoc. Member)	
(Father was Peter Newton)	*Repulse*
Nicholls, T.H.	*Repulse*
Nilen, A.	*Prince of Wales*
Noel, Eric le Brun	*Prince of Wales*
Norton, D.	*Prince of Wales*
O'Hare, P.J.	*Repulse*
Oldfield, J.B.	*Repulse*
Osborne, R.	*Prince of Wales*
Ough, A.J.	*Repulse*

Paton, P.J.	(Father was on *Prince of Wales*)
Patterson, Peter	*Prince of Wales*
Payne, J.D.	*Prince of Wales*
Peacey, C.J.	*Prince of Wales*
Perry, C.H.	*Prince of Wales*
Pownhall, K	*Prince of Wales*
Price, Mrs. E.	
(Husband, 'Bob')	*Prince of Wales*
Pritchard, K.R.	*Repulse*
Portlock, N.	*Prince of Wales*
Portman, B.	*Repulse*
Rhodes, C.C.	*Prince of Wales*
Robbins, W.J.	*Repulse*
Robson, R.S.	*Repulse* (POW)
Rogers, W.D.	*Prince of Wales*
Rothwell, F.	*Repulse*
Selby, W.F.	*Repulse*
Simmonds, G.	*Prince of Wales*
Smalley, Phillip	*Prince of Wales*
Sutton, Clive (Chairman)	*Prince of Wales*
Tout, C.	Not known
Treble, A.J.	*Repulse*
Turner, J.	*Prince of Wales*
Turner, L.J.	*Repulse*
Ward, E.	*Repulse*
Walker, A.	*Prince of Wales*
Watts, W.T.	*Prince of Wales*
Williams, Mrs. I. (Assoc. Member)	
(Wife of Commander, DGV)	
Williams, Rev. Peter	
(Assoc. Member)	
Wood, R.	*Repulse*
Wren, J.	*Repulse*
Wright, C. (Shiner)	*Prince of Wales*

LIST OF DEVONPORT MEN LOST ON HMS *REPULSE*, 10 DECEMBER 1941

RANK	NAME		AGE	HOME
Ord Seaman	William Douglas	Adamson		S. Africa
L/Stoker	Frank James	Adkins	34	Birmingham
L/Stoker	Pat	Ahern	21	Ireland
R Marine	Frank	Alder	31	Liverpool
R Marine	Bill	Allcock	36	Devon
Ord Seaman	Dennis E.	Andrewes	18	Devon
?1st Cl	Bill C.	Angus	30	Aberdeen
?1st Cl	Vincent C.	Ankers	22	Swansea
PO Stoker	Thomas	Annis	?	Lancs
Boy, 1st Class	Peter R.	Anstey	17	Devon
AB	Sydney	Anton	?	?
AB	John J.	Ashton	42	Devon
L/Seaman	Eric	Ashworth	?	?
L/Seaman	Jack	Ashworth	31	Lancs
Supply Off	James	Atkey	47	?
L/Stoker	Charles	Ayres	26	Barrow in Furness
PO Stoker	Walter G.	Bailey	28	Devon
PO Stoker	Donald	Bain	29	East Lothian
Sto 2nd Cl	Ernest	Barlow	?	?
1st Cl Stoker	Norman	Barnes	35	Salford
1st Cl Stoker	Charles	Barnett	21	Cornwall
PO Cook	Bill	Barron	41	Plymouth
CPO Writer	Harry	Barwis	42	Kent
AB	Cyril	Baxtar	20	St Helens
ERA 4th Cl	Arthur	Bennett	21	Plymouth

Sub Lt.	Peter	Bennett	24	Cambridge
Plumber 4th Cl	Leslie A.	Bennetts	28	Cambourne
AB	Clifford	Benson	19	Lancs
Sto 1st Cl	Ken B.	Berry	19	Lancs
R Marine	Fred	Blank	30	Devon
PO Stoker	Bill	Bolton	31	Devon
Boy, 1st Class	Tom	Bond	17	Lancs
PO	Fred	Bord	?	?
Sto 1st Cl	Frank	Bower	?	?
Ord Seaman	John M.	Boyd	18	Glasgow
ERA 1st Cl	John E.	Boyde	?	?
Mech	Arthur	Brewer	35	Portsmouth
PO Cook	Cecil R.	Bromham	?	Glamorgan
ERA Chef	Herbert W.	Brown	34	Plymouth
ERA 1st Cl	Percy	Brown	44	Plymouth
AB	Robert	Brown	?	?
Sto 2nd Cl	Vivian	Brown	?	?
L/Stoker	Arthur	Burrows	27	Cornwall
Sto 1st Cl	Bill	Cadman	?	Co. Durham
Sto 2nd Cl	Cyril	Cairns	18	Carlisle
CH Stoker	Hugh	Cameron	41	Glasgow
Cant. Asst.	Alex	Campbell	?	?
CWO S/Master	Henry	Cambell	43	Fife
Sto 1st Cl	John	Canty	26	Glamorgan
Sto 1st Cl	Cyril	Capper	20	Yorkshire
Sto 1st Cl	Ken C.	Carratt	22	Middlesex
Surg. Ltd.	Bill	Cavanagh	?	?
Comm Elec	Arthur	Cavell	36	Southsea
Sto 1st Cl	Ron	Cawdrey	21	Yorkshire
PO Reg	Harry	Cawte	35	Warwickshire
Teleg	Ron	Chafer	21	Grimsby
Cant. Asst.	Norman	Chamerlin	20	Devon
Sto 1st Cl	Alewyn	Chard	29	Glamorgan
Teleg	Leonard	Chester	22	Wirral
Sto 1st Cl	Charles	Chinn	?	?
AB	Raymond	Christmas	18	Manchester
R Marine	James	Clarke	19	N. Ireland
AB	Thomas	Cleaves	?	?
Ord Tiff.	Leonard	Clough	24	Cheshire

Lt. Cdr.	Charles	Cobbe	34	Yorkshire
R Marine	James	Clarke	19	N. Ireland
R Marine	Albert	Cockram	25	Bristol
R Marine	Ken	Combstock	20	Monmouthshire
Teleg	Charles	Conlan	?	?
AB	Richard	Cookson	20	Garstang
L/Seaman	James	Cooper	25	Plymouth
R Marine	Ron	Coote	21	Middlesex
Cook	Cecil	Cottle	29	Somerset
L/Stoker	Jeremiah	Coughlan	36	Cork
L/Stoker	Charles	Cowan	27	Liverpool
Sto 1st Cl	Bill	Craddock	21	Cornwall
Sto 1st Cl	John	Craft	?	?
Mech	Harry	Crowson	30	Devonport
Mas at Arms	Charles	Cummins	?	Devon
R Marine	George	Curtis	30	Plymouth
Ord Seaman	Jack	D'Alpuget	25	Middlesex
PO	Arthur	Daly	27	Essex
PO Stoker	Denis	Daly	?	?
Shipwright	Wally	Daniels	24	Plymouth
AB	Robert	Davies	24	Caernarvonshire
Midshipman	Robert	Davies	18	Australia
R Marine	Fred	Dawe	20	Plymouth
Mech	Thomas	Day	34	?
PO Stoker	Bert	Deacon	41	Somerset
AB	Thomas	Deacon	26	Gloucestershire
Sto 1st Cl	Tom	Dennehy	22	Cork
AB	Henry	Dewhurst	20	Keighley
Sto 1st Cl	Bruce	Dixon	21	Liverpool
AB	Reg	Dobson	24	Warrington
AB	Tim	Donovan	19	Warrington
AB	Andrew	Doolan	19	Garston
Cook	Wilfred	Douglas	?	?
Boy, 1st Class	Daniel	Downie	?	?
Boy, 1st Class	Fred	Dowrick	?	?
PO Stoker	Pat	Duffin	38	N. Ireland
Sto 1st Cl	Pat	Duffy	34	S. Ireland
Sto 1st Cl	Bill	Dunn	21	?
L/Stoker	Bill	Dunne	23	?

AB	Norman	Durnell	19	Somerset
PO Stoker	Randolph	Easterbrook	36	Cornwall
Sgt. RM	Joe	Edwards	?	Kent
AB	Doug	Eggleton	20	Cardiff
Cook	James	Eke	25	Norfolk
Sto 1st Cl	Frank	Evans	35	Preston
Ord Seaman	Reg	Evans	18	Cornwall
Sto 1st Cl	Frank	Evans	22	Plymouth
AB	Bill	Ewen	?	?
PO Stoker	Tom	Farley	26	Pontefract
R Marine	Frank	Fine	19	Middlesex
Cant. Mgr.	Fred	Finlayson	39	Edinburgh
Sto 2nd Cl	Fred	Fish	21	Darwen
?1st Cl	Henry	Foster	25	Plymouth
R Marine	Jeff	Fox	19	Derbyshire
AB	Lee	Francis	?	Glamorgan
Sto 1st Cl	Henry	Franklin	26	?
Painter 1st Cl	Charles	Frost	36	Devon
Cook	Bill	Fudge	25	?
Sto 1st Cl	Wilfred	Galvin	20	?
PO/Cook	Sid	Garnsworth	37	Devon
R Marine	Brian	Gavin	20	?
ERA 1st Cl	Laurence	Geddes	21	Co. Durham
Boy, 1st Class	George	Gibbs	17	Llandudno
Lieut	John	Gifford	40	Edinburgh
AB	Alex	Gilchrist	34	Ayrshire
Cpl	Fred	Gill	29	Somerset
Sto 1st Cl	Edward	Girvan	23	Ireland
Sto 1st Cl	Isaac	Gordon	24	Devon
Boy, 1st Class	Bert	Goodman	17	Derby
AB	Reg	Gordon	19	Ireland
R Marine	Edward	Gosden	22	Surrey
Sto 1st Cl	Tom	Gosling	24	Bolton
Sto 1st Cl	Sid	Goss	22	Cornwall
R Marine	Morris	Graney	21	?
R Marine	Bill	Grant	21	Plymouth
Ch. Elec.	Henry	Gray	41	Devon
Painter	John	Greaves	?	?
Sto 1st Cl	Sam	Greenham	35	Exeter

223

Writer	John	Griffith	25	MID
R Marine	Bill	Griffiths	21	?
Steward	Frank	Groenenberg	26	Glamorgan
AB	George	Gunnel	22	Hertfordshire
PO Stoker	Frank	Hadfield	?	?
Boy, 1st Cl	Bert	Hall	17	N. Ireland
L/Stoker	Ernest	Hall	21	Yorkshire
Sto 1st Cl	Harry	Hall	?	?
Sto 1st Cl	Tom	Halshaw	?	?
Sto 1st Cl	Alex	Hamill	?	?
Ch. teleg.	Arthur	Hamley	?	?
Boy, 1st Class	Edward	Hampson	17	Blackpool
Ord Seaman	Ray	Hannis	18	Somerset
R Marine	Henry	Hardy	21	?
R Marine	Bert	Harland	21	Blackpool
PO	Sam	Harris	34	Devonport
AB	Sam	Harrison	20	Belfast
CH/Stoker	Charles	Havell	?	?
Sto 1st Cl	James	Hawke	?	?
Sto 1st Cl	Bert	Hawkins	?	?
Midshipman	James	Hawkins	19	?
R Marine	Sid	Hawkins	22	Suffolk
Sto 1st Cl	Joe	Hawthorne	25	Lancs
R Marine	Eddy	Hayson	19	Hull
AB	Leonard	Heath	22	Birmingham
ERA	George	Heathcock	26	Crewe
Cant. Asst.	George	Henderson	16	Edinburgh
R Marine	James	Herkes	18	Lothian
Sto 1st Cl	James	Hewitt	25	Bootle
PO Stoker	Kenneth	Hewitt	?	Co. Durham
Sto 1st Cl	Ernest	Higginbottom	?	Lancs
AB	James	Hill	35	Surrey
AB	Bill	Hindley	21	Everton
ERA	Charles	Hiscox	21	Gifford
PO Stoker	Bill	Hitchen	38	Plymouth
L/Stoker	John Hoe	Richerden	23	Hull
AB	James	Holden	19	Liverpool
Tel	John	Holt	?	?
PO	Fred	Hooper	40	Devon

Rate	First	Surname	Age	County
PO	John	Holt	?	?
Mech	Fred	Horsley	27	Yorks
Boy, 1st Class	Bill	Howard	17	Cheshire
Sto 2nd Cl	Fred	Howe	20	Bristol
Lieut	Dick	Hunting	?	?
PO	Charles	Hutt	34	?
Sto 2nd Cl	Alec	Ireland	27	Lancs
Shipwright	John	Jackson	38	Devonport
Writer	Les	Jackson	21	Lancs
AB	Bill	James	29	Glamorgan
Blacksmith	Bill	Jennings	20	Caernarvonshire
AB	Howard	John	20	Pembrokeshire
AB	Leonard	Johns	19	Bristol
Sto 2nd Cl	Ernest	Johnson	29	Sunderland
Sto 1st Cl	Harry	Johnson	23	Cheshire
OS	Robert	Johnson	?	?
Ch/Stoker	Edwin	Jones	?	?
Ord Seaman	Henry	Jones	18	Bootle
PO Stoker	Bert	Jones	33	?
AB	Maldwyn	Jones	26	Denbighshire
R Marine	George	Joshua	34	Plymouth
Shipwright	Bill	Keast	41	Plymouth
Ord Seaman	Dennis	Keat	17	Cornwall
Cook	Fred	Keeling	18	Manchester
Sto 1st Cl	Ray	Kent	20	?
AB	Hugh	Kerr	23	Belfast
Sto 1st Cl	Cornelius	Keslake	?	?
L/Stoker	Bill	King	23	?
R Marine	Arthur	Kirkland	26	Plymouth
L/Seaman	Fred	Kyte	33	?
Tiff?	Cliff	Ladd	36	?
Ch/Stoker	?	Lagor	39	St Austell
Commd	?	Lang	49	?
Sto 2nd Cl	John	Leahy	?	?
Sto 2nd Cl	Cliff	Leaver	?	?
R Marine	Les	Ling	23	Devonport
AB	Alex	Lyle	22	Newcastle upon Tyne
R Marine	Dennis	Lissaman	22	Warwicks
R Marine	Frank	Little	24	Ilford

225

Rank	First	Surname	Age	Place
ERA	Bert	Livingstone	23	Doncaster
PO Stoker	Ogwyn	Llewelyn	29	Glamorgan
Ord Seaman	Norman	Long	27	killed 14/11/40, Stretford
Mech	Lionel	Lugger	50	Devon (MID)
Sto 1st Cl	John	McBride	22	Grimsby
AB	James	Mackenzie	22	Ross & Cromarty
Sto 1st Cl	Bill	Mackie	?	?
ERA	Ken	McLaren	23	Bradford
Sto 1st Cl	James	McNeill	20	Stirlingshire
L/Seaman	Pat	McStravick	21	Belfast
Sto 1st Cl	James	Mannion	?	?
Mech	Bert	Markey	41	?
L/Writer	James	Marsh	?	?
Sto 1st Cl	Bill	Martin	24	Lancs
Sto 1st Cl	Norman	Matthews	21	Bristol
AB	William	Matthews	19	Cornwall
L/Stoker	Stan	Mead	35	Cornwall
AB	Joseph	Megahey	21	Belfast
Sto 1st Cl	Ernest	Mellor	21	Staffs
Sto 1st Cl	James	Mercer	31	Blackburn
Steward	Ron	Miller	?	?
L/Stoker	Bill	Mills	?	?
ERA	George	Mitchell	?	?
AB	George	Morgan	23	Lancs
Sto 1st Cl	Peter	Morse	?	?
Sto 1st Cl	John	Mowbray	37	Ledbury
AB	Tom	Murch	41	Devon
Sto 1st Cl	Arthur	Murphy	23	Liverpool
AB	John	Murphy	18	S. Ireland
Sto 1st Cl	John	Neagle	35	Bristol
L/Seaman	Charles	Nelson	38	London
Ord Seaman	Robert	Nesbitt	24	Lancs
L/Seaman	John	Newall	24	Llandudno
Surg. Cdr.	Douglas	Newberry	39	Winchester
L/Seaman	Harold	Newby	24	Lancs
Sto 1st Cl	Haydyn	Newman	21	Swanage
Ord Seaman	Sam	North	18	Preston
L/Stoker	Tom	O'Donohue	25	Ireland

Rank	First Name	Surname	Age	Place
PO Stoker	Pat	O'Leary	?	?
L/Stoker	Alfred	Oliver	?	?
AB	Sid	Orme	22	Poole
AB	James	Orme	?	?
Supp. C.P.O.	Charles	Osborne	41	?
Sub Lieut	?	Page	23	London (RNVR)
L/Stoker	Charles	Parker	24	Devon
AB	John	Parkes	19	Northwich
PO Stoker	Harry	Parsons	31	Plympton
Sto 1st Cl	Cecil	Pascoe	?	?
Ele/Tiff	Donald	Pascoe	22	Plymouth
Ch/Stoker	Urbane	Pascoe	39	Devon
AB	Charles	Paul	40	?
L/Seaman	Eric	Pearce	?	?
Sto 1st Cl	Les	Pearce	23	Bristol
ERA	Harry	Pearson	22	Yorks
O/Tel	Reg	Pease	23	Plymouth
Ch/Stoker	Robert	Peck	33	Devon
Cook	Max	Pengally	?	?
Ord Seaman	Norman	Perry	17	Exmouth
Warr/Eng	Sam	Perry	31	Sussex
Sto 1st Cl	Arthur	Pickles	?	?
Sto 2nd Cl	William	Pitman	31	Somerset
Sto 2nd Cl	Ronald	Pocock	19	Glos
Sto 1st Cl	Edward	Pompey	32	Somerset
Sto 1st Cl	John	Pownall	23	Lancs
Sto 1st Cl	Richard	Price	29	Bolton
Cpl/R Marine	Reg	Prue	37	?
Gunner (T)	Cyril	Pudifoot	38	Devon
Ord Seaman	Sam	Pyne	18	Dartmouth
Cook	Tom	Quayle	?	?
Sto 1st Cl	Bill	Rae	?	?
AB	Fred	Randell	19	Nottinghamshire
Boy, 1st Class	John	Rees	17	?
L/Cook	Lawrence	Regen	?	?
L/Stoker	Arthur	Richards	?	?
Blacksmith 3rd Cl	Howard	Biddle	25	Falmouth
Sto 1st Cl	Bill	Robb	21	Liverpool
ERA (4) Cl	George	Roberts	21	Lee-on-Solent

CPO Stew	Percy	Robertson	38	Devon
Ord Seaman	Robert	Robertson	?	?
AB	James	Robinson	30	Ireland
R Marine	James	Robinson	28	Nottinghamshire
L/Stoker	George	Robson	21	Co. Durham
Lieut	?	Rowe	26	Glamorgan
Joiner 2nd Cl	Bert	Rowe	?	?
Sto 2nd Cl	Fred	Rowlands	37	Wolverhampton
PO Stoker	James	Rumble	31	Plymouth
Sto 1st Cl	Leslie	Rundle	21	Plymouth
CPO Stoker	?	Russell	41	Dorchester (MID)
Joiner 2nd Cl	Bill	Salisbury	31	Torquay
PO Stoker	Ben	Sandcock	42	Cornwall
PO Stoker	Cyril	Sanders	34	Plymouth
L/Stoker	Alfred	Sargent	47	Devon
Shipwright	Harry	Screech	23	Cornwall
Sto 1st Cl	Alex	Semple	?	?
L/Stoker	Bill	Sharples	40	Chester
AB	Robert	Shaw	27	Lancs
PO Stoker	Norman	Shears	?	?
R Marine	Horace	Shread	22	?
Supp. Asst.	Norman	Sinclair	27	?
Ch/Stoker	?	Slater	41	Devonport (MID)
PO	Reg	Slatter	25	Plymouth
Ord Seaman	Alex	Smith	24	East Lothian
Cook	Edwin	Smith	21	Gloucestershire
L/Stoker	Roy	Smith	25	Plymouth
Sto 1st Cl	Henry	Smitherham	21	Cornwall
Sto 2nd Cl	James	Southwell	24	Manchester
L/Stoker	Tom	Spink	?	Devonport
R Marine	Harold	Spray	20	Derbyshire
L/Stoker	Leonard	Sprigg	47	Somerset
PO Stoker	Douglas	Stadon	25	Bristol
Sto 1st Cl	Bert	Stansfield	25	Cheshire
S/Berth PO	George	Stevens	32	Plymouth
L/Cook	Reg	Stevens	22	Newport
AB	Charles	Stewart	19	Edinburgh
Sto 2nd Cl	George	Stillwell	24	London
Sto 1st Cl	John	Strachan	21	Dundee

Supp. Asst.	Alex	Stuart	27	Aberdeen
R Marine	Arthur	Stubbings	23	?
Ord Seaman	Arthur	Sturrock	?	?
Sto 1st Cl	Walter	Swift	24	Lancs
Boy 1st Class	William	Symonds	?	?Devon
S/Man	Robert	Teasdale	32	?
AB	Edward John	Thomas	22	Flintshire
Sto 1st Cl	Ernest James	Thomas	?	?
R Marine	John	Thomas	19	West Kirby
Tiff	John	Thomas	21	Glamorgan
PO Stoker	Percy	Tonkin	35	Plymouth
Ord Seaman	Allinby	Trigger	18	Devon
Sto 1st Cl	Ernest	Tucker	?	?
ERA	Sidney	Tucker	22	Pembroke Dock
Sto 1st Cl	Harold	Turner	?	?
L/Seaman	Herbert	Turner	19	Dorsetshire
Ord Seaman	Fred	Tyrell	20	Barrow in Furness
Sto 2nd Cl	Walworth	Vaughan	20	Glamorgan
L/Seaman	William	Vaughan	19	?
AB	James	Wait	19	?
L/Stoker	Alfred	Walker	?	?
ERA 4th Cl	Henry	Walker	?	?
ERA 5th Cl	John	Walker	?	?
Commis/Tiff	Horace	Ward	?	?
R Marine	Ernest	Warren	22	Wiltshire
Supp/PO	Horace	Waters	27	Plymouth
Midshipman	John	Watson	19	Essex
CPO/Cook	Edgar	Watts	34	Plymouth
AB	Alan	Webb	20	Cornwall
Cmdr	Lancelot	Webb OBE	?	?
AB	John	Whitear	39	Somerset
ERA 3rd Cl	Frank	Wilcock	24	Preston
AB	Douglas	Williams	23	?
AB	John	Wilkins	20	Liverpool
L/Stoker	Alfred	Williams	24	?
PO Stoker	Edgar	Williams	33	Cardiff
L/Stoker	Francis	Williams	22	Cornwall
R Marine	Harold	Williams	21	Co. Durham
PO	John	Williams	22	Cornwall

229

L/Stoker	George	Williamson	22	Ireland
Sto 2nd Cl	Ken	Williamson	18	Bristol
AB	Charles	Wills	22	?
ERA 5th Cl	Jack	Wilson	?	?
Sto 1st Cl	William	Wilson	20	Glamorgan
Sto 1st Cl	Frank	Wood	27	Wolverhampton
CPO ERA	Harry	Wood	41	?
Lieut	Leonard	Wood	?	?
Sto 2nd Cl	John	Wookey	33	Bristol
Sto 2nd Cl	Ernest	Wright	31	Gloucestershire
AB	Cyril	Young	?	?